CW01668531

MUSEUM OF MONTSERRAT

Museum of Montserrat

The surprise of art

Published by: Museu de Montserrat
08199 Abadia de Montserrat
Tel. 00 34 938 777 745
museu@larsa-montserrat.com
www.museudemontserrat.com

Text: Josep de C. Laplana

Contributors: Eva Buch, Sandra Rosas, Montse Mur, Rosa Maria Martín, Lluís G. Turell Coll, Josep Maria García Fuentes, Amalia Zomeño, Javier del Barco.

Photographs: Dani Rovira and other photographs from the MDM Photographic Archive

© Albert Ràfols Casamada, Alphonse Mucha, Andreu Alfaro, Hermen Anglada Camarasa, Jean Cocteau, Jean Metzinger, Joan Hernández Pijuan, Joaquim Sunyer, Josep Guinovart, Marc Chagall, Natalia Gontcharova, Pablo Gargallo, Ricard Opisso, Serge Poliakoff, Javier Mariscal, Xavier Nogués, Georges Rouault, Sean Scully, VEGAP, Barcelona, 2013
© Josep Maria Subirachs, VEGAP, Barcelona, 2013
© Salvador Dalí, Fundació Gala-Salvador Dalí, VEGAP, Barcelona, 2013
© Fundació Antoni Tàpies, VEGAP, Barcelona, 2013
© Fondation Le Corbusier, VEGAP, Barcelona, 2013
© Sucesión Pablo Picasso, VEGAP, Madrid, 2013
© Successió Miró, 2013

Translation: Francis Bandin

Graphic Design: www.victoroliva.com

Printing: Ormoprint, Barcelona

Production: Editorial Mediterrània, SL
editorial@editorialmediterrania.cat
www.editorialmediterrania.cat

ISBN: 978-84-9979-006-0
Legal Deposit: B-14.496-2013

All rights reserved. Reproduction of this book, in whole or in part, without prior permission from the publisher, is prohibited.

Contents

The Museum of Montserrat 9

The building 11

The archaeology of the ancient world

- The Middle East 14
- Egypt 19
- Cyprus 24
- Italy and the Hellenic World 25
- The Late Roman Empire and the PaleoChristian culture 28

***Nigra Sum*. Iconography of Our Lady of Montserrat** 31

Joyful light. Icons from the Eastern Church 39

Religious precious metal work 43

Antique paintings (13th-18th centuries) 47

Modern painting (19th-20th centuries) 55

The avantgardes and contemporary painting 73

Modern sculpture (19th-20th centuries) 79

Collection of drawings and watercolours 85

Other reserve collections

- Prehistory and Iberian culture 94
- Amerindian Art 96
- Asian Art 98
- Primitive cultures 100

Hebrew Culture 102
Islamic Culture 104
Medieval Art 106
Sculpture from the 16th-18th centuries 108
Ceramic, Porcelain and Decorative Art 110
Clothing, Textiles and Embroidery 112
Coin, Medallion and Stamp Collections 114
The Collection of religious prints 116
Modern and Contemporary Graphic Work 118
Posters and *Ephemera* 120

The Museum of Montserrat at the service of culture 122

Bibliography 124

The Museum of Montserrat

The Museum of Montserrat showcases a selection of the most outstanding artistic and archaeological heritage at the thousand-year-old Abbey of Montserrat. However, these treasures are all relatively recent since, due to the consequences of the Napoleonic War (1811-1812) and its disastrous aftermath, Montserrat lost all sits medieval and baroque art. Nonetheless, generally speaking, the current heritage is significantly larger and more valuable than the old. Most of the works in the museum come from private donations. It was their donors' wish that the artworks they had collected in life should be exhibited in Montserrat in order to promote culture.

Most works in the Museum of Montserrat are private donations.

The Museum of Montserrat aims to offer the visitor an opportunity to enjoy art and culture. It is also intended to provide an arena for dialogue, which the Abbey of Montserrat offers civil society in the field of studies of antiquity and of ancient and modern fine art.

It offers visitors a unique opportunity to enjoy the world of art and culture.

To this end, as well as exhibiting the collections appropriately, the Museum also seeks to provide a forum for researchers and a place where leading art critics and artists from different movements, approaches and tendencies can meet to share their opinions and views in a broad, all-embracing humanist atmosphere.

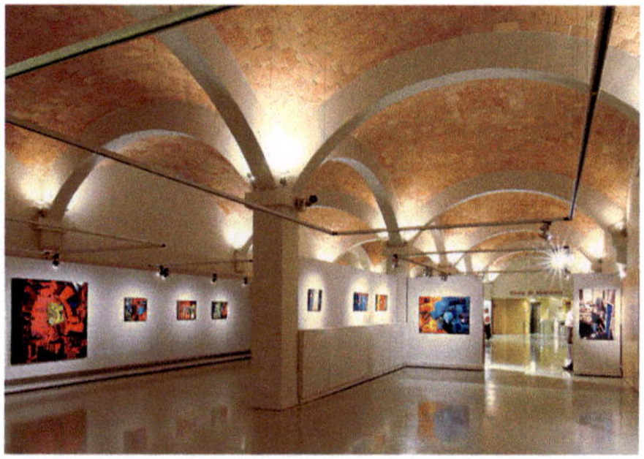

It is also a meeting point for dialogue among artists, scholars and art professionals.

Our Museum is constantly growing.

All this cultural activity reflects the Benidictine secular tradition as well as a tacit pact between the monastery and civil society. Montserrat, with its thousand-year history, has been and is considered one of the most permanent and emblematic elements of the singular personality of Catalonia, its fraternal links with other peoples of the Iberian Peninsula and its opening to Europe and the rest of the world.

The Museum of Montserrat was declared of national interest by a Government of Catalonia decree dated 3 October 2006.

We present a quality exponent of our country's culture to the public.

It is an entity which is full of life, new interests and projects.

The Museum of Monserrat wishes to thank their main donors: Josep Sala i Ardiz, Pere Sensat i Maristany, Xavier Busquets i Sindreu, Caja Madrid Foundation, Josefina Cusí in memory of her father Joaquim Cusí i Furtunet, Montserrat Carreras i Jané.

And also many others who have helped to increase our heritage with their generous and valuable contributions.

The Museum of Montserrat has its own statute as a church institution, since it belongs to the Benidictine Abbey. This institution has always been unique due to its wide range of criteria. Even in the hardest of times, it aimed to offer room for freedom of speech and respect to others. This is why we intend the rigorous study of History, Archaeology and Art to go beyond frontiers and barriers that cause empoverishment. Without detriment to the above mentioned and according to our traditional deep-rooted devotion to our country (the characteristic Benedictine *stabilitas*), we intend that the general public can contemplate selected exponents of the best art which has ever been produced in Catalonia, within Montserrat. We are interested in the past as it is there where we find the roots and the core of human development but we are also passionate about modernity, the avant-garde and the serious attempts to scan and open up new horizons.

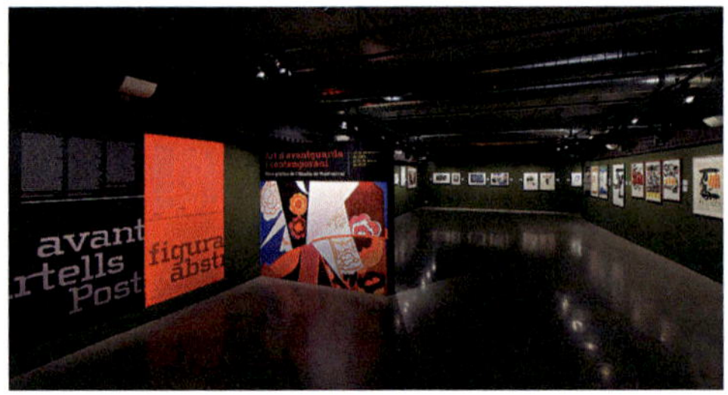

The Museum of Montserrat is a living entity. It experiences a constant transformation and continuous and renewed exhibitions of its collection. Only a small part of it is exhibited permanently. This is why temporary exhibitions follow each other non-stop in the **Pere Daura Room** and the **Pere Pruna Art Space**. These temporary exhibitions make up the best complement to the Museum's visitors and stand for the real efforts of this institution.

THE BUILDING

The Museum of Montserrat takes up all the space under the surface of the three squares which precede the monastery and were built by the famous Catalan architect **Josep Puig i Cadafalch** (1867–1956), in a comprehensive project for the architectural and urban reform of Montserrat, between 1928 and 1933.

The spacious hall is framed by pillars which divide the space into twelve areas. These are covered by a 'groin vault' of typically Catalan ceramic tiles.

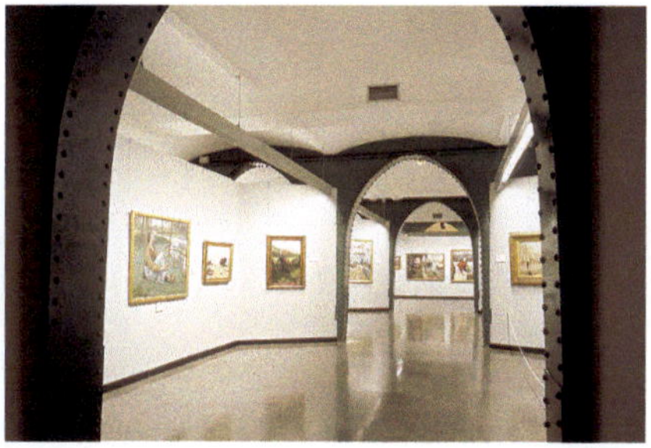

The original purpose of this space was to house a wash-house and airing places. Another area was used to accommodate the Sanctuary staff.

The building which houses the Museum's permanent exhibition is very interesting due to its architectonical quality and unique structure. The upper floor of the Museum, which was initially used as a restaurant, is supported by sturdy Vierendeel main beams. Their steel parabolic arches lean on the rock and the façade, covering the distance between the squares. The lower floor hangs from these main steel beams by very thin steel braces. In this way, the ground floor, which was used as a garage, is free of pillars or other supporting elements.

The architect Puig i Cadafalch designed this structure in 1929 in collaboration with the engineer and building constructor Joan Torras, who was known as the Catalan "Eiffel" within the profession.

The famous Catalan architect Puig i Cadafalch originally designed the space which currently makes up the Museum of Montserrat as a restaurant. Forty years later, the building became too small and another one had to be built. In 1982, the space created by Puig i Cadafalch was renovated to be used as a museum and in 2004 and a new entrance was added which communicated with other adjoining rooms.

The current collection of the Museum of Montserrat takes up some two thousand square metres of exhibition space.

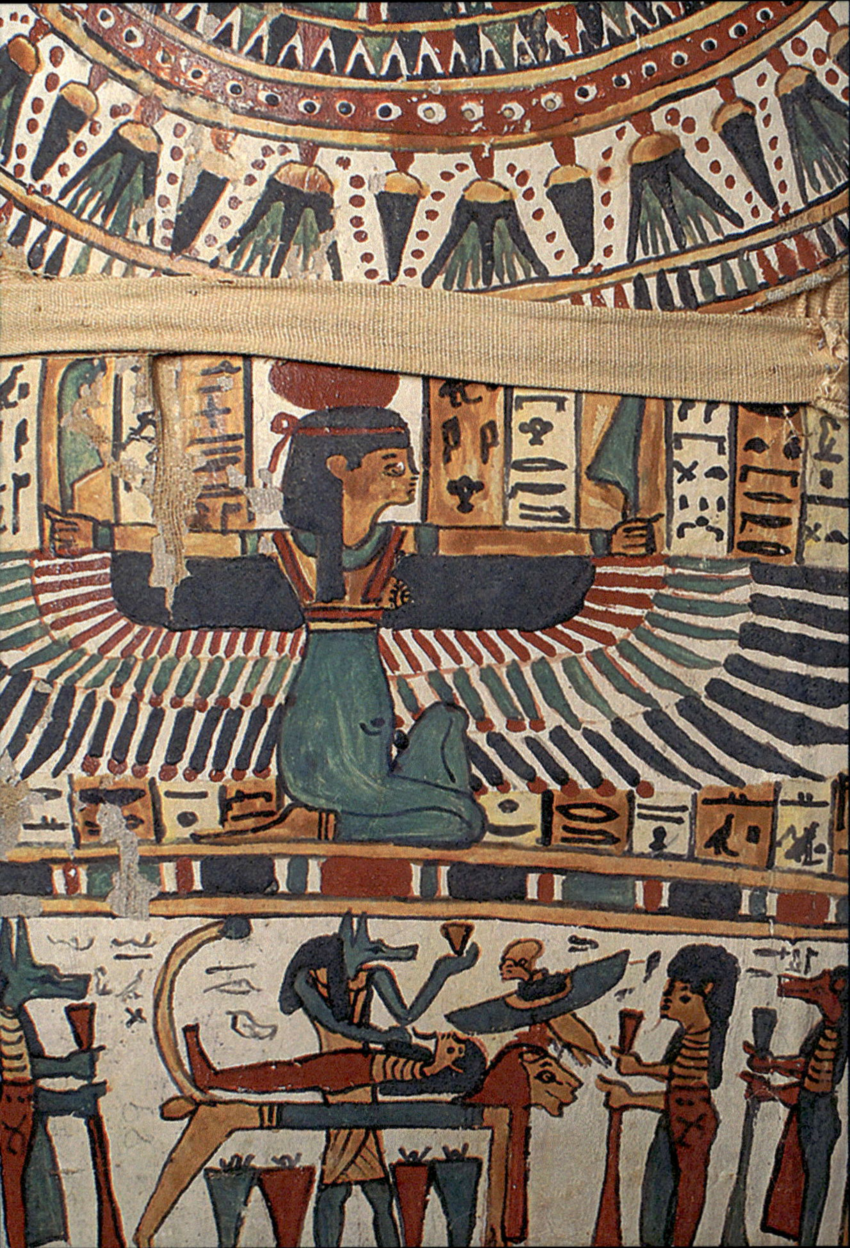

The archaeology of the ancient world

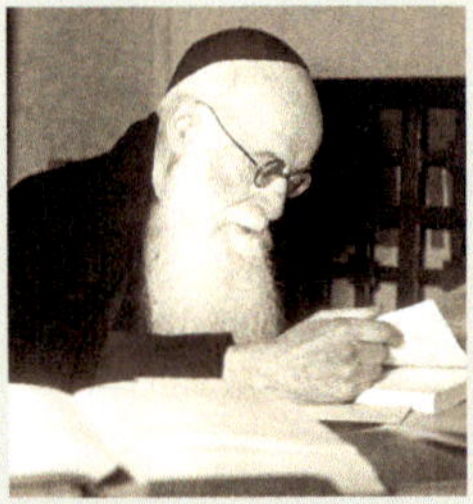

Dom Bonaventura Ubach was a Bible scholar and his devotion also led him to become an explorer. An outstanding philologist, he studied the Semitic languages. He belonged to a small group of Catalan adventurers who chose the Middle East as their operational base and collected a great quantity of materials and photographs. B. Ubach went beyond all of his peers, especially for his dedication and tenacity.

The original basis of the Museum of Montserrat was the so-called 'Biblical Museum', a huge, admirable work by the monk Dom Bonaventura Ubach (Barcelona 1879 - Montserrat 1960), who spent long periods of his life in Jerusalem and Beirut from 1906. He embarked on great travels and exploratory journeys in search of topographic, anthropological as well as natural and archaeological scientific data, with the purpose of understanding the Bible and making it better understood with reference to the cultural atmosphere in which it was written. This Biblical Museum of Montserrat was inaugurated on the 27 April 1911.

In 1962, the old Biblical Museum was reorganised according to strictly archeological criteria. The materials acquired by P. Ubach in Jerusalem, Baghdad, Beirut and Cairo have been currently enriched with new contributions of very relevant pieces which had been donated by the architect Xavier Busquets (1990) and the Caja Madrid Foundation (2003).

The archaeological materials from the Ancient World are located in a very different architectural environment from the rest of the Museum. It is also covered with a typically Catalan brick groin vault. The colour tone is designed to evoke the Egyptian and Middle Eastern sandy areas.

The different cultures which make up this section in a permanent way can be easily identified and a more or less chronological order is followed.

The Middle East

In the immense deserts of the Middle East, there was an area which was irrigated by the great Tigris and Euphrates rivers and together with other oasis, became one of the original centres of culture and history. This country was called Mesopotamia from time inmemorial. The Museum of Montserrat holds a numerous collection of archaeological material from this region, which became a great agricultural empire. It included the huge territories of Syria and the interior of the Middle East beyond Persia and its culture extended for a long period from the year 3400 until the year 200 BC.

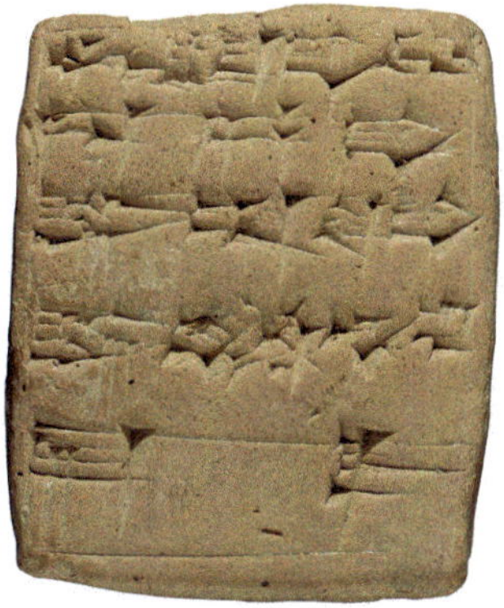

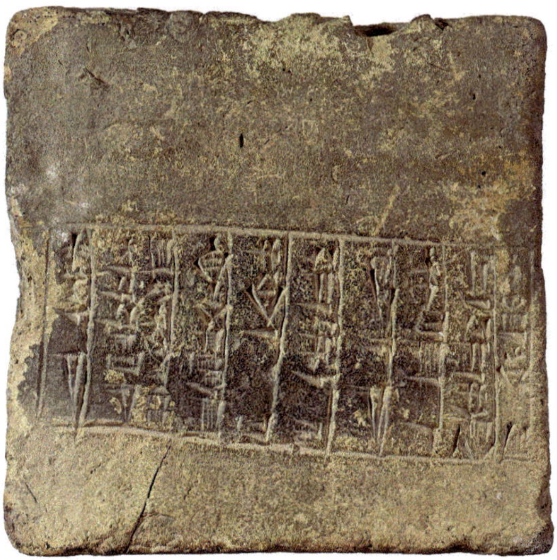

Tablets with cuneiform script *in Sumerian, Akkadian, Elamite, Hittite and Canaanite languages. The collection of Montserrat consists of a thousand two hundred pieces and is well-known among experts all around the world. Most of them are commercial documents but there are also letters, lists of locations, diseases and medicines, an astrological calendar, a Sumerian-Akkadian vocabulary and even school dictations.*

Apart from the tablets, the keys of construction from the old Sumerian kings Urbaba, Gudea and Singasid of Uruk, and the large pavement stones stamped by Gudea, viceroy of Lagaix (c. 2050 BC), Salmanasar III, Nabucodonosor II (600 BC) and Nabonid (550 BC) are of particular interest.

Mesopotamian culture was mainly agricultural and commercial; this is why coins had a special importance. In the Museum of Montserrat, there is a small collection of them. Some have a pear shape (prior to the third millenium), others have a date shape (3000-2600 BC) and others have a duck shape. The ***mina*** *coin was made of black calcite bearing the inscription by Naram-Sin, king of Accad (2250 BC).* ***The talent*** *coin also had a duck shape and weighed approximately 30kg.*

Syrian / Babylonian statuettes*. Many of them are fertility charms or amulets to ensure the flow of breast milk in order to feed a baby. There are also priest figures which perform ritual kissing of a large glass of water, a female figure in prayer position (2000 AD), etc.*

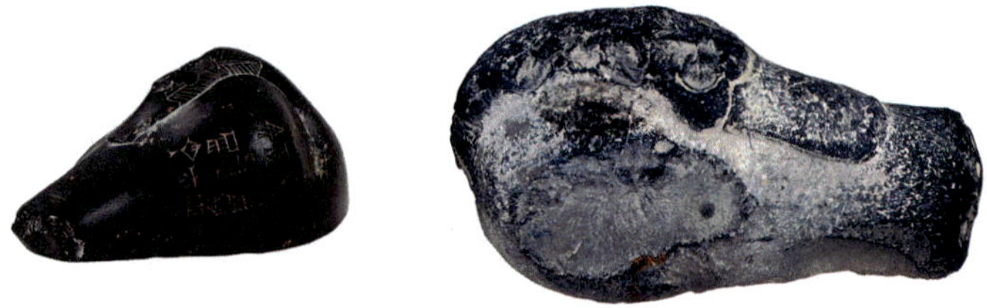

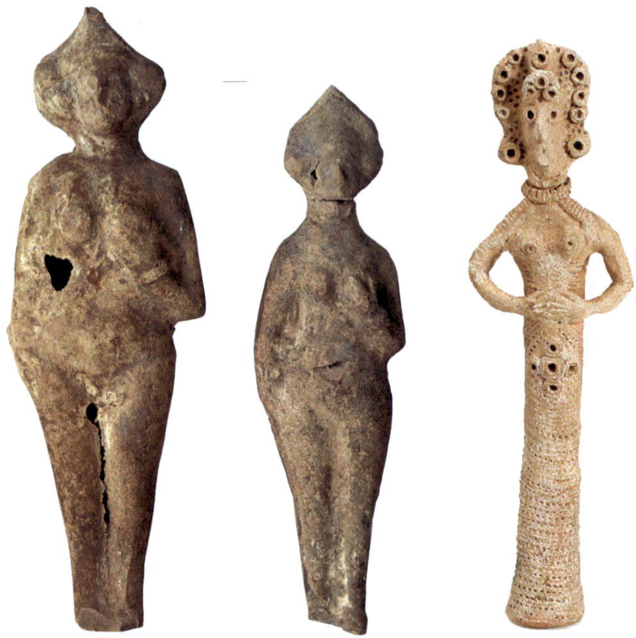

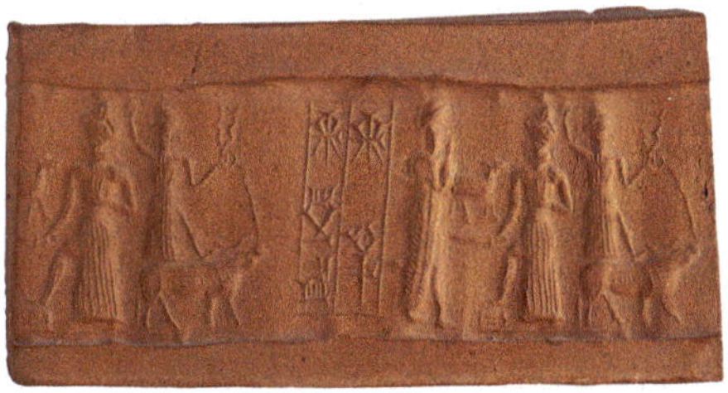

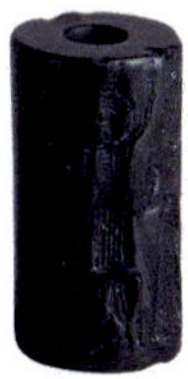

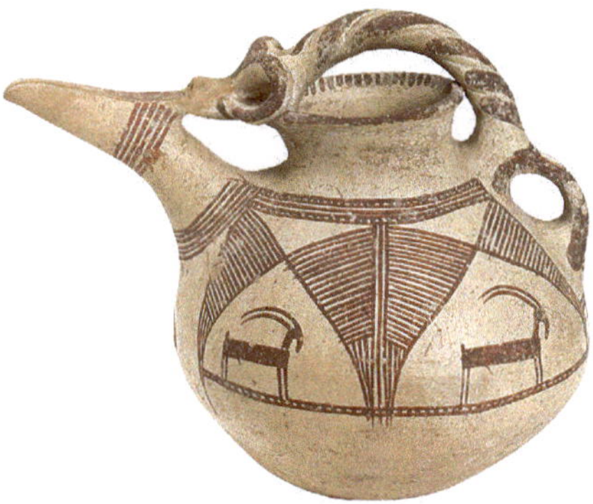

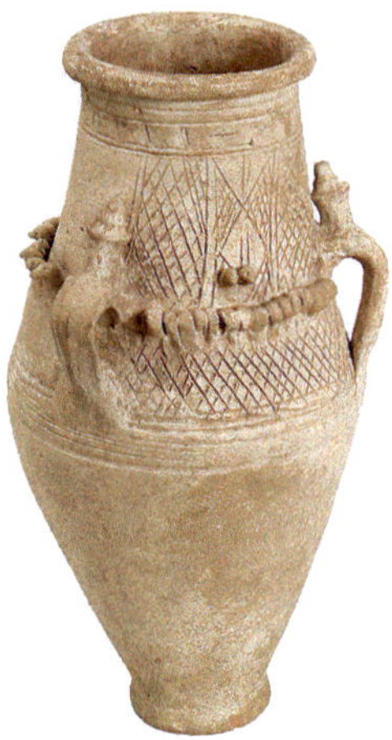

Cylinder Stamps.
The collection of Montserrat consists of 159 Sumerian, Babylonian, Assirian and Neo-Babylonian stamps (3400-600 AD), which provide insight into the symbolic and religious world of these cultures.

Alabaster and ceramic vessels.
They have very different shapes and decorations according to the areas and periods. The collection of Montserrat includes alabaster works and a terra-cotta amphora with engraved decoration and animals in relief, from Sumeria (2nd millenium AD), a jug with a large peak and goats painted as decoration from Luristan (1100 AD), a red ceramic glass decorated with goats from Gilan (1000 AD) and different ceramic objects from Amlash, among which were two rithon jugs in the shape of a bull (1200-1000 AD) and which are the most interesting pieces.

Kudurru, upper fragment.
It was a type of boundary stone used to divide royal property which was being managed by a tenant. The one in Montserrat is from the Kassite period (1500 BC). We can see two temples which hold two mounds, a quadruped and star signs. Behind, there is another temple supporting a tree and the sun. The remains of an inscription can also be seen.

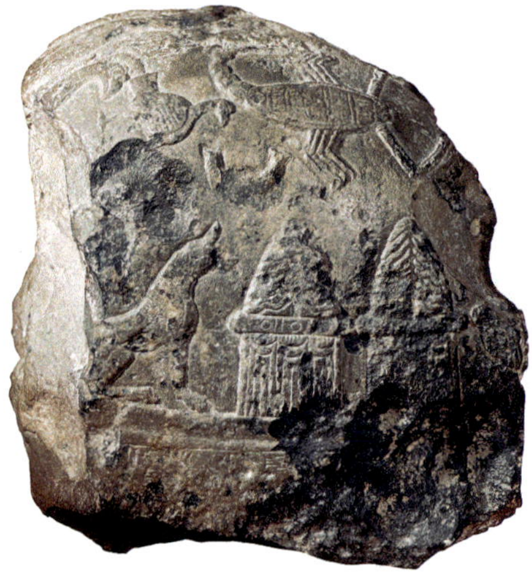

Hittite and Luristan Bronze materials.
The Hittite population settled in Anatolia (Turkey) and their history covers the period from 1750-1180 AD. The production of Hittite metalwork was very famous; an outstanding piece in the exhibition is a two-headed deer from the third millenium. Luristan was another country, in the north of current Persia, which produced and exported bronze materials. The materials related to this culture which are found in the Museum of Montserrat can be dated to around the year 1000 BC.

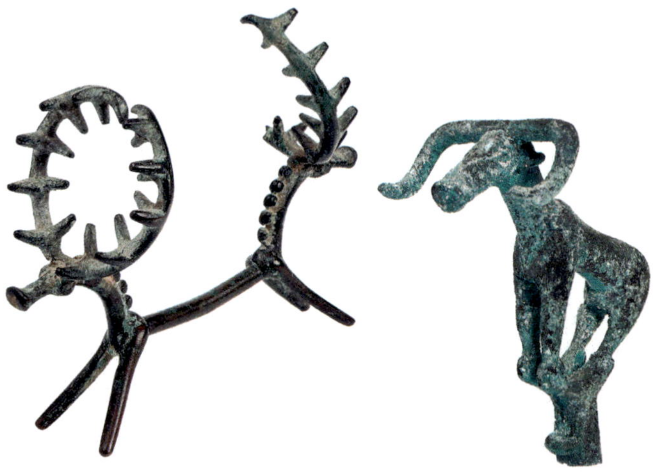

EGYPT

The Egypt collection of the Museum of Montserrat is especially rich and varied, since apart from pieces of great interest it has all kind of materials which illustrate the life, customs, culture and religion of the Egypt of the Pharaohs.

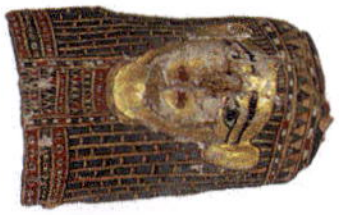

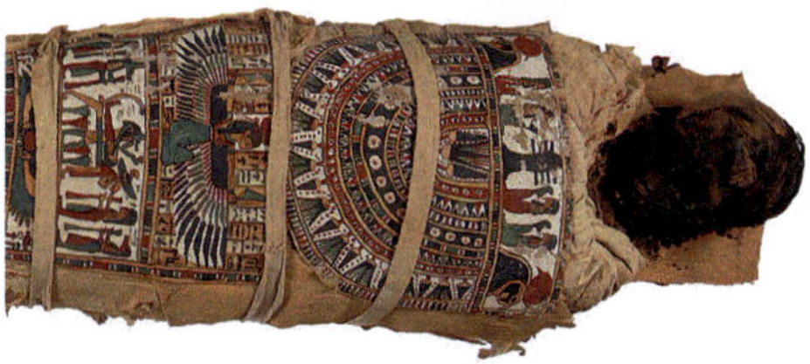

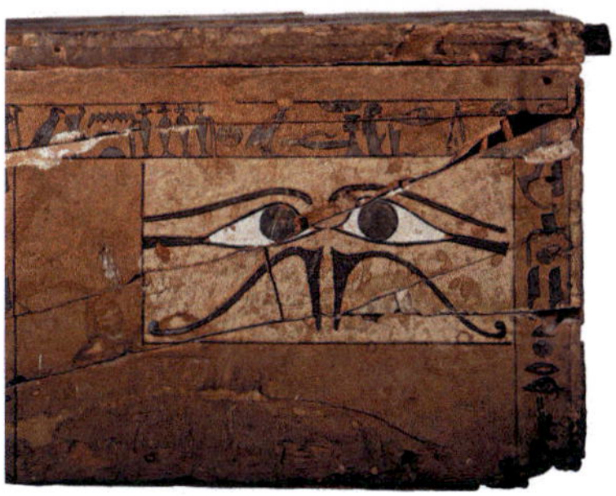

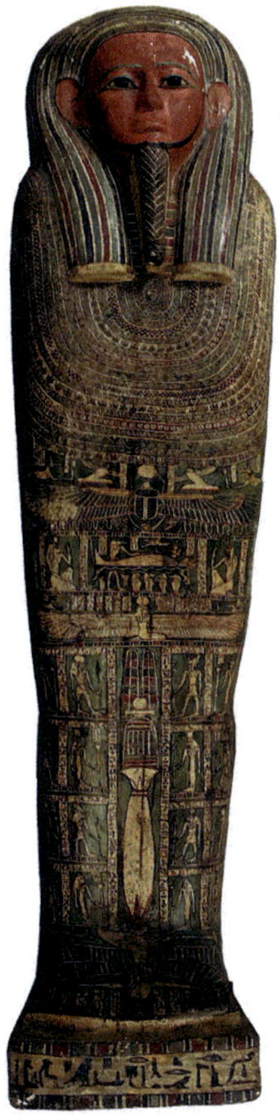

Adult mummy *from the Ptolemaic period (303-30 BC). With its golden death-mask and very well-preserved bandaging, this piece allows us to imagine and interpret the ritual and the religious motivations of mummification.*

Polychrome rectangular cedar wood sarcophagus *(9th century, end of the 3rd millenium BC), with painted detail of Horus' (wedjat) eyes and hieroglyphic inscription related to the deceased.*

Antropomorphic sarcophagi *of Naisenetniut and Padiherpakhered, most likely brother and sister, from the beginning of the Ptolemaic period (600-200 BC). Donated by Caja Madrid.*

Portraits for sarcophagi and mummy masks. *The anthropomorphic sarcophagus was intended to reproduce the deceased´s features, but given the difficulty to carve a real portrait, their faces were made to a standard type applied to them all. The Montserrat museum has four of them, one being of great beauty (18th-20th Dynasty), and also two impressive mummy masks, the last one being from the Roman period.*

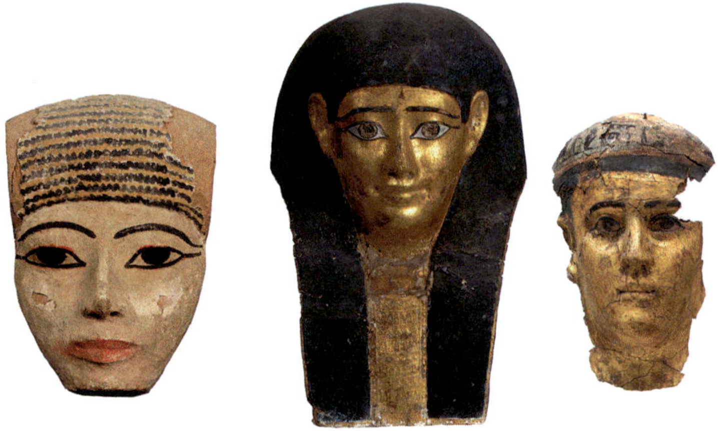

Canopic vases. *They were used to preserve the entrails of an embalmed body and they invariably came in sets four. Their lids were shaped like the heads of the four sons of Horus: Amset, Hapi, Duamutef and Qebehehsenuf, which covered the liver, the lungs, the stomach and the intestines. In one of these glasses, the following inscription could be read: "Neit's words: I spend day and night making Duamutef's protection thrive in my inner self". All of them date from the Dark Ages (1085-341 BC).*

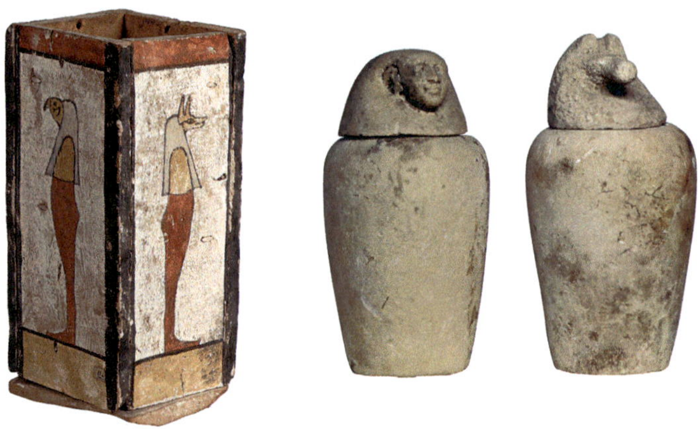

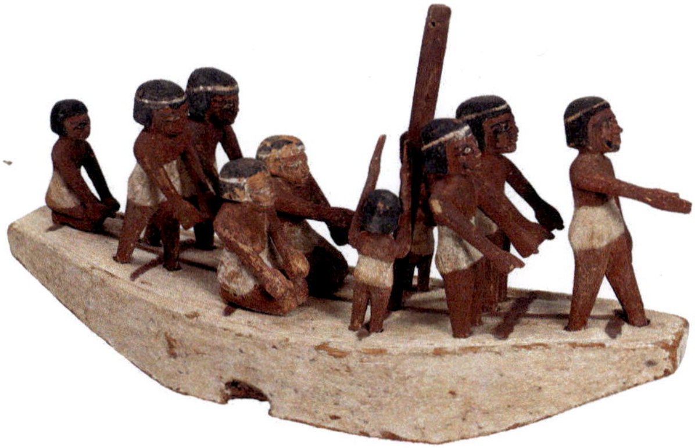

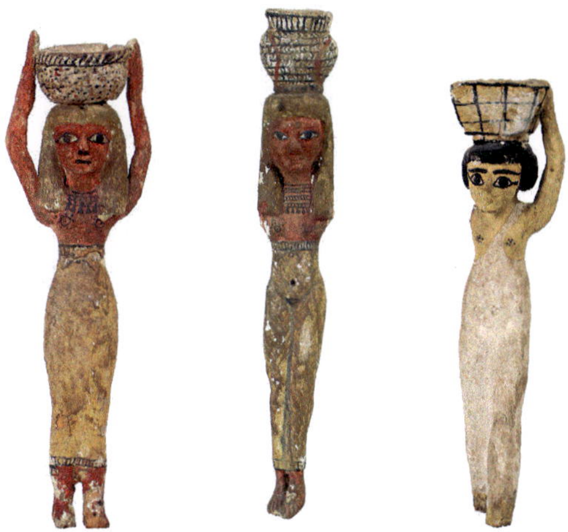

Funeral barges. *They represent the sun's course and this is why they are related to the god Amon-Ra. He shares his journey through the night with the deceased, during which he will have to overcome all kind of dangers. The best examples of these funeral boats have little figurines featuring the crew and the division of labour on their voyage along the Nile. The young man we can see kneeling in the stern is the helmsman; the one in the bows is the pilot. He has his arm outstretched and should carry a long cane to measure the river depth; we can also see the oarsmen and two cabin boys who are in charge of the sail. This particular boat dates from the Middle Empire (2000-1750 BC).*

Offering bearers. *Their purpose was to continue their work of serving corn, beer, water, ostrich eggs, etc, inside the tomb. These particular ones in the Museum of Montserrat are dated between the years 2130 and 1786 BC.*

Polychrome jar
from the Palace of Amenhotep III (18th Dynasty, 1402-1364 BC) of extraordinary quality, donated by Xavier Busquets.

Tamiu's tablet.
The deceased woman in a semi-kneeling position with her hands outstretched, prays to Osiris and the goddess Neftis. The inscription mentions this goddess and calls on "Osiris, lord of eternity and the earth". It also mentions the deceased woman's name: "Tamiu, singer of Amon". It dates from the Ramesid era (c. 1292-1069 BC).

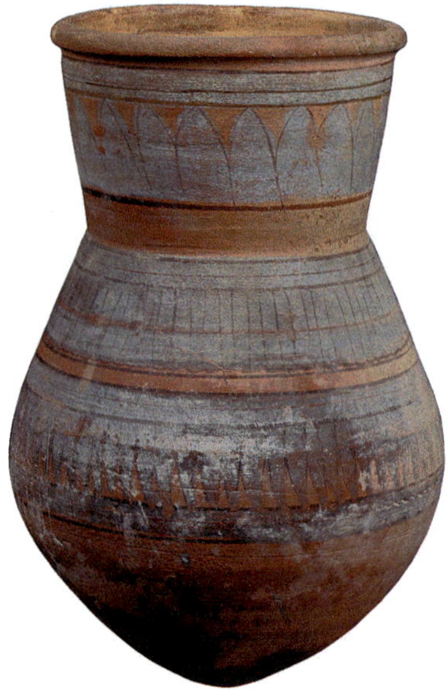

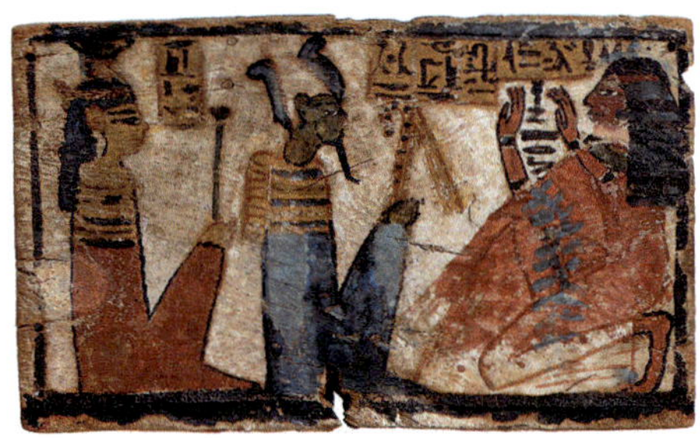

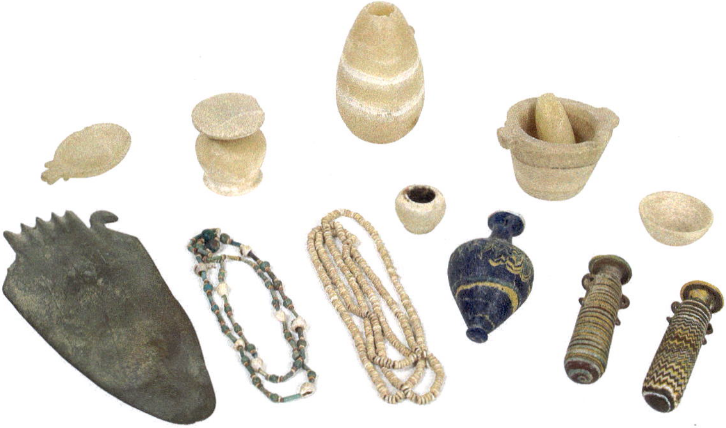

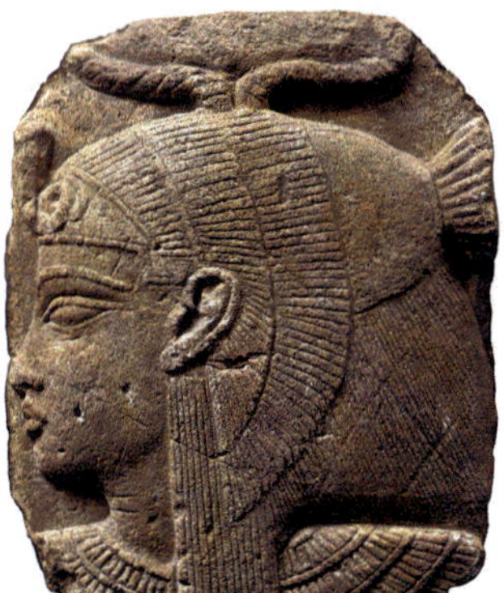

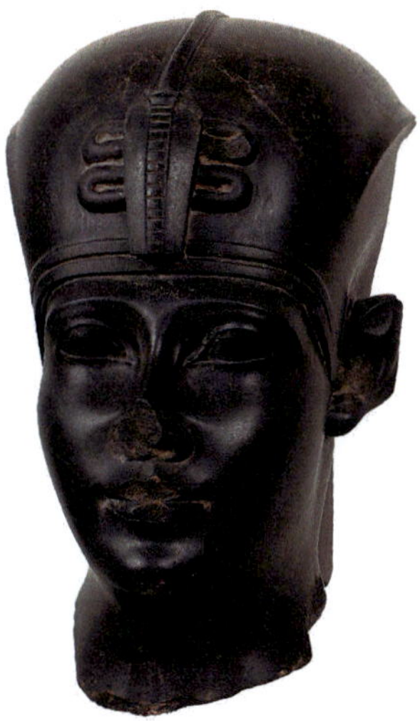

The Egyptian boudoir. *The Egyptians were very fond of cosmetics and beauty care. The little alabaster receptacles were used to contain perfumes. We can also see little mortars which were used to produce essences, palettes for the mixtures, necklaces and lucky charms.*

Sculptures. *Montserrat houses a large collection of small figurines. Many of them were used as lucky charms and represent almost all the Egyptian pantheon, together with other bigger ones which are made out of stone. The extremely beautiful Hathor or Isis' profile in limestone (from the Ptolemaic period, c. 304-30 BC, donated by X. Busquets) and a black diorite royal head with a blue crown and the ureus, a piece belonging to a pharaoh sculpture from the Saita period (665-625 BC, donated by X. Busquets) are the most outstanding pieces in the exhibition.*

CYPRUS

Given its geographical location, the island of Cyprus was always a crossroads for the ancient cultures of the Eastern Mediterranean. The collection of Cypriot ceramics in the Museum of Montserrat is particularly rich. It allows us to follow this culture's evolution from the Cyprus-Geometric I (1050-950 BC) until the Archaic period (750-600 BC).

__Cypriot ceramic materials__ vary in shape: semi-spherical bowls, with or without handles or with a tubular conduct, jars with handles and polychrome decoration, amphoras, oinochoes or wine jars, a skyphos, a lèkythos, dishes of various sizes, perfume jars and opium substances to combat pain, bottles, water containers, etc.

The most characteristic decorative motifs which can be observed are simple lines, zig-zags, waves, die, little chains, diamond shapes, animals such as birds, ducks, goats; concentric circles, cross-shaped circles, stars and even swastikas, all of them solar symbols.

Among the most curious objects, we can notice two __rhìton shaped bulls__, a third one in the shape of a male goat and a fourth, which is a horse (Middle Bronze Age, 1900-1650 BC); __a warrior leading a chariot__ (700-600 BC), donated by Caja Madrid.

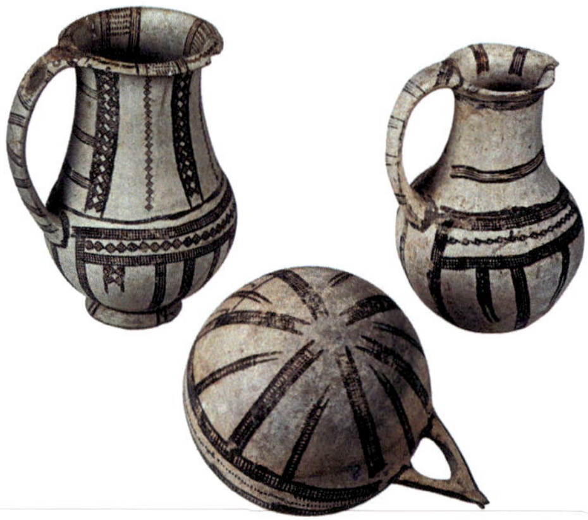

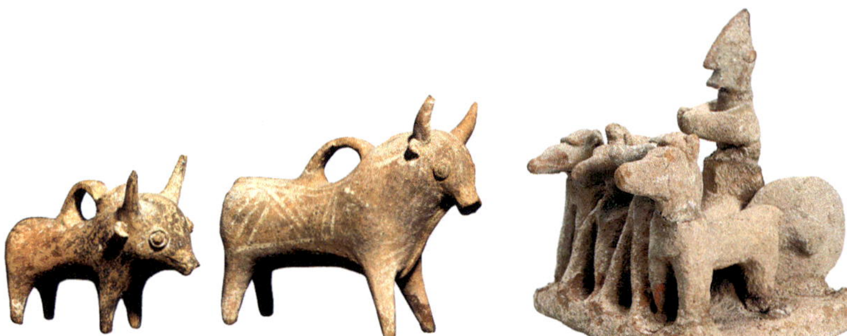

Italy and the Hellenic World

Pre-Roman Italy consisted of a mosaic of local cultures which were later absorbed by the Etruscans. The donation by the Caja Madrid Foundation has contributed to an interesting collection of ceramics from the so-called villanoviana culture" (9C-8C BC), from Daunia, c11-4 BC, and from Bucchero: three kylix, and an oinochoè or wine jar (6C BC).

Greek culture is represented in Montserrat by a small collection of jars of great beauty, from the Archaic and Classical periods. Some of them consist of black figures; others are already red, together with some sculptorical fragments.

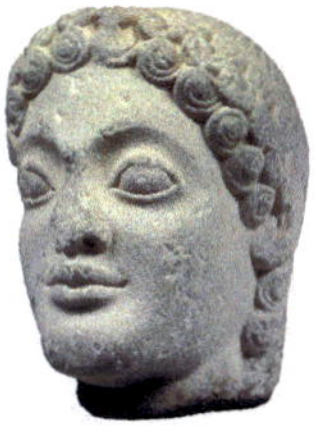

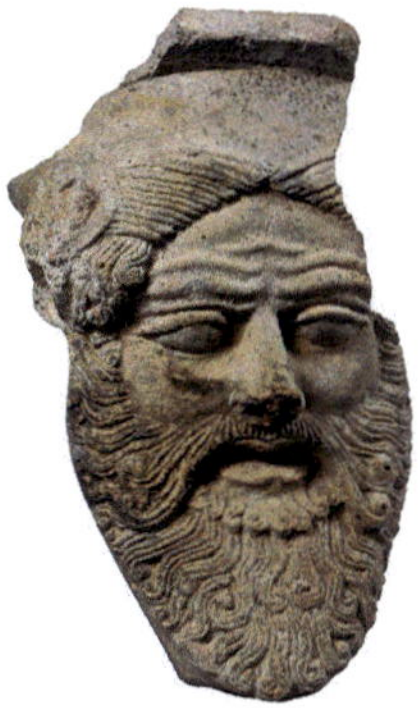

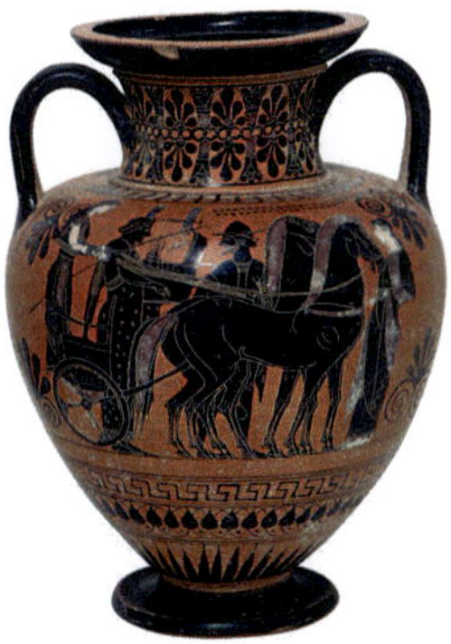

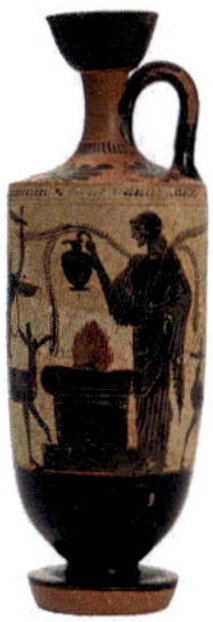

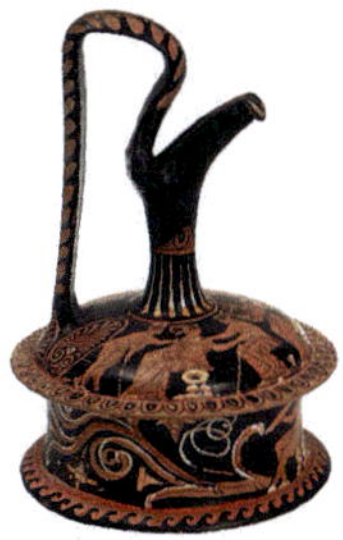

Head of kourós *or athlete, Pentelicus marble, from the Archaic period (6th-5th C BC), donated by X. Busquets.*

Head of Aquelous*, the most emblematic piece of work from the Etruscan culture we can find in Montserrat. In fact, it is a great glazed ceramic piece in the shape of Aquelous, the river god (4th C BC), donated by X. Busquets.*

Attic amphora *(c. 520 BC) The face depicts the black figure of Hera on a cart and the reverse, Zeus with Heracles and a satyr, donated by X. Busquets.*

Attic Lékithos *(4th C BC) depicts black figures and a sacrifice scene. Corynthian* ***Olpe*** *and* ***Aryballos*** *(c. 590 BC) shows gorgons and fantasy animals.* ***Procous*** *originally from Magna, Greece with red figures which represent the men's and women's toiletries (4th C BC), donated by Caja Madrid.*

Tanagra figures. *The Museum of Montserrat has a great and beautiful collection of over two hundred terracotta figurines from Alexandria and El Fayum, from the Greek-Roman era which presents a great variety in shapes and iconography. We can observe ancient Egyptian deities, which have been already Hellenized, religious scenes, customs, grotesque masks, animals... However, the most frequent ones are female heads with huge hairstyles and pierced ears where beautiful gold and silver earrings used to hang. A Tanagra figure from Beocia is of particular interest (3rd C BC), donated by X. Busquets.*

Roman glass*. It consists of a valuable collection of a hundred and eleven pieces from the first four centuries of the Christian era. They are mainly from ancient Palestine. Their shapes vary: bottles, flasks, cups, glasses, ointment bottles, small amphoras, balm receptacles, etc.*

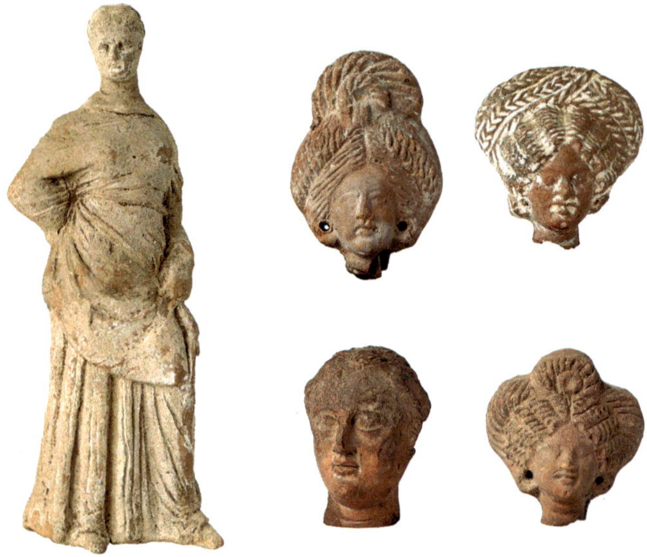

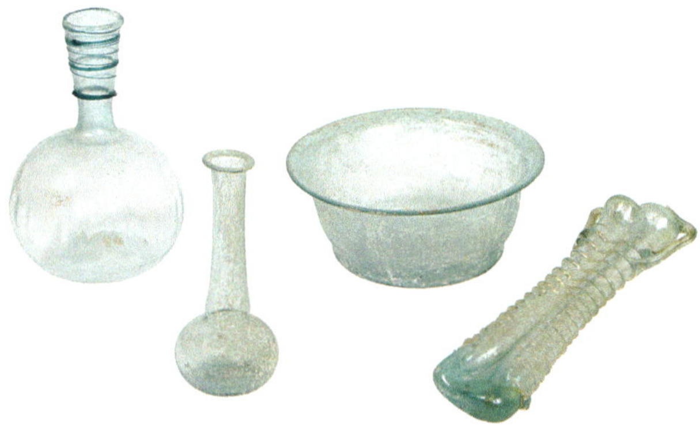

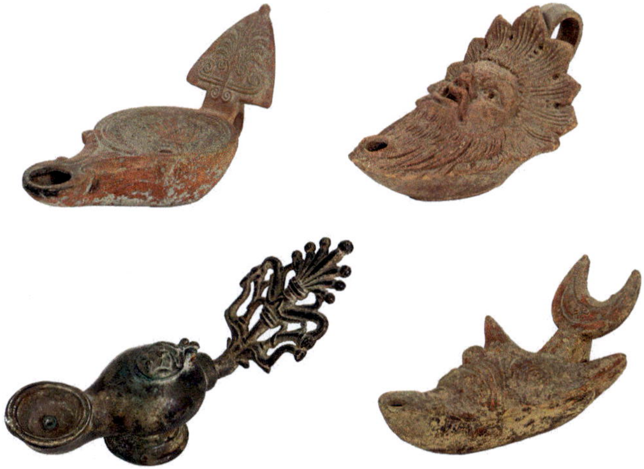

Roman lamps. *This collection is also outstanding. There are some items from the Hellenic period and some others from the Roman Empire which come from the East Mediterranean. Some have figurative decoration: the horse, the wild boar, a death mask, a woman's bust, Venus with her cloak blown out by Zephirus, Aphrodite Anadiomene, etc. Only the four largest and most luxurious ones are noted (1st – 4th C AD, donated by X. Busquets and Caja Madrid).*

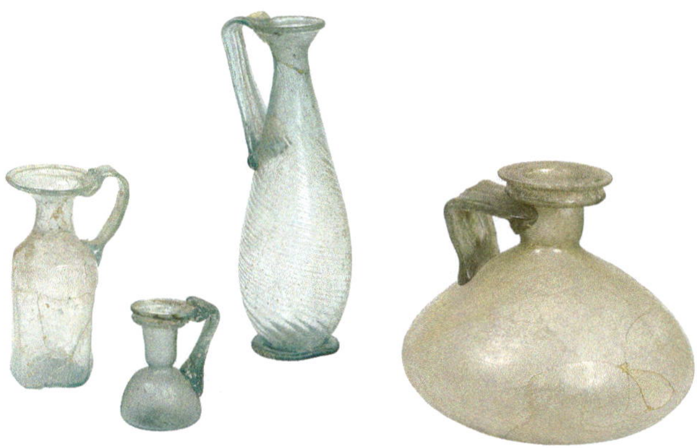

The Late Roman Empire and PaleoChristian culture

The decline of the Roman Empire at the end of the 3rd century and the active presence of Christianity which would dominate the 4th and 5th centuries strongly marked the history of Western culture.

The materials from this period in the Museum of Montserrat came almost exclusively from ancient Palestine and Egypt.

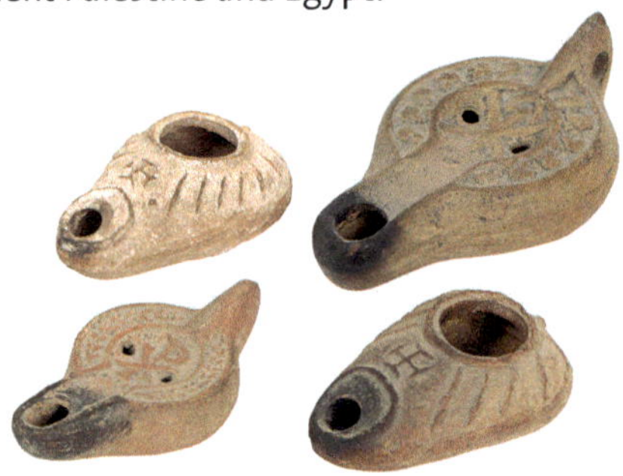

PaleoChristian and Proto-Byzantine Lamps *(4th-5th century AD). They date from the early Islamic period (6th-7th century). The first ones show the fitted anagram XP (christós) or IX (Ihesus-Christos), and the second ones feature the abbreviated inscription phos Christou fainei pasi (the Light of Christ enlightens us all), or Tês Theotókou (from the Mother of God).*

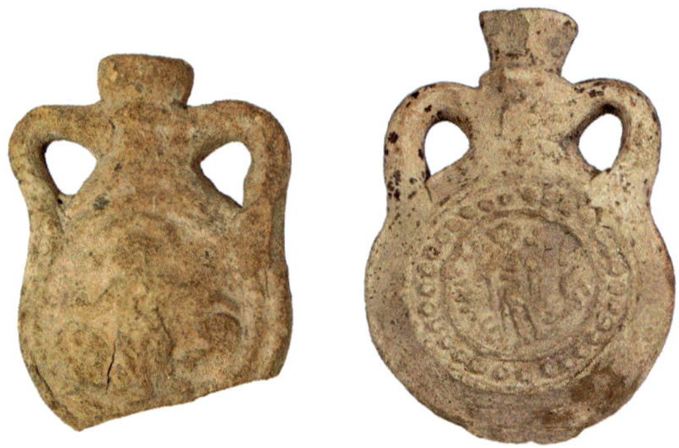

Ampullae *of Saint Menes*. *They were used as eulógya or souvenirs that the pilgrims could buy at the famous pilgrimage centre of the Abu Mina sanctuary, in Egypt. They were filled with the oil from the lamps which were burning in front of the saint's tomb and they took them home as a relic and a remedy. Saint Menas, the Coptic knight, was very popular. He is featured in a praying position, with a camel kneeling on each side, since he was the patron saint of camel riders as well as the protector of travellers and pilgrims on the way to the Holy Land. They date from the 6th and 7th centuries.*

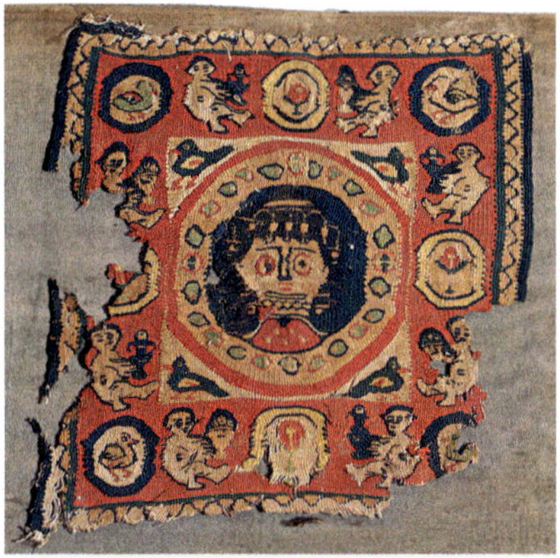

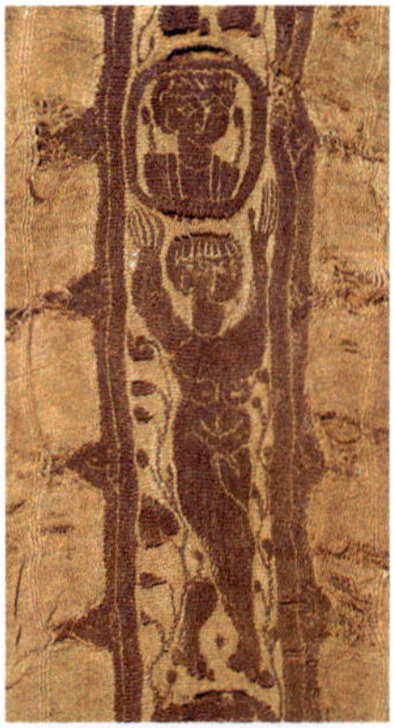

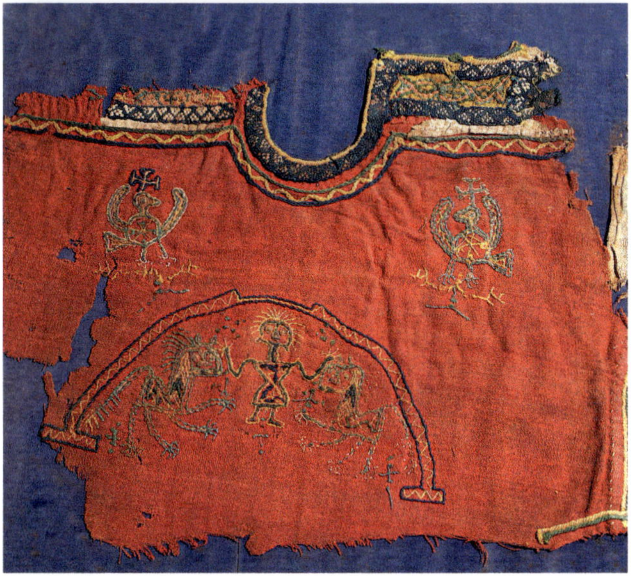

Coptic textiles. *From a scientific point of view, the most important elements of this section are without doubt, the Egyptian textiles from the Soler Vilabella collection. It consists of five full-size tunics, four large pieces and many pieces of outstanding textile and decorative value. The most outstanding pieces are a tabula from the 6th century, with imagery of a bust placed centrally and Nile wildlife, a piece which represents a coribante dancing with an imago clipeata (5th-6th centuries). A piece of red tunic bearing the scene of 'Daniel in the lions' den (6th century) is embroidered in a particularly bright and colourful way.*

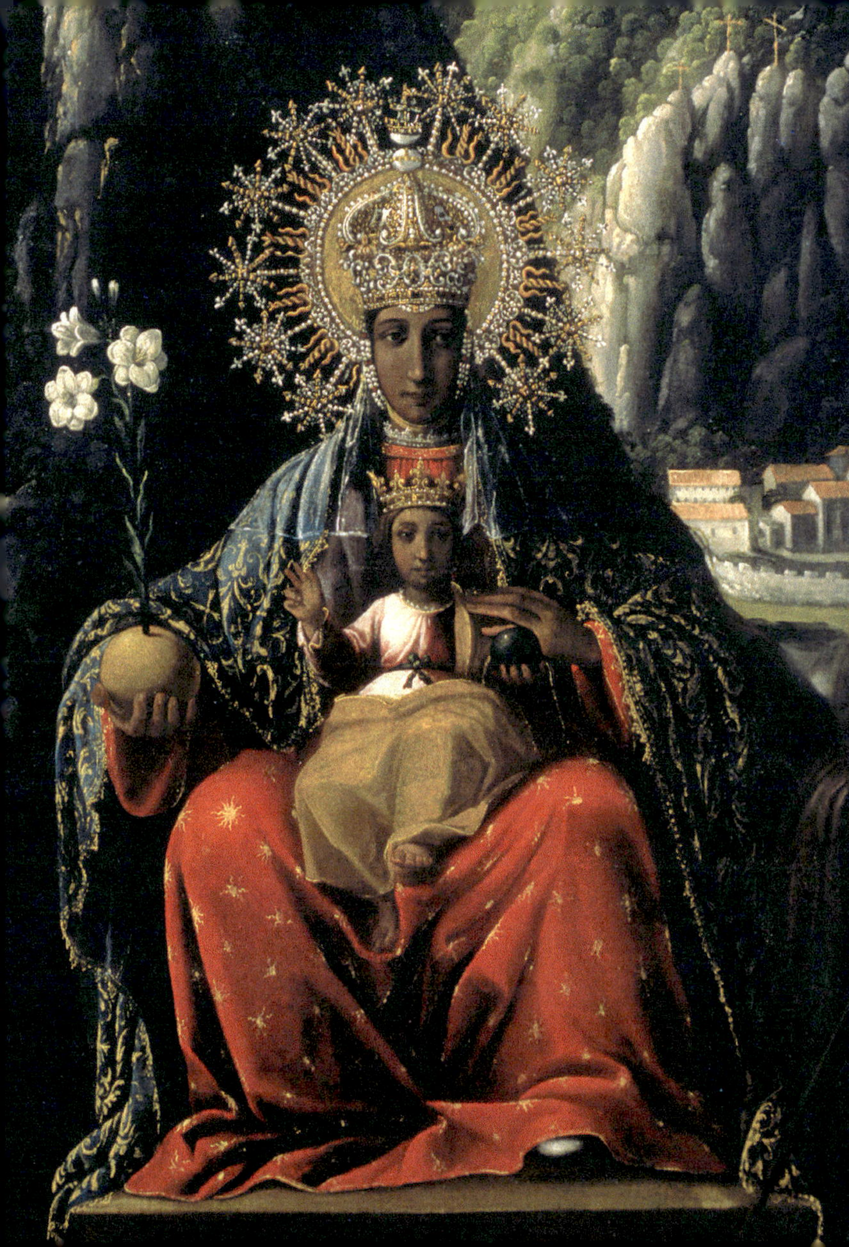

Nigra Sum. Iconography of Our Lady of Montserrat

This section offers a very diverse sample of artistic and popular materials which explains the iconographic evolution of this holy image and its expression in various art works. The pieces which are exhibited in the museum are only a tiny part of the total amount that there are in Montserrat. However, they allow us to state the old great universal devotion to the *Moreneta* (the affectionate name by which the Virgin is popularly known), who was declared Patron Saint of Catalonia in 1881. This is the reason behind the wealth of the national Catalan emblem (the four red bars on a golden background) which combines with Montserrat's (the mountain range with prominent peaks).

The location of all the material in a single room provides the visitor with a chance to appreciate in one place the permanent elements and the iconographic variations of the image. This exhibition has the educational purpose of showing how a single image can reflect a whole variety of tastes and artistic styles through the centuries.

The image of the Our Lady of Montserrat *is made out of poplar wood, polychrome and gold. It is 92.2cm high and weighs 17.1kg. It was made by an artist at the end of the 12th century and shares common traits regarding style and clothing with other similar images which are worshiped in Benedictine monasteries, such as Sant Cugats', and other exceptional ones such as the bishoprics of Vic, Girona and Occitania.*

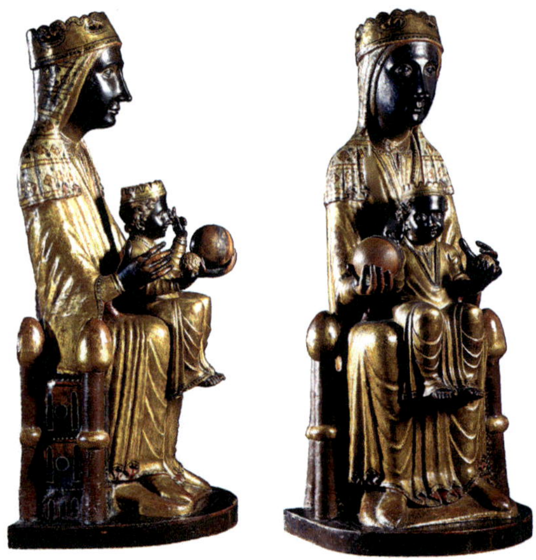

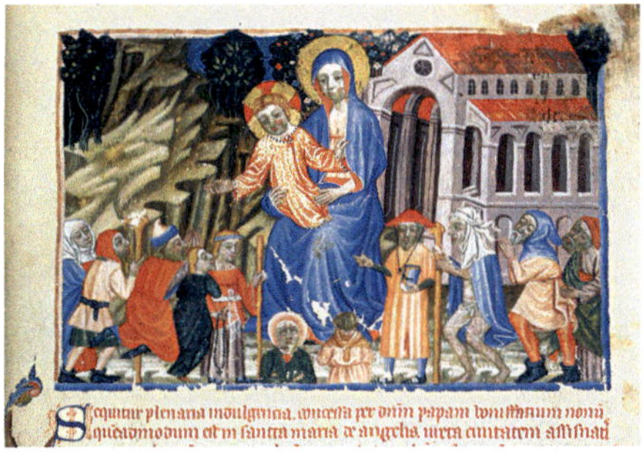

Our Lady of Montserrat with pilgrims.
A miniature from the Red Book dates from the beginning of the 15th century. A totally idealized image of the Virgin in relation to the original image in Montserrat welcomes and blesses pilgrims of various kinds and social classes. She is sitting on the rocks and the church of Montserrat can be seen in the background.

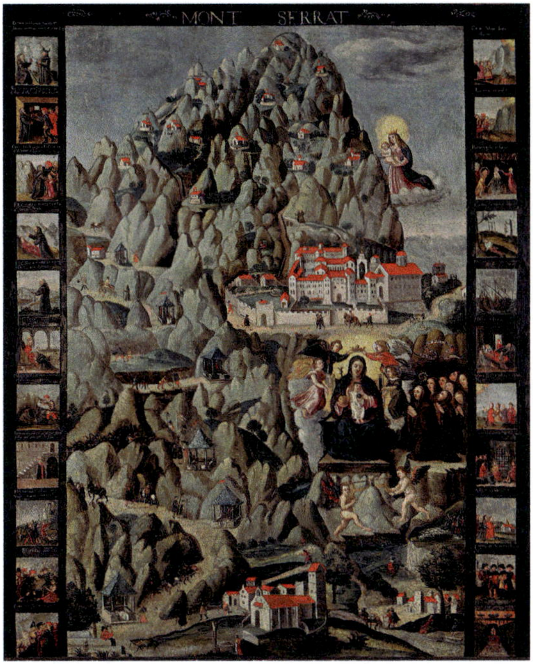

Montserrat.
Oil on canvas, 100 x 81cm. This is a version of a print from the beginning of the 17th century. It was an update of another one that Antonio Lafreri had thrown away in Rome in 1572. It features the Montserrat path to the walled monastery and the newly built church. Further up, the chapels can be seen. The figure of the Virgin Mary is placed where, according to tradition, her image first appeared.

Our Lady of Montserrat

by an unknown Madrilenian artist, c. 1639 (oil on canvas, 189 x 144cm). The accuracy with which the artist renders the monastery buildings, the clothing and the decoration of the image, known from older inventories, is surprising here. Though it has been suggested that the praying figure represents Saint Benedict, it is most likely to be a portrait of Abbot Juan Manuel de Espinosa (1637-1641), accompanied by his brother. The two characters portrayed on the other side are thought to represent Montserrat hermits. Below is the famous Montserrat school choir, organised into two in accordance with the original canons of baroque music: a vocal choir which is reinforced by a bassoon and another wind instrument. This excellent painting is the best graphic document we have from the magnificent Montserrat from the 17th century.

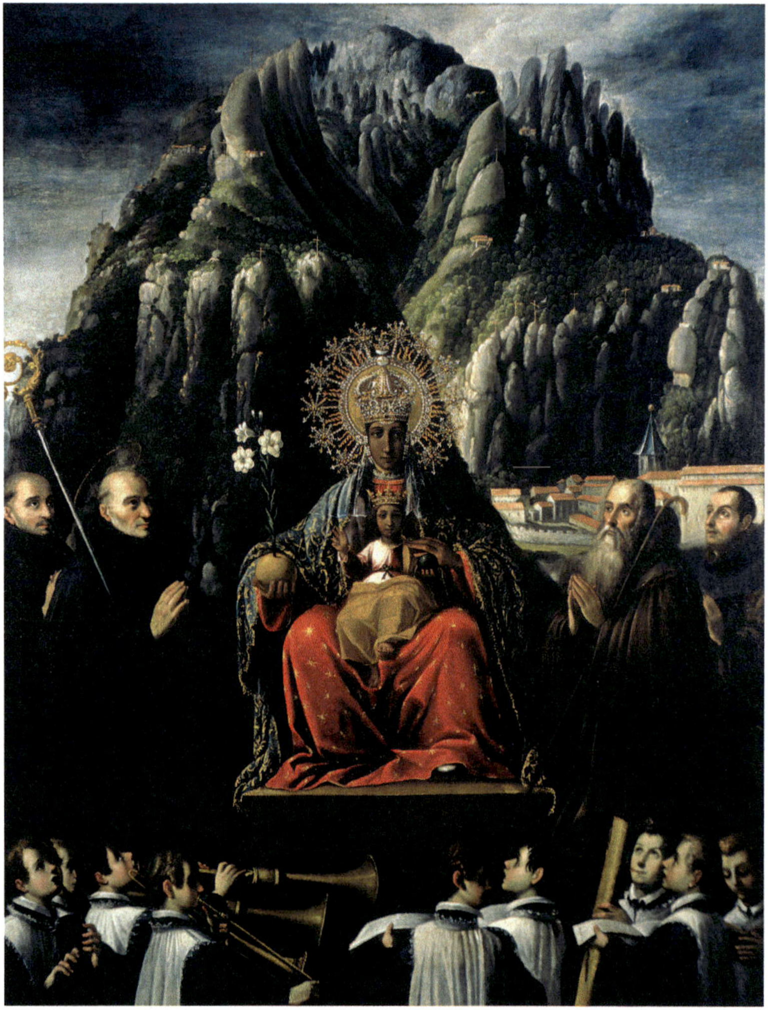

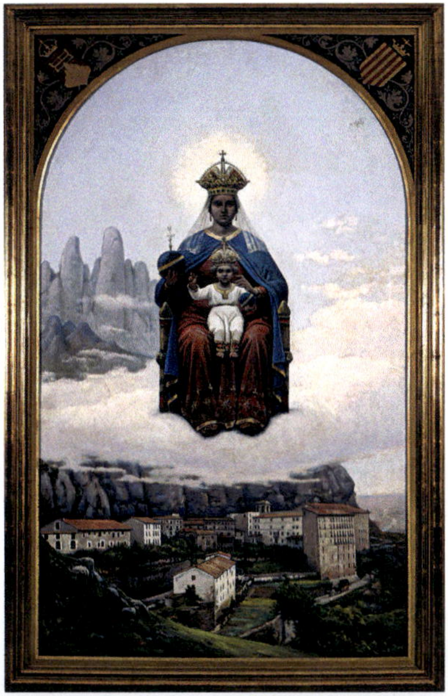

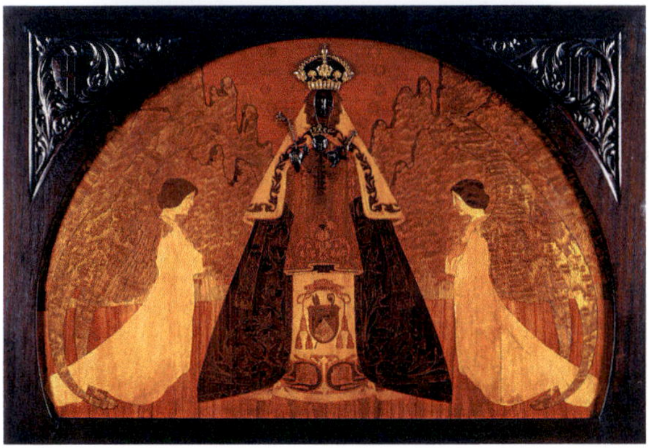

Virgin Mary of Montserrat *by* ***Joaquim Vayreda*** *(1883) Oil on canvas, 190 x 110cm, donated by Gas Natural, 2003. It comes from the chapel of the Palace of Graz (Austria), which was the residence of Prince Alfonso de Borbón y Este, from the Carlista branch of the Spanish royal family. It portrays with great accuracy the beautiful crown which Catalans offered by popular subscription to the Virgin image on its canonical coronation in 1881 and proclamation as the Patron Saint of Catalonia. This painting is another example of the collective enthusiasm which was caused by that celebration.*

Modernist Marquetry, Gaspar Homar *c. 1905. It has a bronze frame, 85 x 125cm, donated by the Espar Ticó brothers. The image is represented with rich flared clothing which was typical of the iconography of the 19th century and first third of the 20th century.*

With all the pieces which were recovered from the remains of the destroyed monastery, only this ***alabaster image*** *(60 x 38 x 34cm) which represents the Virgin of Montserrat sitting in a monk seat, could be restored. It was made by an Italian or perhaps an Italian inspired artist from the latter third of the 16th century.*

Devotional statuettes *from the Our Lady of Montserrat present diverse shapes which often have nothing to do with the original image which is worshipped in Montserrat. However, the mountains become the emblem which fully identifies the image. As an example, we present the image of the Virgin bearing white scars. She is sat straight and holds the Child who is busy sawing the mountain of Montserrat. This looks like a pillar featuring its old chapels, (polychrome wood, 61.5 x 32 i 17cm), 18th century, donated by Celestina Terré, Widow of Farré.*

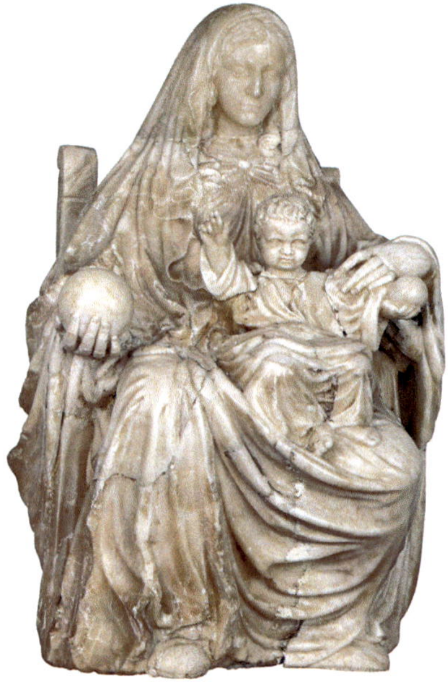

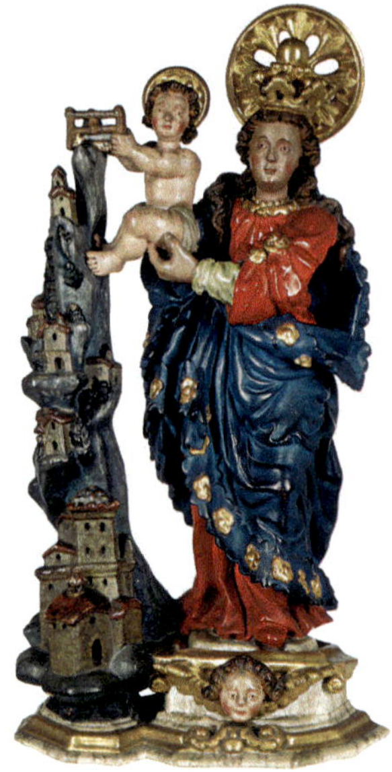

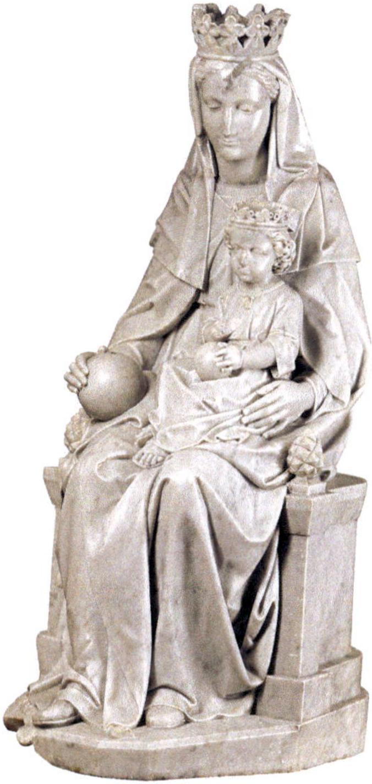

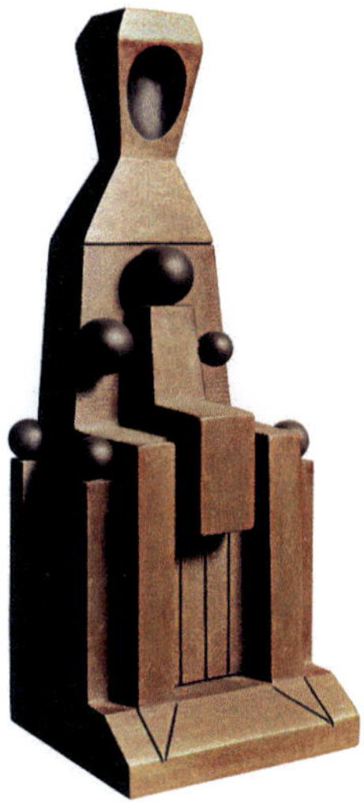

Romantic representations of the Our Lady of Montserrat usually stress her sweet face, disregarding the original model. This beautiful image is made out of marble (96 x 62 and 60cm) and presided the so-called Festivities of the Millenium of 1880 in the ***Holy Cave****.*

Our Lady of Montserrat *by* ***Josep Maria Subirachs****, 2001, slightly polychrome wood (70 x 22 and 22cm, donated by Caixa del Penedès). Modern artists have never stopped representing the most emblematic religious image of the Catalans. This is the reason why it can be immediately identified from a collection of geometrical shapes.*

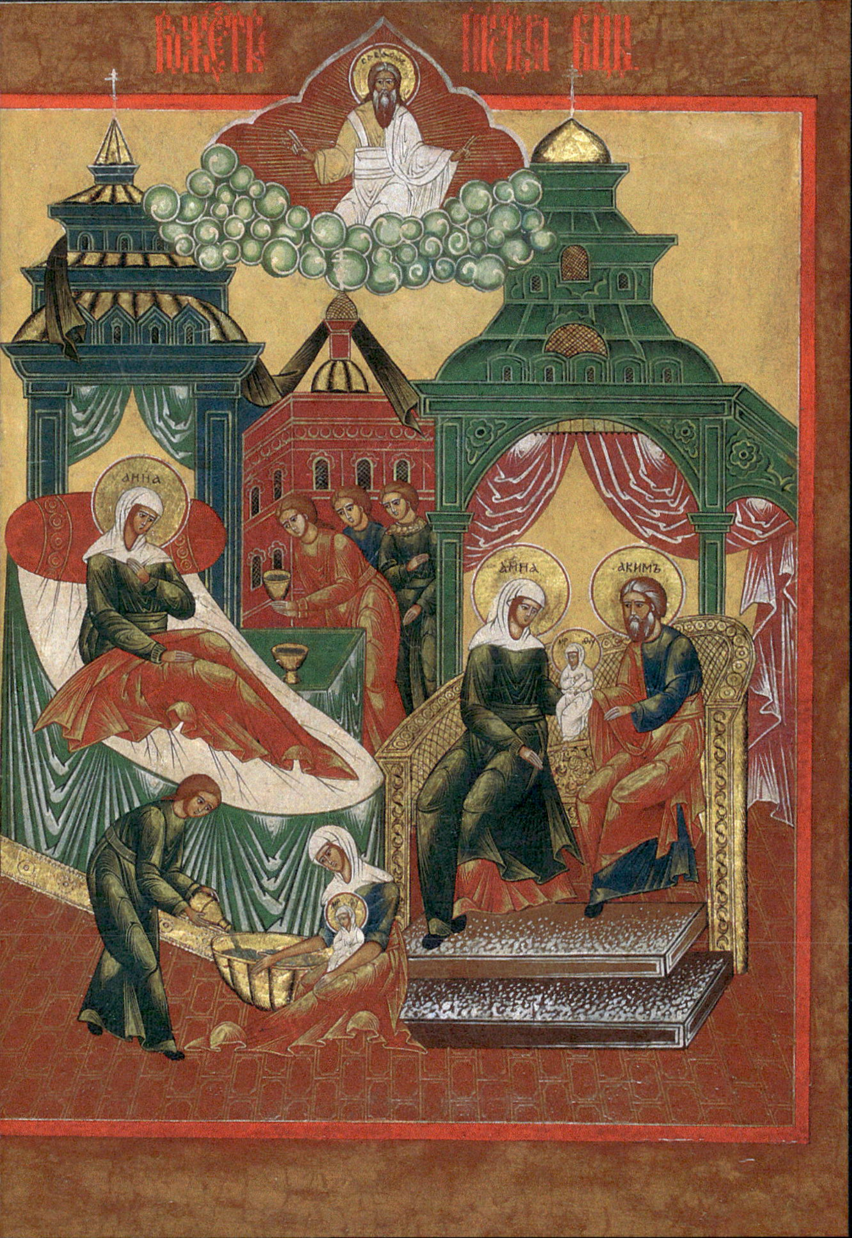

Joyful light
Icons from the Eastern Church

The **Mandylion** *and the history of the* **Holy Face**, *(53.5 x 45cm). Russia, 18th century.*

The face ***acheiropoietós*** *(which has not been made by human hands) of Jesus Christ is the logical principle of every iconic exhibition. The three lower medallions narrate the double origin of the image according to tradition (the Veronica, and the portrait of Jesus by order of King Abgar) and its discovery and later veneration in the old city of Edesa.*

The small icon of the **Crucifixion**, *Russia, school of Paleh, 18th century (24 x 19.5cm), is incredibly beautiful and gracefully combines the Byzantine tradition and Italian Naturalism.*

Phos Hilaron (Joyful light) is a beautiful chant and the most typical from the Hesperinón (Evening Service) of the Byzantine liturgy. It is sung whilst lighting up the church or house lamps at sunset. The "Joyful Light" is Jesus Christ "the Light of the World". The exhibition of iconography of the Eastern Church aims to present the faces and mysteries, the glory of Jesus Christ, fos ek fotós (Light of Light) according to the Creed of Nicea (325), the glory of the Virgin Mary (la Theotokos), the glory of the Saints and the religious calendar festivities. This is achieved by representing the saint icons, wrapped in a golden light which is so typical of the Byzantine churchs. The whole collection makes up a very homogeneous, holy and sacramental collection, set in our world in order to reflect the glory of the 'Uncreated Light', as the Eastern Church believes it to be.

This section of icons from Byzantine-Slavic Churches has a totally special character in the message of the Museum of Montserrat. It is a world which is outside our world, where the golden light of Byzantium shines. This light allows us to see and contemplate the icons in an environment which is typical of a holy space, rather than an art gallery. It is only here where the icons find their own place and communicate a message which transcends simple, human nature and creativity: it is theology in practice.

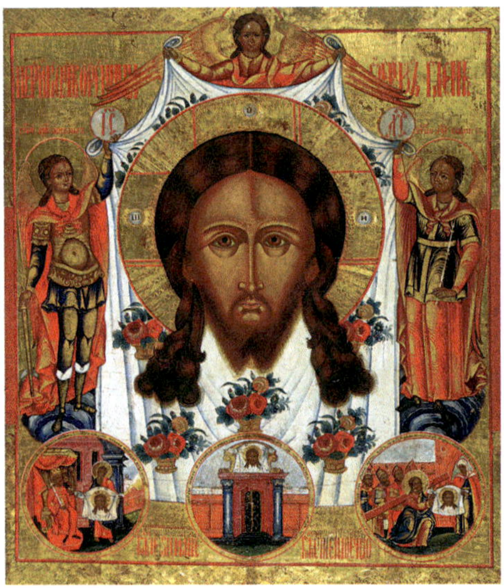

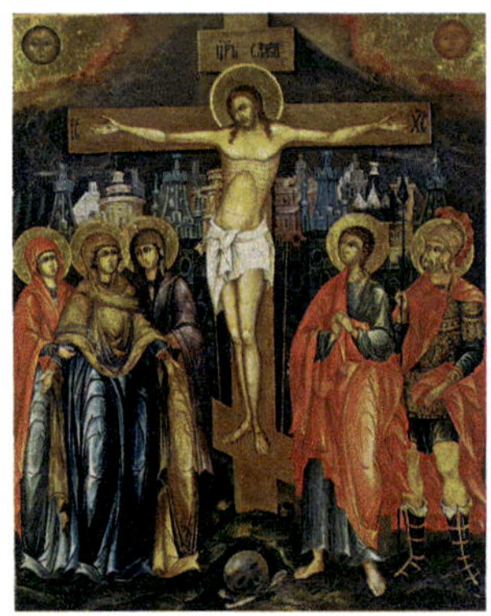

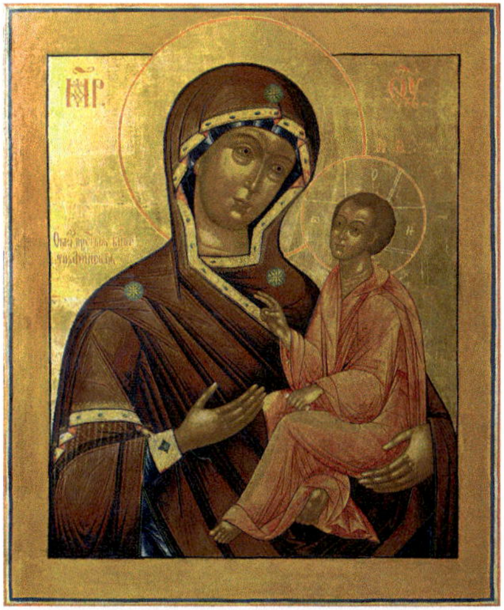

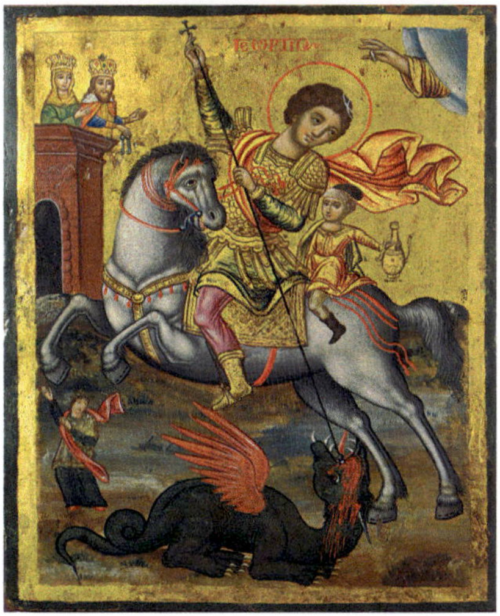

Virgin Hodighitría *(which shows the path), Russia, 19th century (89 x 74cm). This is the most common way of representing the Virgin Mary: as an empress, with a purple cloak and three stars on her head and on each of her shoulders, which symbolizes her virginity. With her left arm she supports the blessed child and with her right, she indicates the path.*

Saint George *riding a horse (Hágios Georgios éphippos), Greece, 18th century (22.5 x 18cm). The Eastern Church considers Saint George to be a Megalomàrtir (the great martyr) a martyr worthy of 'special' worship. The icon features the legend of the fight with the dragon in order to free the princess. A little boy with a small jar is on the horse's posterior. This is a reference to the famous miracle by which an emperor's son was healed by the oil of the martyrion of the saint, which is in Lidda (currently in Israel).*

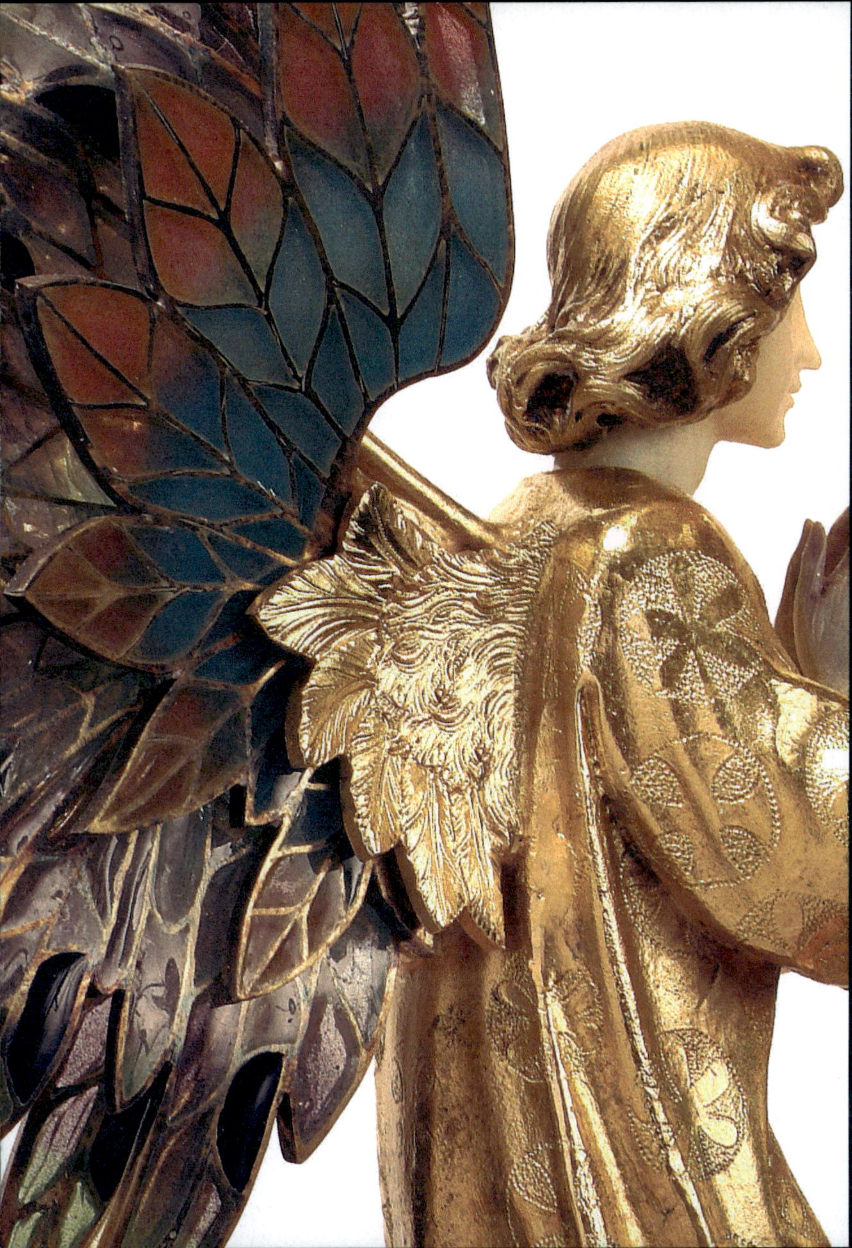

Religious
precious
metal wo

In the old Montserrat, prior to the 19th century revolutions, the religious precious metal work made up the main artistic collection of the Monastery and the Sanctuary. Unfortunately, most of that treasure was lost. However, since the Monastery was restored, a new collection of work from the 19th and 20th centuries of great material and artistic value, has been built up. Other old pieces have been added to form a beautiful collection, from which only a small part is exhibited.

By its very nature, the religious precious metal work is a living element of the liturgy, which is the axis of monastic and sanctuary life. Its natural exhibition place would be the Main Vestry, next to the ceremonial clothing, but for practical reasons the most important pieces are in the permanent exhibition space of the Museum.

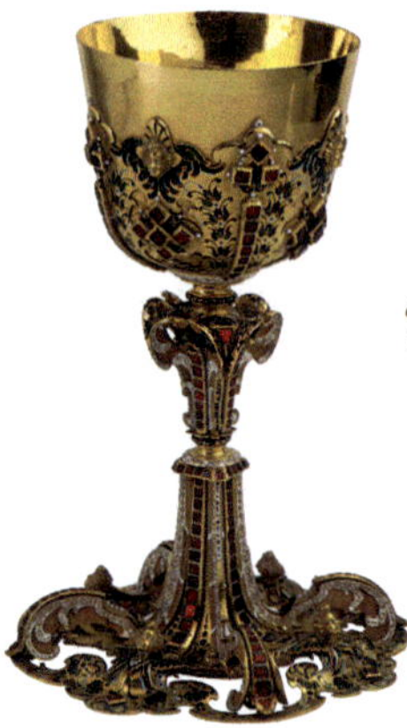

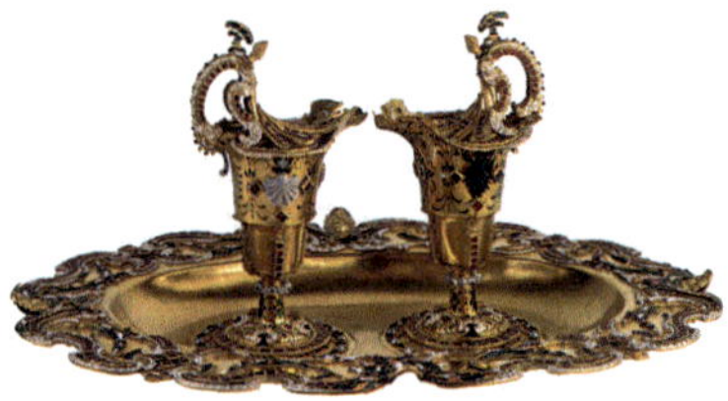

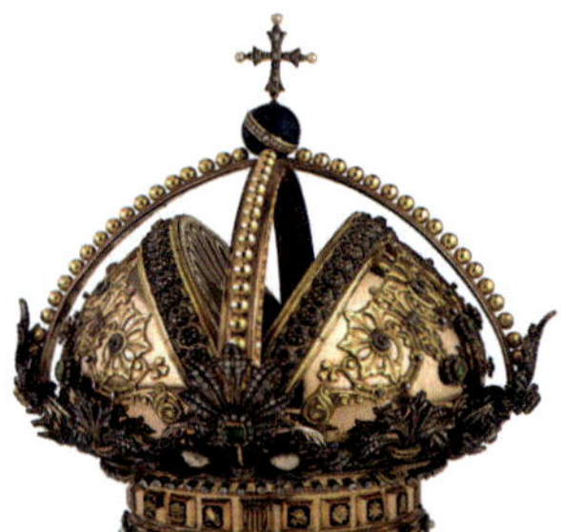

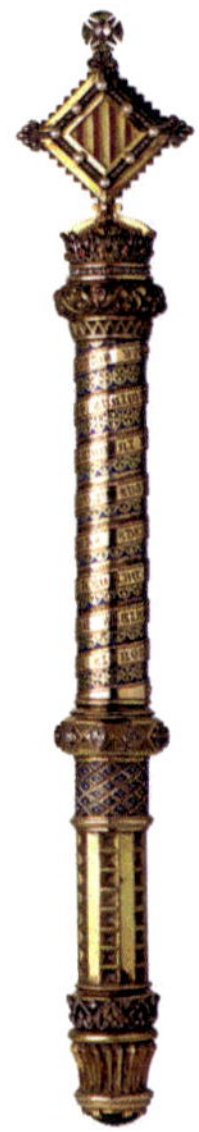

***Emperor** Fernando III of Austria's **chalice and wine glasses**, offered in gratitude for the imperial troops' victory over Gustavo Adolfo of Sweden in Nordlingen (1634). This has always been one of the most beautiful jewels of the Vestry of Montserrat, having survived many wars and confiscations.*

***Precious Crown** and scepter of the Virgin Mary of Montserrat, by the Barcelona artists Joan Sunyol and Francesc Cabot (1820-1895). They were paid for by popular subscription on the occasion of the formal coronation and proclamation of the Moreneta as the Patron Saint of Catalonia (1881).*

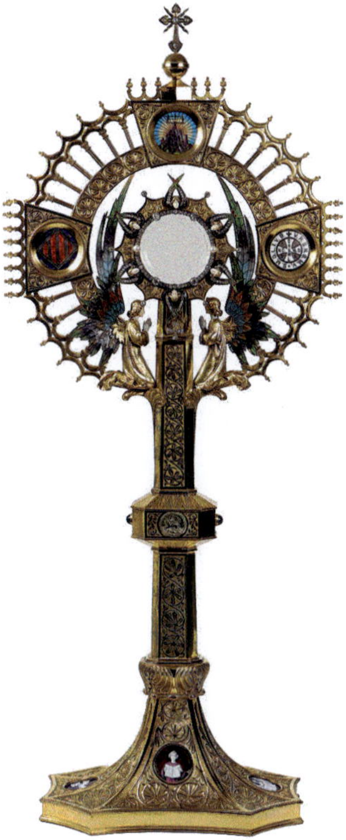

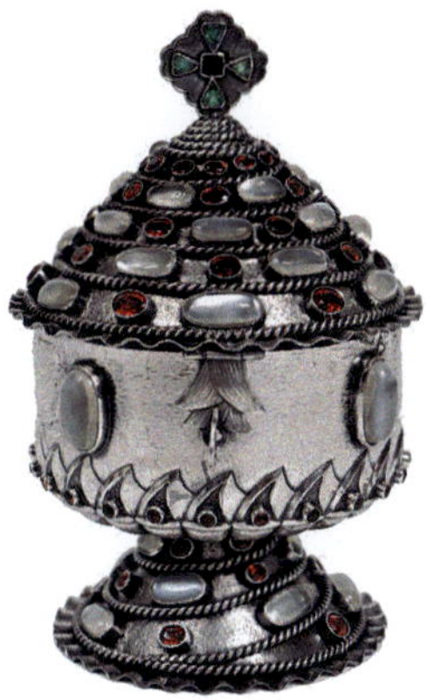

The Basilica Vestry contains an extraordinary collection of mobile and fixed displays as well as processional ones. The most outstanding ones are those by ***Joaquim Cabot Rovira*** *(1891) in a pre-modernist style and by* ***Lluís Masriera*** *(1872-1958), which is fully modernist from 1903 and shows some beautiful angel figures with translucent, enamelled wings.*

The prestigious master ***Jaume Mercadé i Queralt*** *(1887-1967) is the author of an entire altarpiece collection (cross, candelabra, holy cups) in Art Deco style, which represented an original innovation within religious art at the time (1922).*

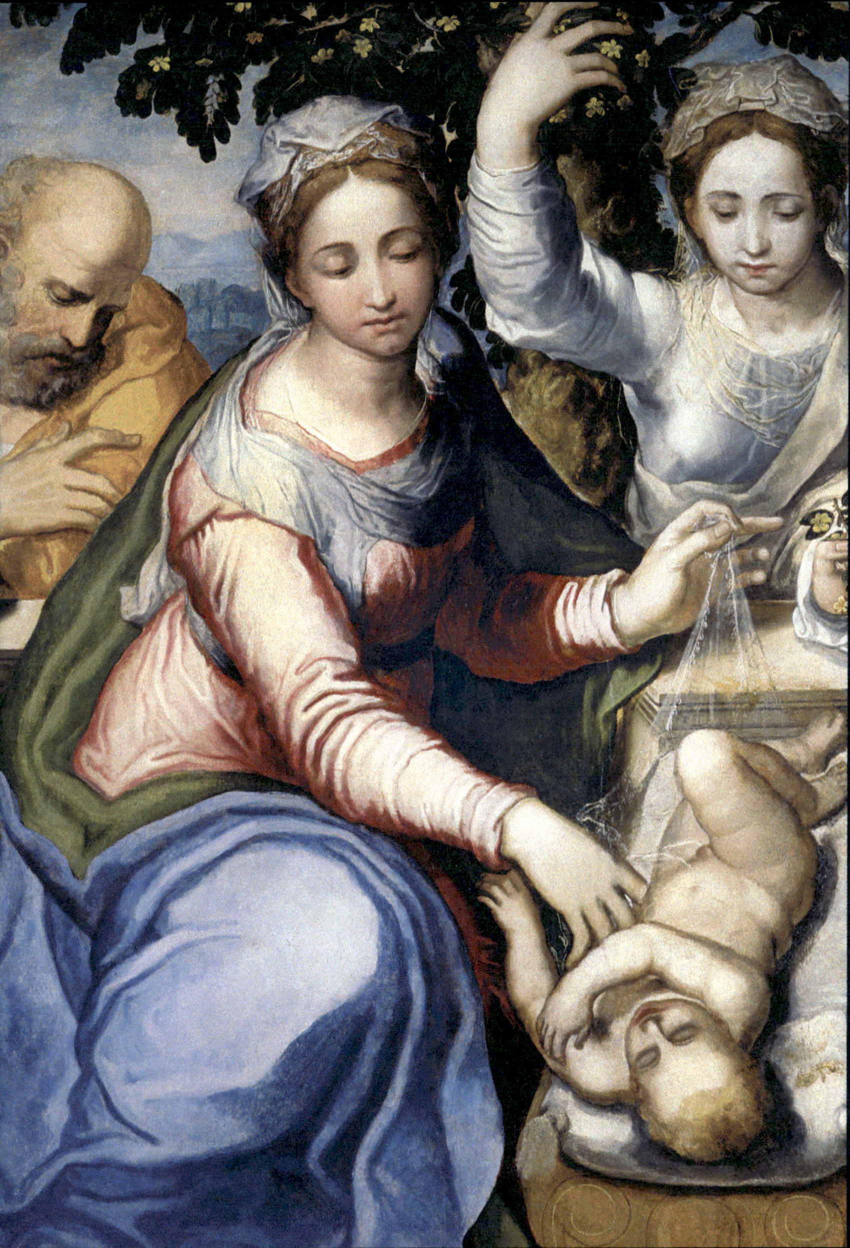

Antique paintings (13th–18th centuries)

Most of the collection of antique paintings of the Museum of Montserrat was recently acquired. Abbot Antoni M. Marcet (1878-1946) ordered it bought in Rome and Naples between 1911 and 1920. Later on, Abott Aureli Mª Escarré (1908-1968) tried to enrichen the collection with new acquisitions and donations. It consists of about 250 pieces, from which only a third are exhibited.

In spite of the fact that many of the paintings were acquired with attribution to authors of great prestige, the critical study of the collection has clearly demonstrated the considerable standard of more than half of the bought paintings.

There are original paintings by premiere artists. Good and relevant work by second class artists is common. Very interesting original paintings by unknown or yet to be known artists can also be seen.

The acquisition of this small art gallery illustrates a very characteristic facet of the magnanamous character of Abott Marcet, who spared no effort to turn Montserrat into a high quality cultural centre in the international Benedictine world.

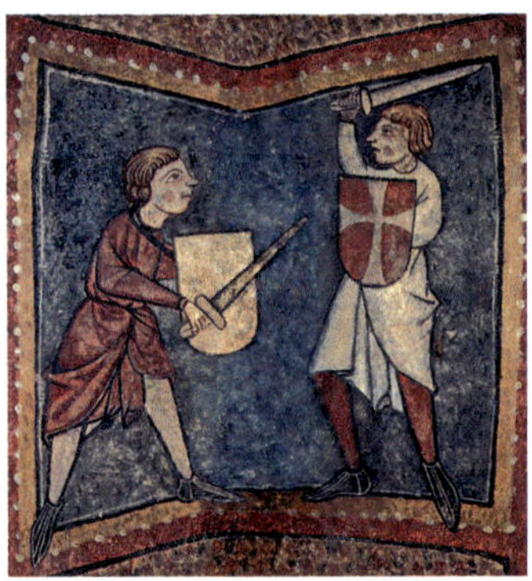

Training of a Templar, *fragment of wall painting from the 13th century (109 x 100cm), donated by X. Busquets.*

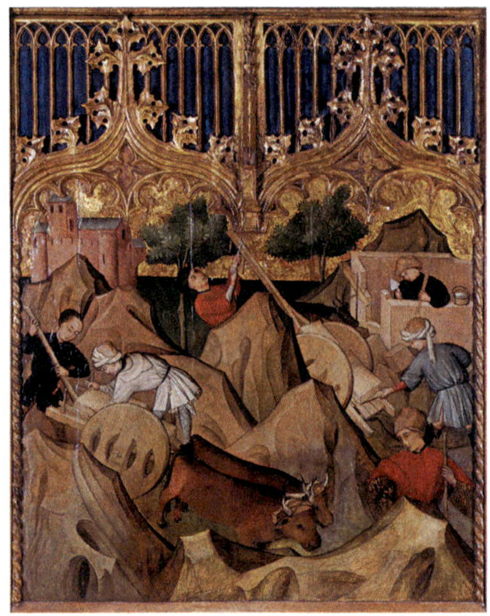

Maestro Nicolás Francés, *(actively working in León between 1434 and 1468).* **Construction scene** *(118 x 91.5cm), donated by X. Busquets.*

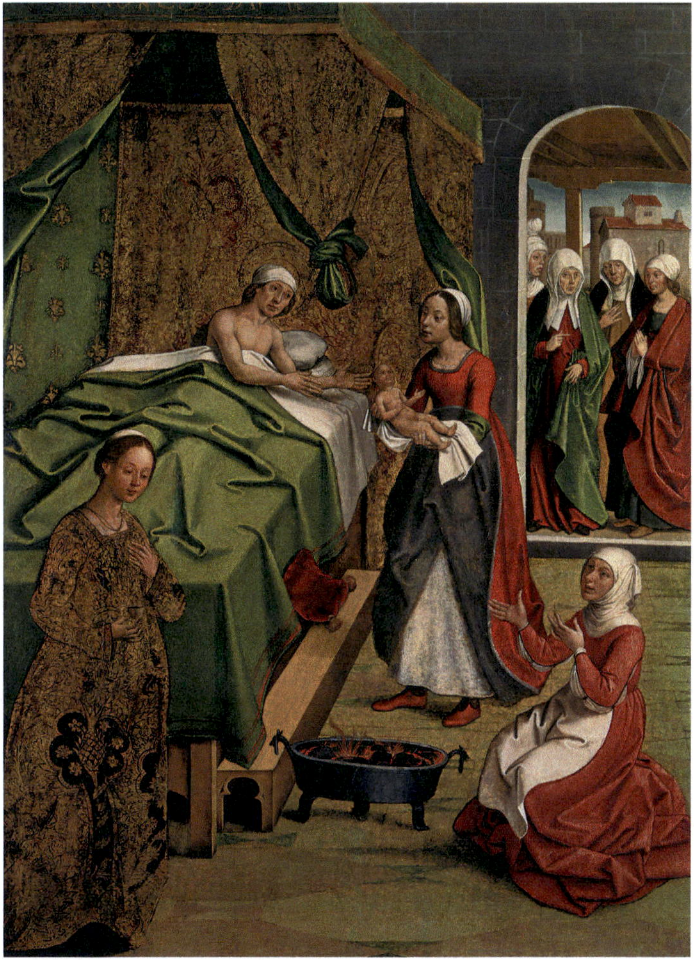

Birth of the Virgin, ***Pedro de Berruguete*** *(c. 1450-1504), yet another tablet featuring the* **Death of the Virgin**, *from the same altarpiece (128 x 95cm). Berruguete is one of the best Castillian masters and he introduced the Renaissance in the Peninsula. He integrates diverse elements: his characteristic Spanish realism flows together with the narrative detail of Flemish art that shows its links to the Italian Renaissance.*

The collection of antique paintings of Montserrat also consists of a great series of Flemish paintings. The following ones should be noted: **Jan Bruegel de Velours** (1564-1625), all the series of the passion by **Frans Francken** (1542-1616), and several by unknown artists which have yet to be studied. The two portraits of the fable writer **Jean Lafonaine** and his wife by the Perpignan born painters **Jacint Rigau** (1659-1743) and **Gabriel Revel** (1643-1712) are also remarkable.

The best pieces in the collection belong, without a doubt, to the Italian school. There is work from the Quattrocento, such as the sides of a triptych by Siena born artist **Benedetto Bonfigli** (Unknown-1496). There is also work from the Cinquecento, by influential painters such as Raphael or Michaelangelo, **Marco Pino** (1512/1522-c. 1579), or **Andrea da Salerno** (c. 1480-1530/1531) such as the centre piece of Montecasino altarpiece, which is devoted to *Saint Bertrario* and dates from the year 1513. The best painting from the whole collection is undoubtedly the '*Saint Jerome Penitent*' by **Caravaggio**, which is worthily accompanied by tens of his followers' paintings.

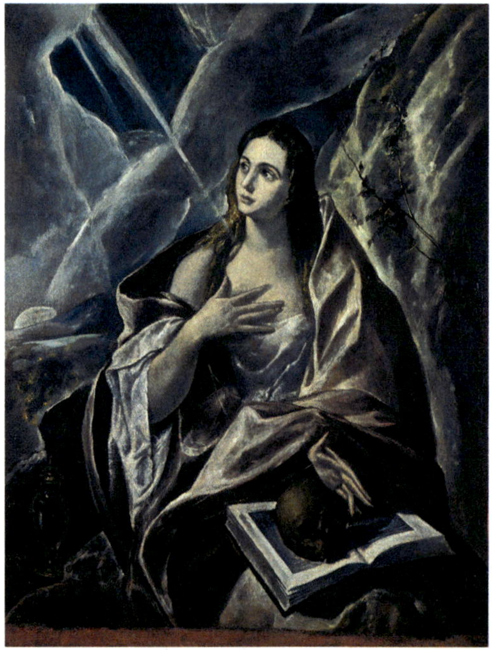

El Greco *(1531-1614) is the foremost Spanish Mannerist painter. His work of* **Penitent Saint Magdalene** *(57 x 44cm) is a grisalla painting in the Venetian style, which was most likely painted at the time he moved to Spain. Later on, it was used for larger and brighter pieces.*

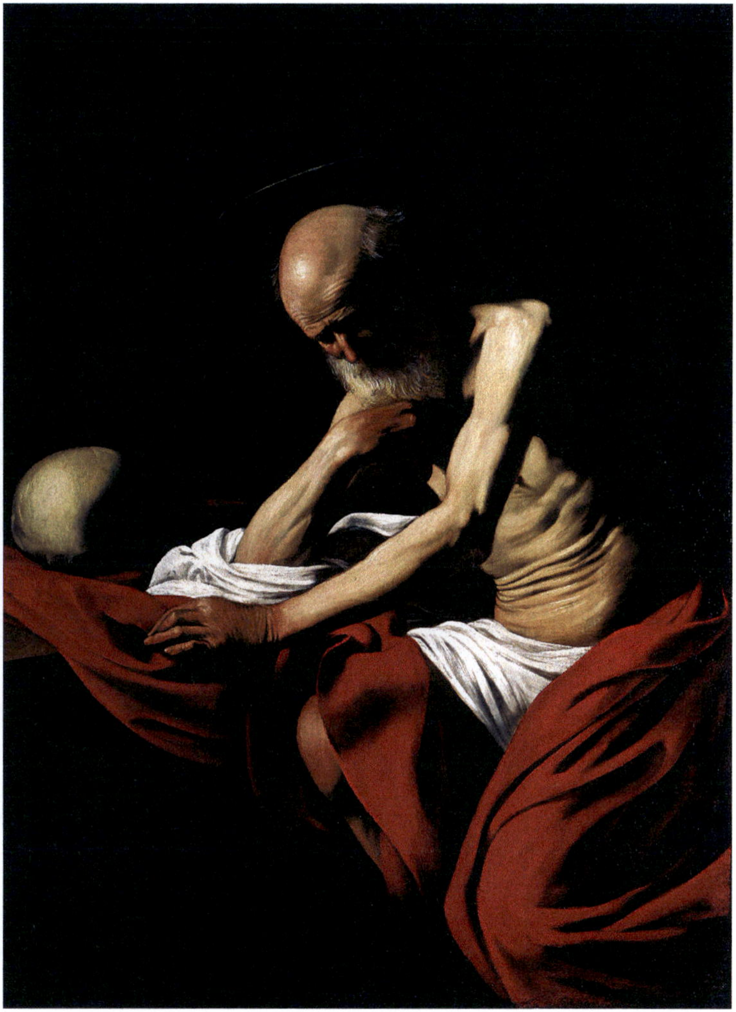

Saint Jerome Penitent
c. 1605 (oil on canvas, 140.5 x 101.5cm).
Michelangelo Merisi da Caravaggio *(1571-1610) innovated the painting of his time with a new naturalistic sensitivity and a vision which was based on the chiaroscuro. The figure of an old man in pensive mood, roughly illuminated by a single light and barely covered with a white loin cloth and a red robe, stands out from the dark background and takes on a great prominence and evocative realism.*

Jesus in the Garden of Getsemani *(174.5 x 125cm) by the Naples born artist* ***Andrea Vaccaro*** *(1604-1670) is a signed copy and one of the most important ones by this painter. Among Caravaggio's followers, whose work is exhibited in the Museum of Montserrat, the following ones are worth mentioning:* ***Rutilio Manetti*** *(1571-1639)* **The Last Supper** *(173 x 232.5cm),* ***Matthias Stomer*** *(c. 1600-c. 1650)* **The Adoration of the Shepherds** *(127 x 180cm),* ***Giovanni Battita Spinelli*** *(working between 1630-1660),* **Saint Sebastian Tended by Saint Irene,** *(102 x 130cm),* ***Luca Giordano*** *(1634-1705)* **Head of a Martyr** *(early age, 60 x 50cm),* ***Corrado Giaquinto*** *(1703-1766)* **Jesus Tied to a Pillar,** *(95 x 70cm), etc.*

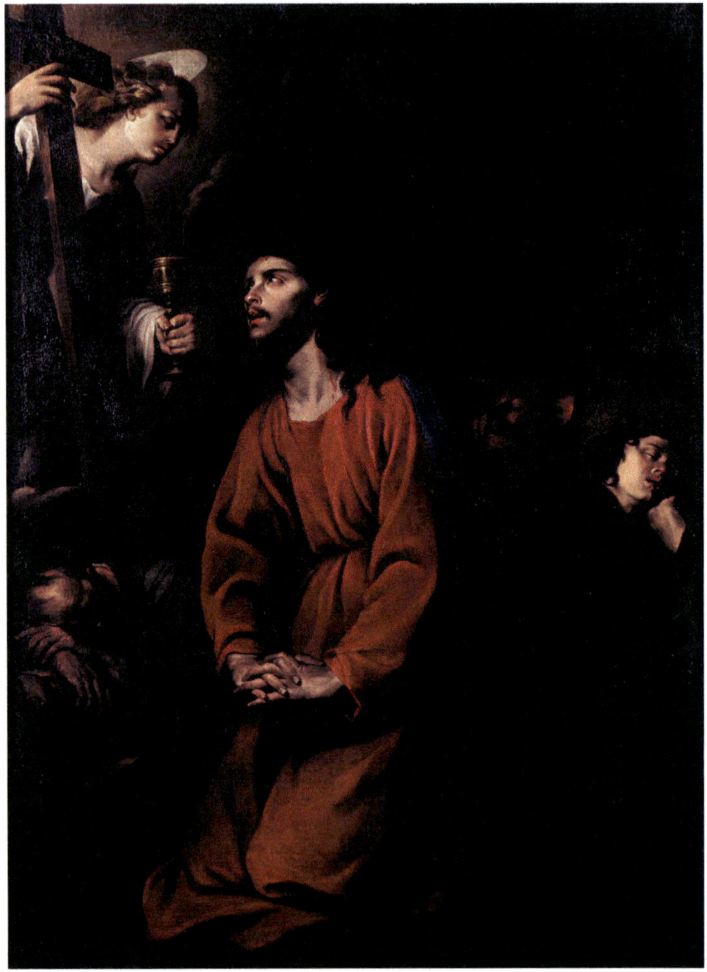

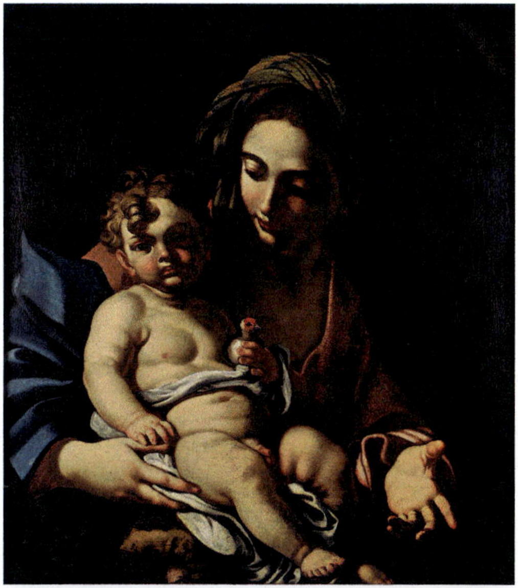

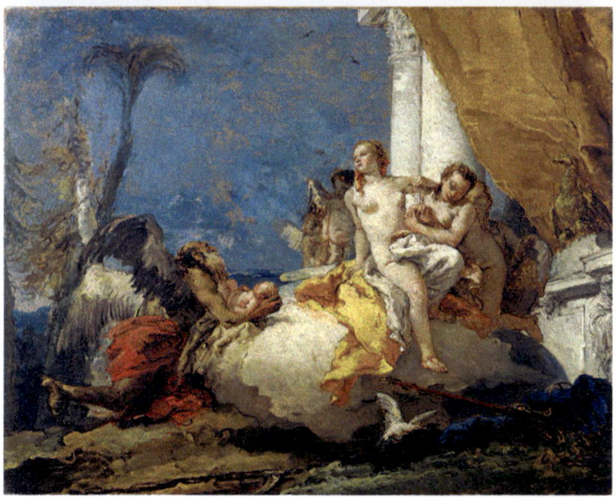

Francesco Solimena *(1657-1747) is another artist from Naples who still used, although partially, Caravaggio's chiaroscuro but his work became complex and theatrical, in the spirit of the 18th century:* **Virgin and Child** *(68 x 59cm).*

Other Italian painters of interest round off the collection: ***Sassoferrato*** *(1609-1685)* **The Virgin in Prayer** *(73.1 x 61cm),* ***Nicolò de Simone*** *(doc. 1636-1655)* **The Adoration of the Shepherds** *(128 x 155cm),* ***Pietro Bardellino*** *(1728-1819)* **Saint Anthony of Padua** *(112 x 87cm),* ***Domenico Corvi*** *(1721-1803)* **Lament over Hector's Body** *(159 x 220cm).*

Gianbattista Tiepolo *(1696-1770),* **Happiness for the Birth of Francis I of Austria***, 1768 (46 x 57cm), painted during the painter's Spanish period. Chronos (Time) introduces to Venus, who personifies the Augsburg Royal House, the newborn, Francis, who is destined to become emperor.*

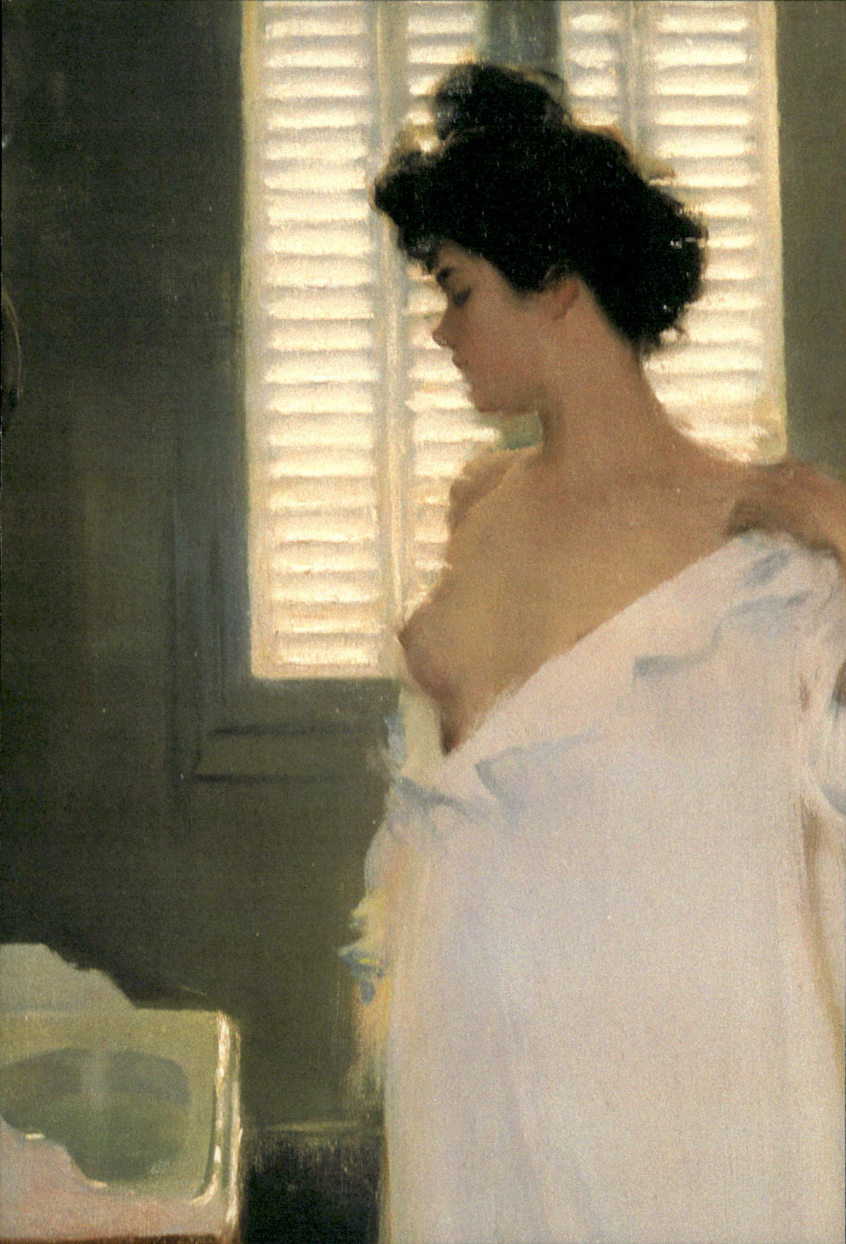

Modern painting (19th–20th centuries)

The Realist movement in painting, which was led by Courbet during the years 1850-1870 in Paris, was echoed by the painter ***Ramon Martí Alsina*** *(1826-1894) in Catalonia. This can be considered as the starting point of the Catalan Modern Painting School; he was also forerunner of a change towards a brighter and more colourful painting style which became successful in the 80s, with the restoration of the Borbons. Good examples of his work from this period are* **Portrait of the Painter Tusquets**, *c. 1865 (124 x 74.5cm), donated by J. Sala Ardiz and* **Fishermen's Pier in Barceloneta**, *(97 x 200cm), donated by J. Gassó Vidal.*

Other realist painters worth noting are also ***Simón Gómez*** *(1845-1880), Antoni Caba (1836-1907) and* ***Ramón Tusquets*** *(1838-1904).*

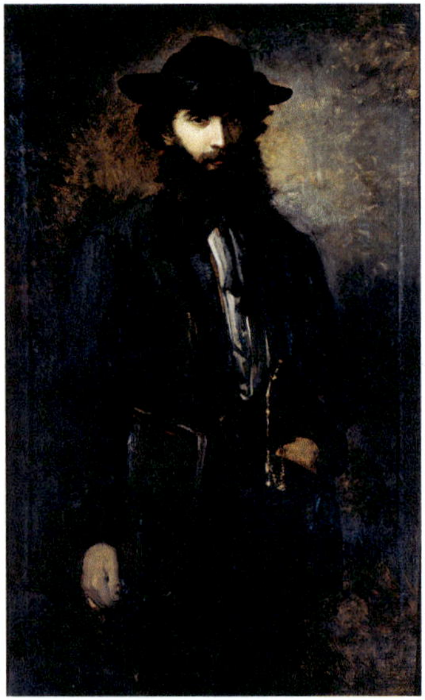

Since 1982, the Museum of Montserrat has exhibited a painting collection from the 19th and 20th centuries, which offers a very comprehensive and selective panoramic perspective of the Catalan painting from this period. This painting is undoubtedly one of the best exponents of Catalan culture and personality. Almost all the art work comes from private donations, mainly from the Ardiz Room collection (1980) and the architect Xavier Busquets i Sindreu (1990). The example of these patrons has been imitated by other people who have regarded the Museum of Montserrat as an ideal place for the preservation, study, exhibition and communication of artwork of public interest.

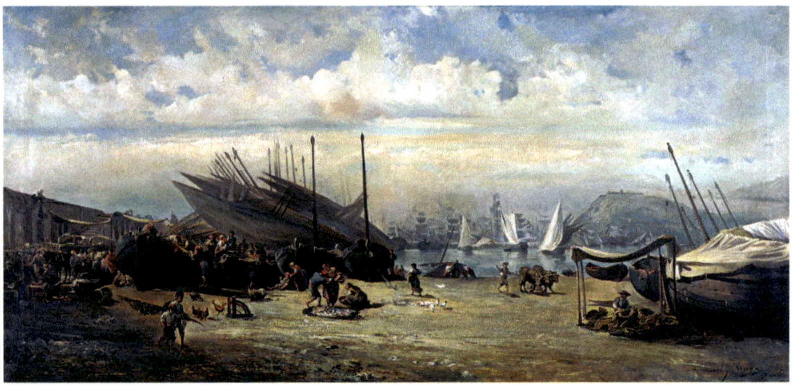

This section of the Museum is the largest and worthy of the highest qualification in the museum world "ranking", especially regarding Catalan painting, since it is difficult to find such an acomplished and balanced selection outside the National Art Museum of Catalonia. It currently consists of about two hundred and seventy figurative paintings which cover the mid 19th century to the mid 20th century.

The exhibition route follows a more or less chronological order, through schools and painters. It covers both floors of the building, with the peculiarity that it starts from the upper floor and it is necessary to go downstairs (or take the lift) to finish the itinerary.

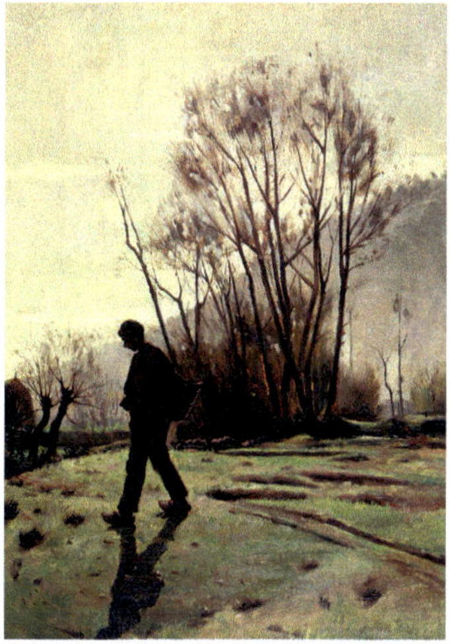

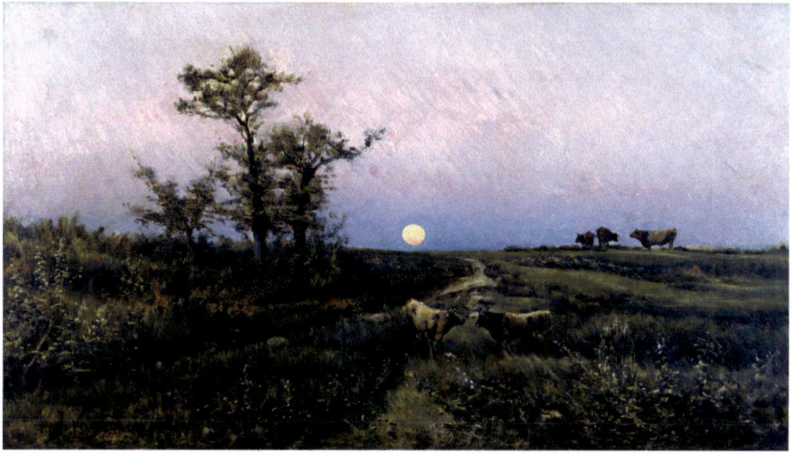

The Catalan equivalent to the French Barbizon or Fontaineblau painting school is the ***Olot School****. It meant a return to nature and an idyllic hymn to rural life and traditions, typical of green Catalonia, with its flourishing springs, quiet waters, cows, sheep, carts brimming with hay, etc.*

Joaquim Vayreda. *(1853-1894)* **Young Peasant Man**, *c. 1871 (55 x 37cm), donated by J. Sala Ardiz,* **Moonrise**, *1883 (75 x 133cm), donated by J. Sala Ardiz.*

It is somehow surprising to find in Montserrat a small collection of paintings by the great masters of French Impressionism, which can hardly be seen in official museums or in painting collections from the Peninsula.

Claude Monet *(1840-1926)* **Etretat. Porte d'Aval** *(73 x 100cm),* ***Alfred Sisley*** *(1839-1899)* **Thaw in Port-Marly** *(38 x 55cm),* ***Camille Pissarro*** *(1830-1903)* **Old Peasant Woman. Indoors in Moret** *(64 x 54cm),* ***Auguste Renoir*** *(1841-1919)* **Pornic Beach** *(62.5 x 72cm), and a pastel painting by* ***Edgar Degas*** *(1834-1917).*

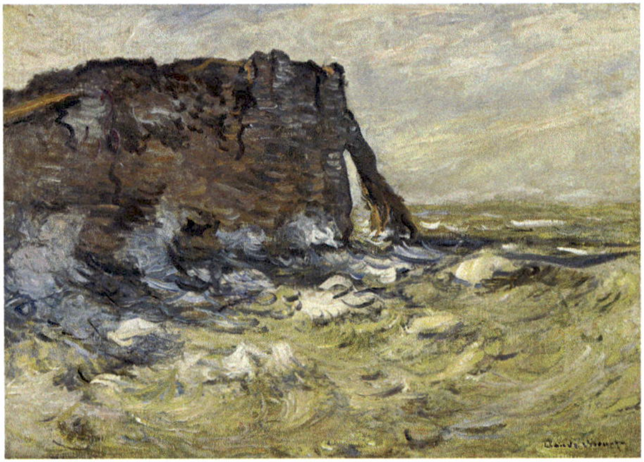

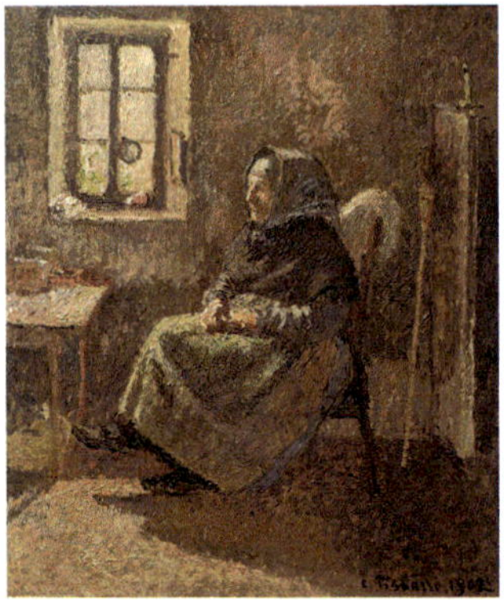

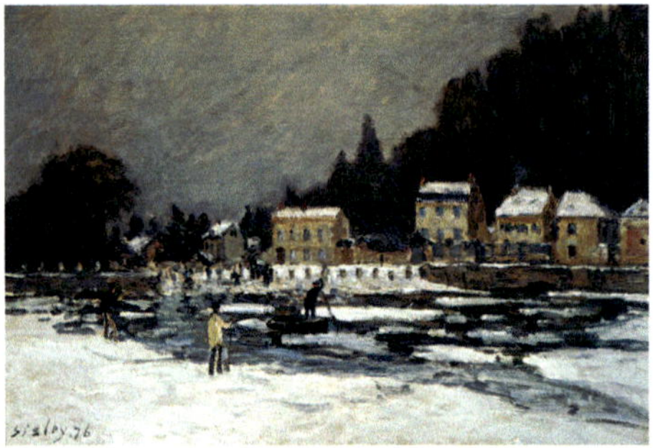

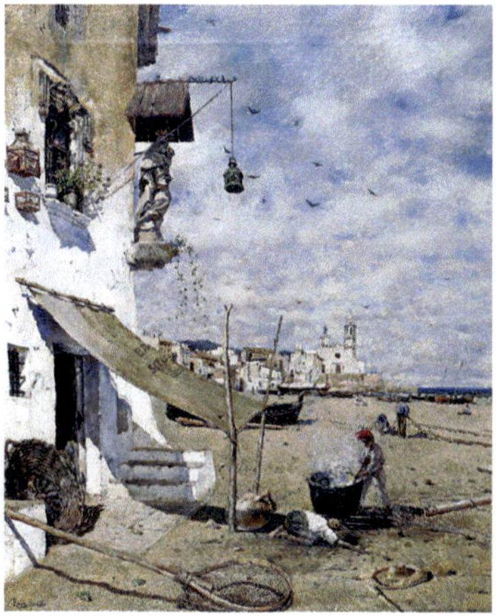

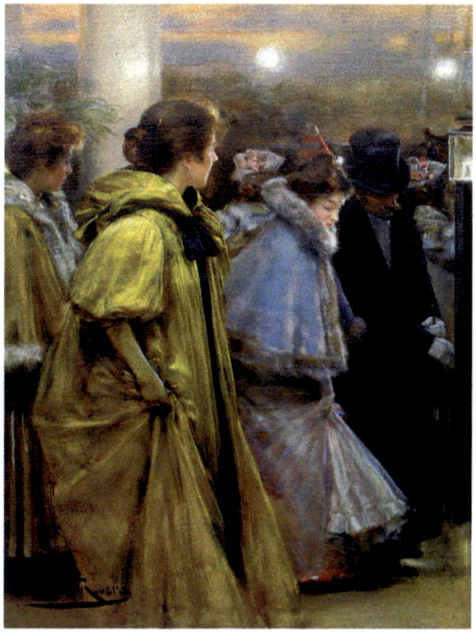

Among the Catalan painters from the 80s, the following ones are worth mentioning: ***Joan Roig Soler*** *(1852-1909), painter of several coastal towns landscapes, such as this one of* ***Sitges****, c. 1885 (57 x 45cm), donated by Pere Sensat,* ***Arcadi Mas Fondevila*** *(1852-1934), who alternated bright landscapes with the genre of church interiors.*

Romà Ribera *(1848-1935) specializing in the female figure, he captured as nobody else could the tactile quality of clothes and clearly illustrated the high society atmosphere. A good example of this is his work* **Exit from the Dance**, *1913, (82 x 62cm), donated by J. Sala Ardiz.* ***Josep Cusachs*** *(1851-1908) was both a career soldier and a painter who specialized in equestrian and military themes.* ***Eliseu Meifrén*** *(1859-1940) was also a fine landscape painter.*

Catalan Modernism *is the most important artistic phenomenon in the twenty five years around the turn of the 19th and 20th centuries. It was a very plural movement. Some artists showed preference for Naturalism while others tended toward Symbolism. There are the very religious ones who were members of the Artistic Circle of Sant Lluc, such as* ***Joan Llimona*** *(1860-1926),* ***Dionís Baixeras*** *(1862-1934) whilst others kept within more secular spheres. The most Symbolist painter, strongly influenced by to Art Nouveau was without a doubt,* ***Alexandre de Riquer*** *(1856-1920),* **Awaiting the Birth**, *c. 1898, (350 x 200cm).*

The best Catalan Modernist artists are well represented in the Museum of Montserrat amongst all the major Catalan paintings.

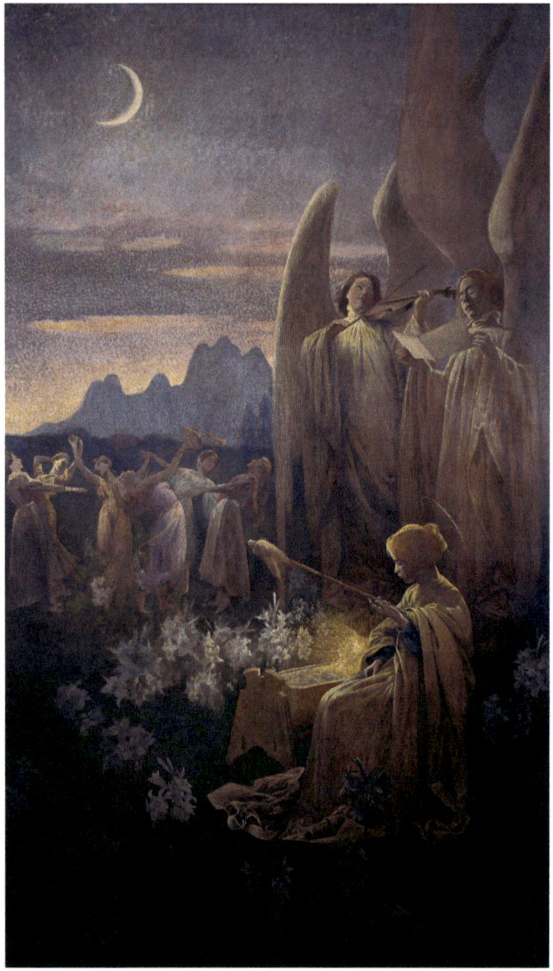

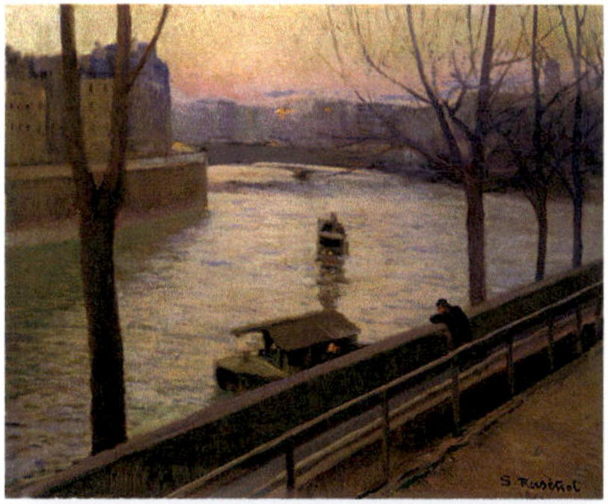

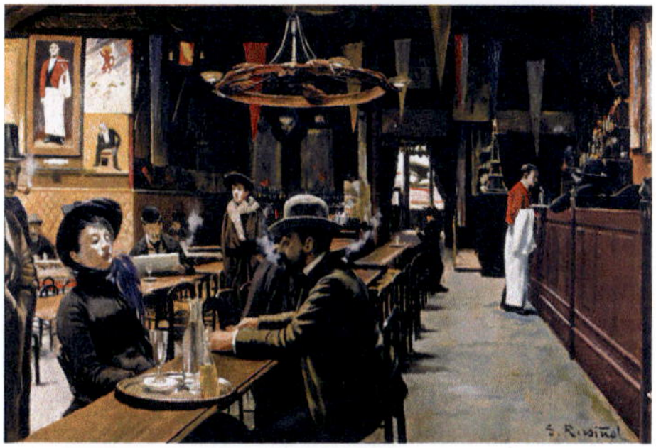

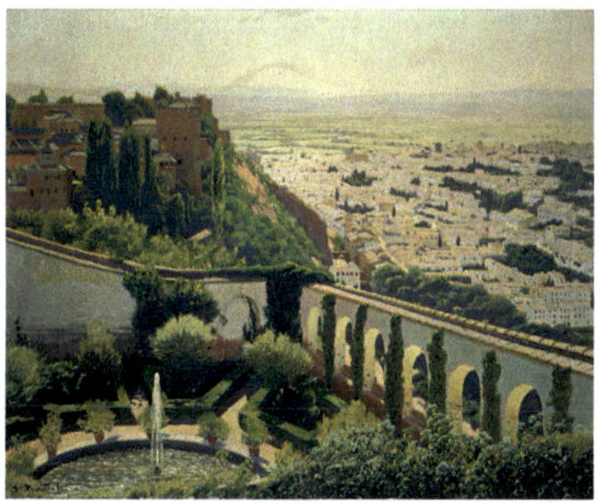

Santiago Rusiñol
(1861-1931) has fourteen outstanding paintings in the Museum of Montserrat. They belong to different periods, from the Montmartre period to the Spanish gardens one. Rusiñol was a comprehensive artist and a cultural agitator, whose influence was felt in the Peninsula as well as in Europe. His paintings **Twilight. Île-Saint-Louis**, *1890 (50 x 60cm),* **Montmartre Café**, *1889/1890 (80 x 116cm) and* **Generalife. Granada**, *1898 (93 x 110cm), donated by J. Sala Ardiz, are worthy of special mention.*

Ramon Casas *(1866-1932) was the Modernist painter with the greatest force and expressive intensity. He was especially interested in the female figure. The collection in Montserrat consists of twenty two oils on canvas. Some of them are his most famous masterpieces. The following are particularly worth mentioning:* **Decadent Young Woman**, *1899 (46.5 x 56cm),* **Madeleine**, *1892 (117 x 90cm) and* **Before Bathing**, *1895 (725 x 60cm), all of them donated by J. Sala Ardiz.*

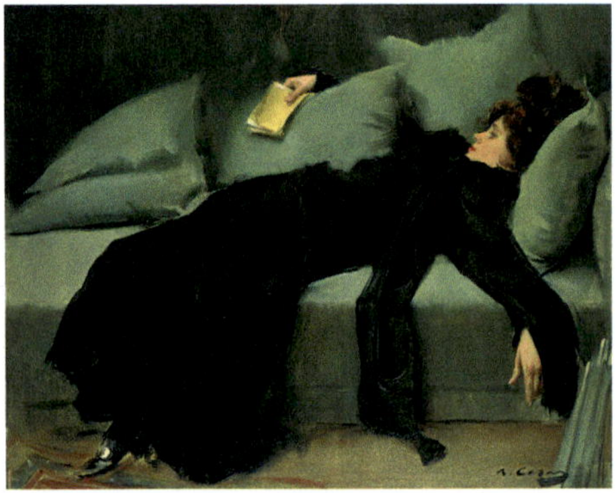

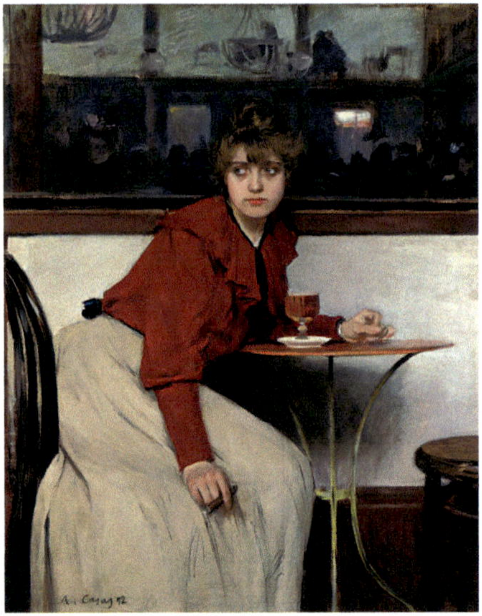

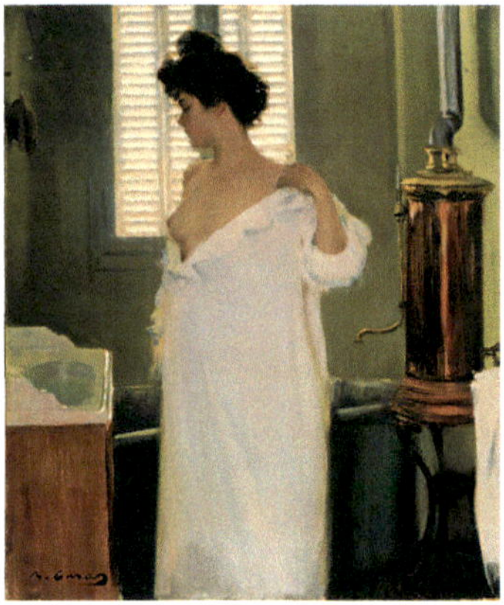

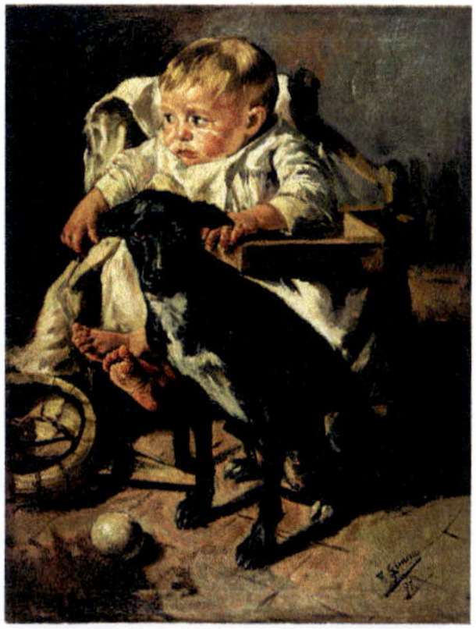

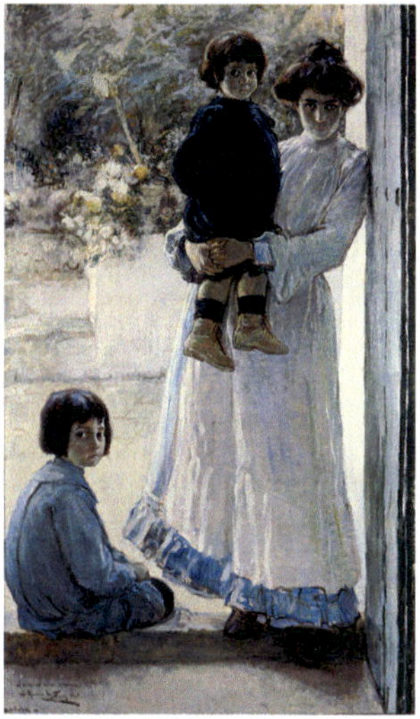

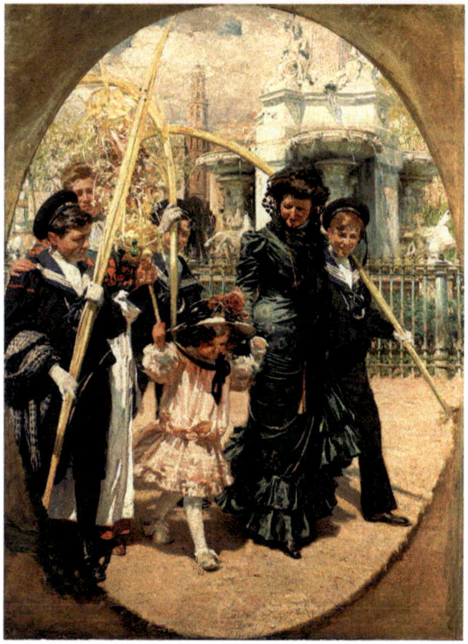

Other painters with special character within the Modernist movement, who had an influence on the Catalan or Spanish artistic scene, are: ***Joaquín Sorolla*** *(1863-1923) and* ***Ignacio de Zuloaga*** *(1870-1945). It is also worth mentioning other artists who can be considered marginally modernist but represented their life and times magnificently.*
Francesc Gimeno *(1858-1927)* **The Little Girl and Her Good Companion**, *1891 (75.5 x 57cm), donated by J. Sala Ardiz,* ***Julio Romero de Torres*** *(1880-1930),* **Waiting**, *1905, (166.5 x 98cm), donated by Xavier de Sagarra) and* ***Fèlix Mestres*** *(1872-1933)* **Palm Sunday**, *1911 (233 x 170cm), donated by the artist's grandchildren.*

Darío de Regoyos *(1857-1913) was the Spanish painter who best understood the splitting technique of French Impressionism. He has six oils on canvas in our collection,* **Chickens**, *c. 1912, (55 x 45cm), donated by J. Sala Ardiz is the most representative.*

The two oils on canvas by ***Pablo Picasso*** *(1881-1973) which reside in Montserrat have been donated by J. Sala Ardiz and belong to the painter's formative years. He was 14 and 16 years old respectively when they were painted in Malaga and Barcelona. The first one,* **The Old Fisherman**, *1895 (83 x 62cm), is signed only with his first surname: Ruiz, while the second one features both of them: Ruiz Picasso.*

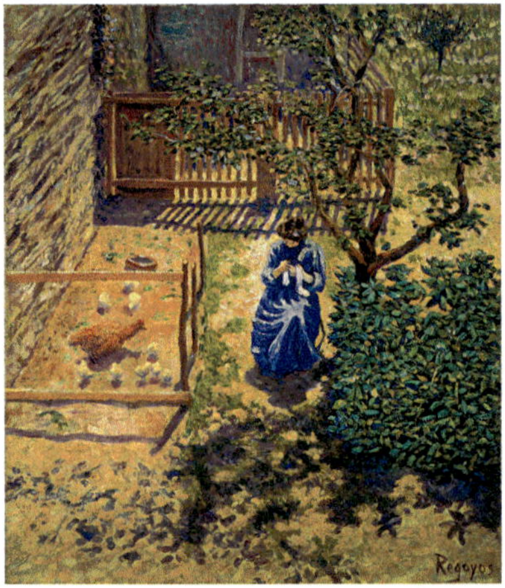

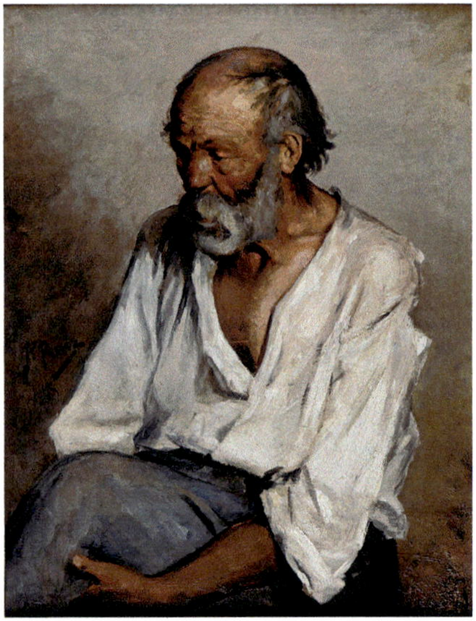

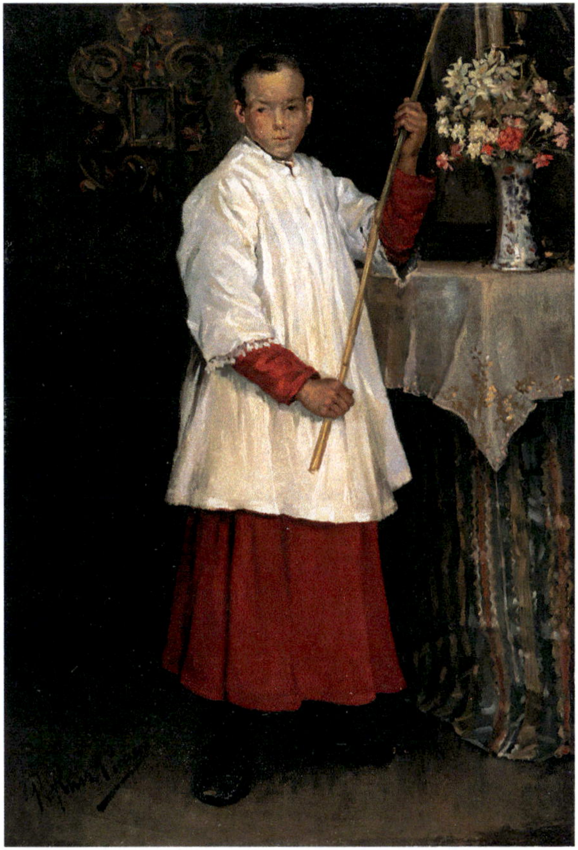

Altar Boy, ***Picasso*** *1896 (75 x 50cm) is a first attempt from which his painting 'The Holy Communion' was created immediately after. The topic of the altar boy, dressed in a red cassock became fashionable in late 19th century painting. Artists enjoyed painting anecdotes about these boys' pranks and funny tricks. Despite his youth, Picasso showed a greater maturity than the average in these portraits. He presented the resigned poverty of this altar boy, which recalled the poor and marginal children that Isidro Nonell was also painting at this time.*

The good taste of our modernist painters', which the well-off and progressive Catalan bourgeoisie liked so much, was followed by a reaction by newer painters who intended to 'épâter le bourgeois' with vulgar themes of poor and marginal characters. They were full of colour, either dark or contrasted, where instinct was valued over moderation.

Isidre Nonell *(1873-1911)* **Poor People Waiting for Soup**, *1899 (51 x 65cm), donated by J. Sala Ardiz,* **A Poor Boy**, *c. 1896, (145 x 94cm),* **Gypsy Woman**, *1904 (118 x 81cm), donated by J. Sala Ardiz.*

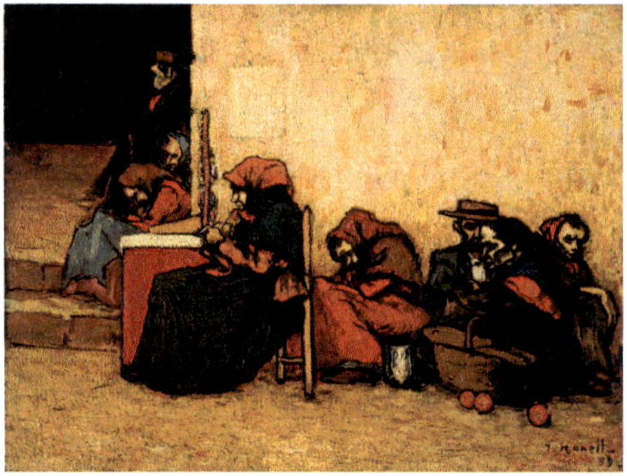

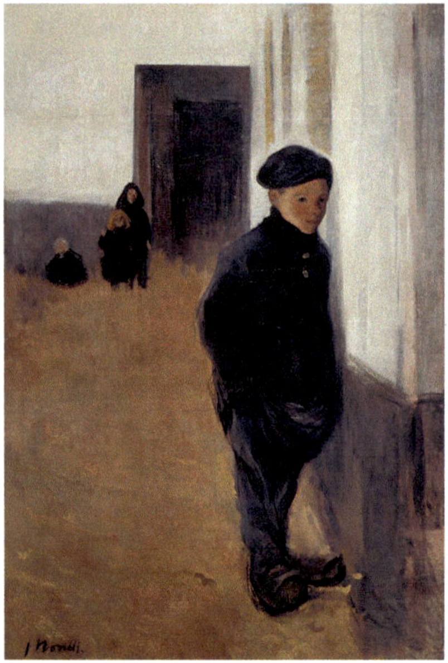

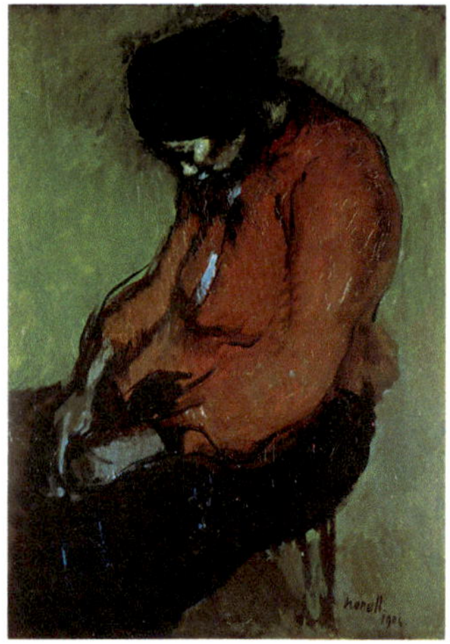

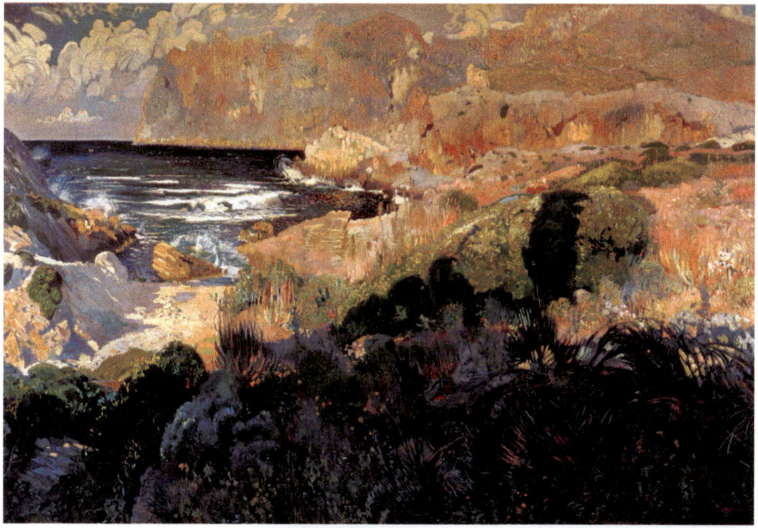

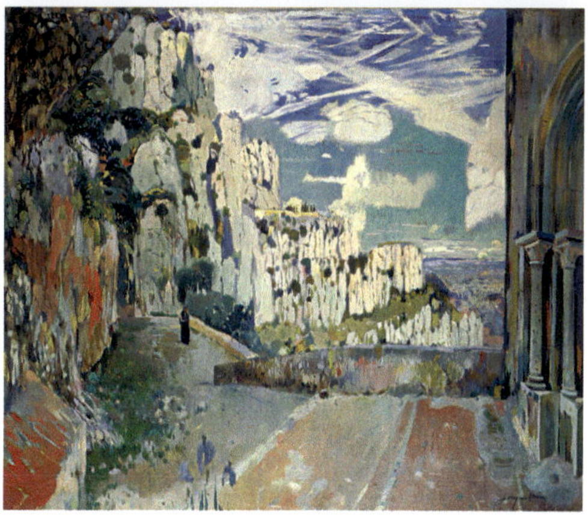

Joaquim Mir *(1873-1940) is the greatest colour master of the Post-Modernist Catalan painting. The collection of Montserrat features most of his work, with first class paintings; it amounts to nineteen oils on canvas, excluding drawings and prints. Mir was a good friend of the Monastery of Montserrat. He was a residential guest many times during his life and he knew how to paint our great mountain with exceptional skill and beauty.*

Cala Saint Vicent. *Mallorca, 1902, (280 x 400cm).* **The Pathway to the Cave**, *Montserrat, 1911 (117 x 134.5cm), donated by J. Sala Ardiz.*

Hermen Anglada Camarasa *(1872-1959) also belongs to the postmodernist generation. He was passionate about colour, Parisian life and the decorative trend in international painting of the first third of the 20th century.* **Champs Elysées** *1904 (81 x 120cm), donated by J. Sala Ardiz.*

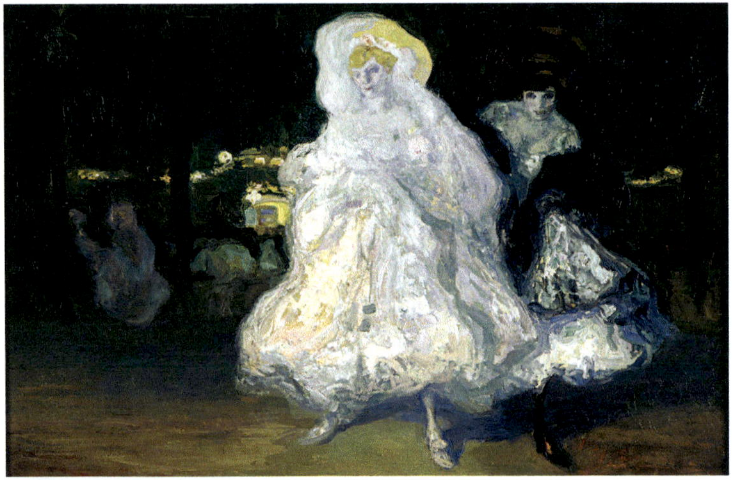

Ricard Canals *(1876-1931) took up residence in Paris and painted in a neo-impressionist style. His painting shows many references to the great masters such as Renoir or Cezanne.* **Maternity**, *1903 (93 x 73cm), donated by J. Sala Ardiz.*

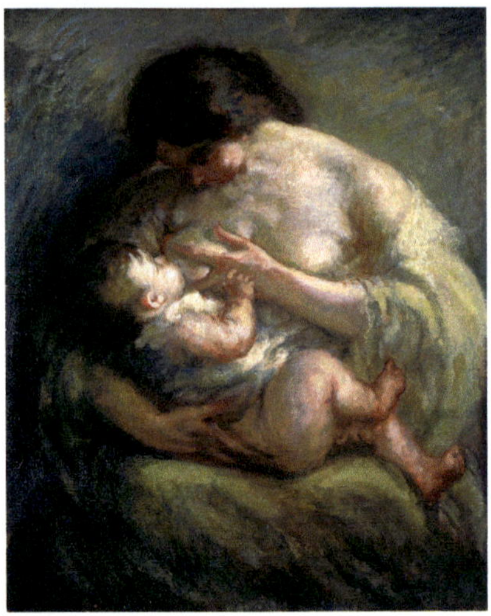

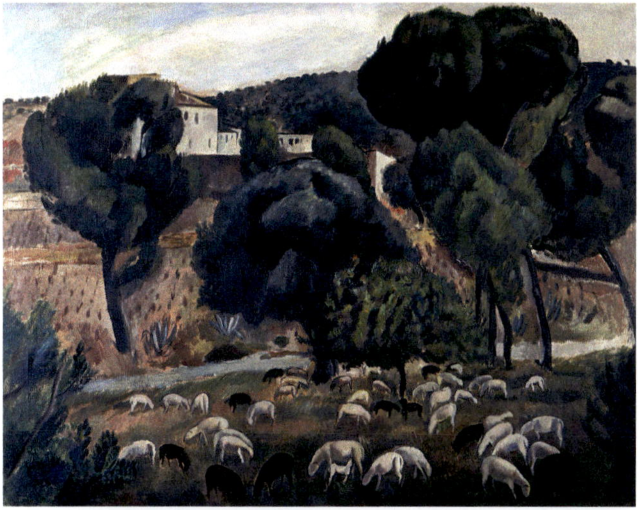

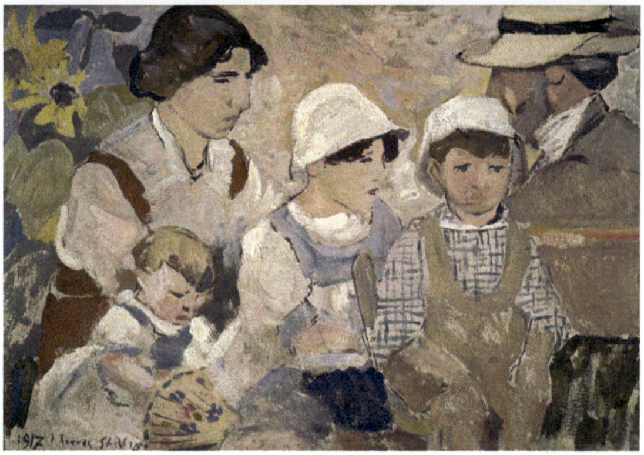

The Catalan cultural movement of ***Noucentista Art*** *represents a reaction against the "genius" and the "instinct" which were predominant in the Modernism. It was a return to rule, the clarity of concepts and well defined shapes by drawing and volume. Its main values were calm and the balance and grace of ordinary life. The artists stopped looking towards the North and returned to the Mediterranean and the classical Greek-Roman spirit. There are many turn of the century and post-turn of the century painters represented in Montserrat. Therefore, here, we only mention some of them:*

Joaquim Sunyer *(1875-1956),* **Flock of Sheep** *c. 1914 (66 x 81.5cm), donated by J. Sala Ardiz.*

Joaquim Torres García *(1874-1949),* **The Painter and His Family**, *1917 (50 x 69cm), donated by J. Sala Ardiz.*

Xavier Nogués *(1873-1940),* **Between Dances**, *1940 (54.5 x 65.5cm), donated by J. Sala Ardiz.*

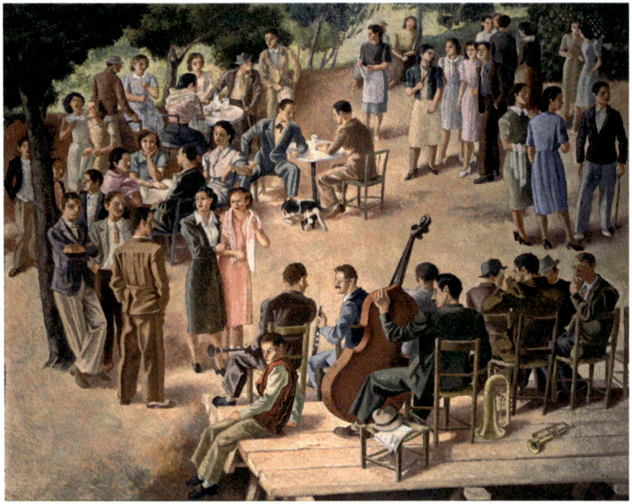

Without contradicting the Noucentista Art spirit but with a different emphasis, there is a group of Catalan painters who are very different from each other but nonetheless, they share the common principle of the "good job" and the predominance of the métier or the good trade. ***Feliu Elias*** *(1878-1948),* ***Iu Pascual*** *(1883-1949),* ***Domènec Carles*** *(1888-1962),* ***Rafael Benet*** *(1889-1979),* ***Olga Sacharoff*** *(1889-1967). They are followed by* ***Josep de Togores*** *(1893-1970),* ***Alfred Sisquella*** *(1900-1964),* ***Antoni Vila Arrufat*** *(1894-1989). Their work as well as many others' is featured in the Museum of Montserrat.*

Josep Obiols *(1904-1977),* **Girl Knitting**, *1938 (61 x 50cm), donated by J. Sala Ardiz.*

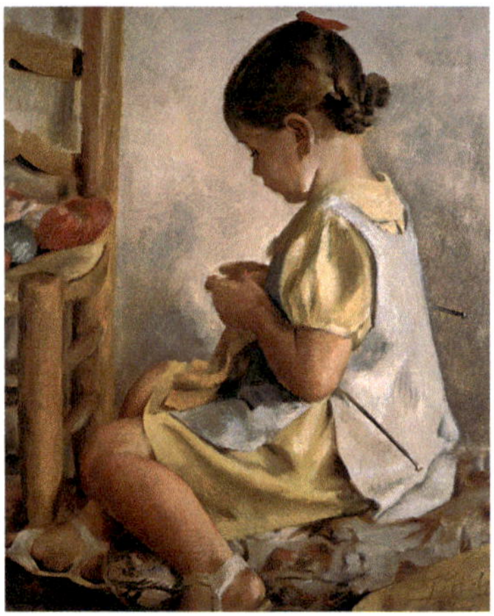

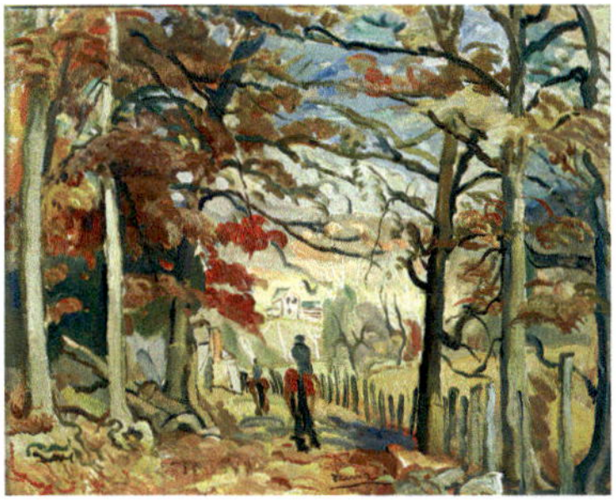

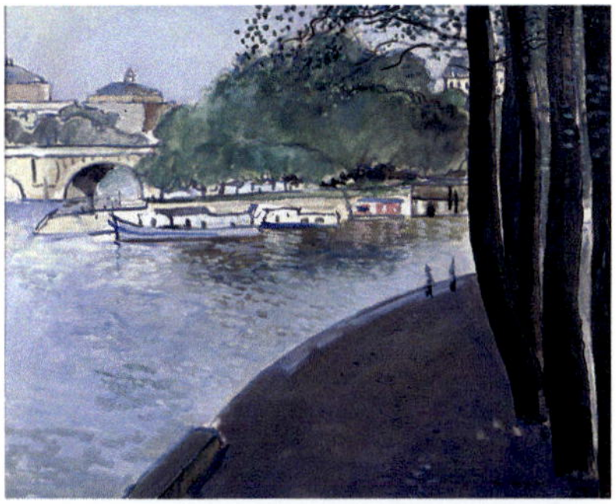

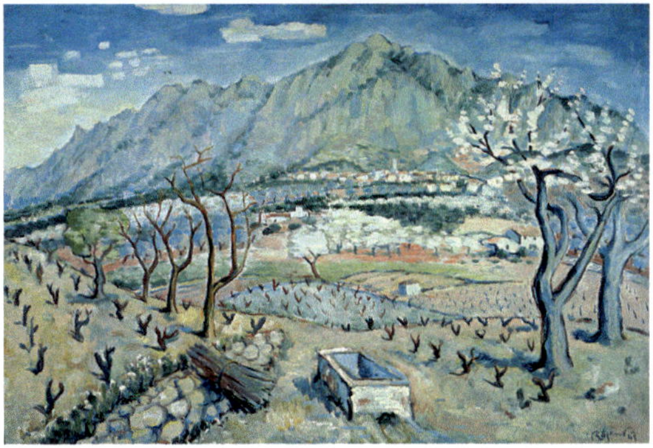

Pere Daura *(1896-1976),* **Return to the Village**, *c. 1935 (50 x 61cm), donated by Calvó Vilardebó.*

Josep Mompou *(1888-1968),* **Le Vert Galant et le Pont Neuf.** *Paris, 1932 (60 x 73cm), donated by J. Sala Ardiz.*

Ramon Rogent *(1920-1958),* **Montserrat seen from Can Martí Joan**, *1947 (80 x 116cm).*

We might mention another generation of Catalan artists who were more or less integrated in the fringe of the avantgarde and others who might only have breathed its scent: ***Josep Amat*** *(1901-1991),* ***Pere Pruna*** *(1904-1977),* ***Miquel Villà*** *(1901-1988),* ***Manuel Capdevila*** *(1910-2006), etc.*

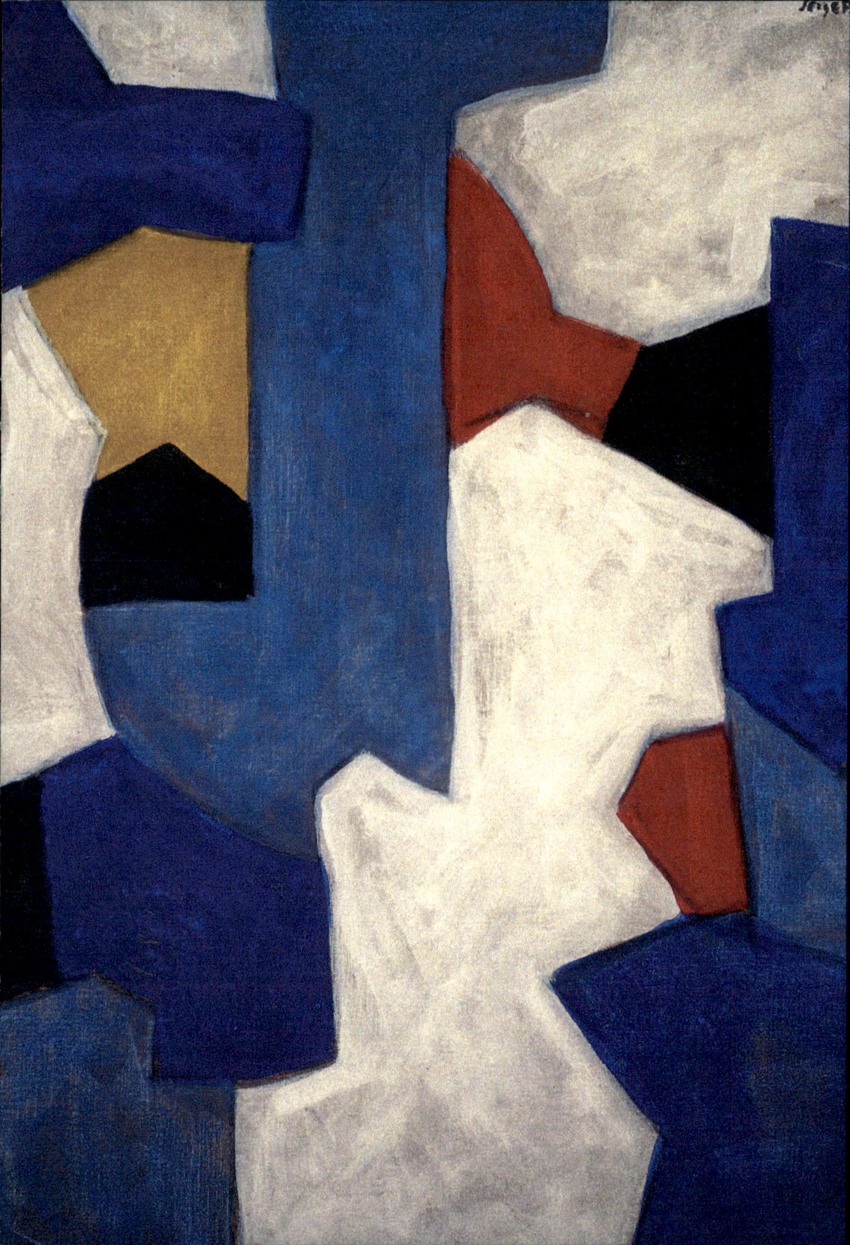

The
avantgardes
and
contemporar
painting

The Montserrat Museum hasn't yet reached its goal of providing a complete and balanced vision of avant-garde and contemporary painting. Nonetheless in this area as well, we offer some very significant work which may become the nucleus of this growing collection.

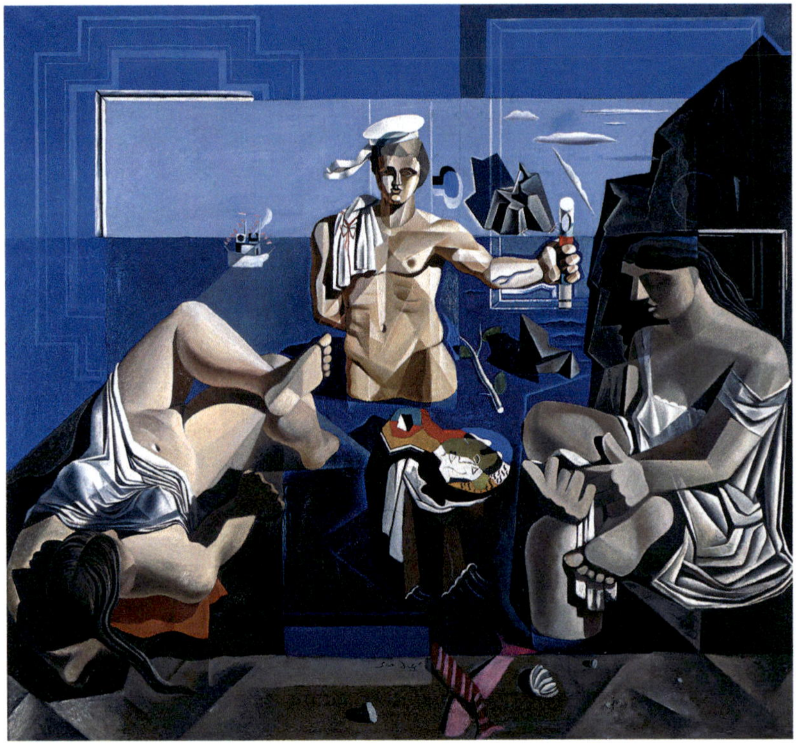

***Salvador Dalí** (1904-1989), **Neocubist Academy**, 1926 (190 x 200cm), donated by Josefina Cusí, is the star piece of the museum regarding avantgarde art.*

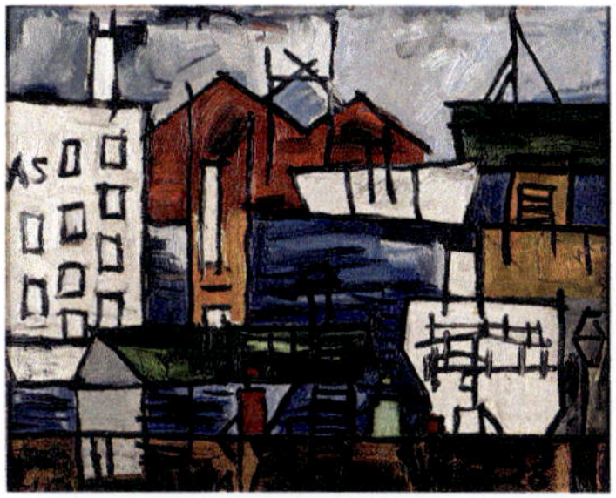

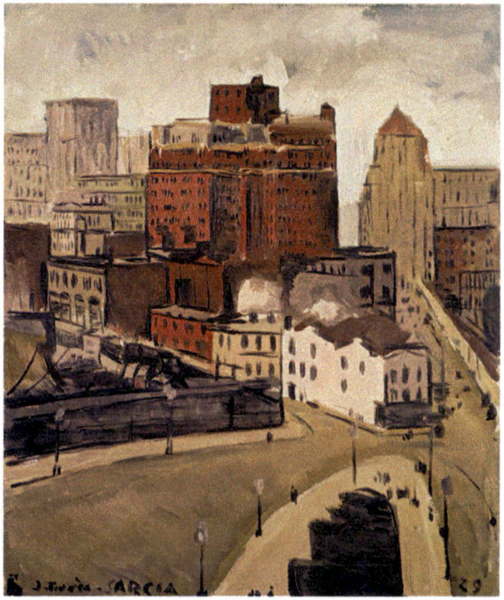

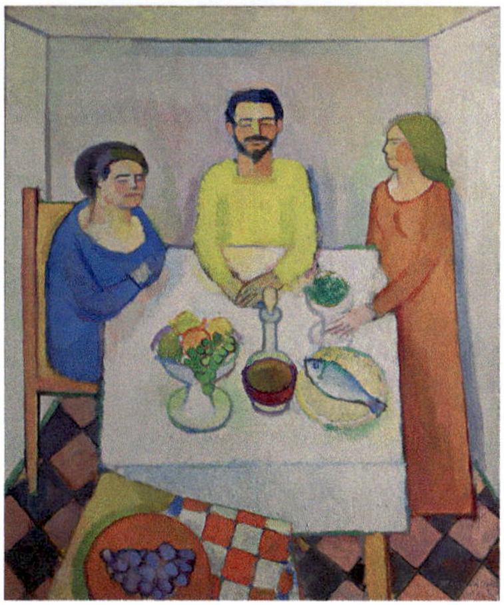

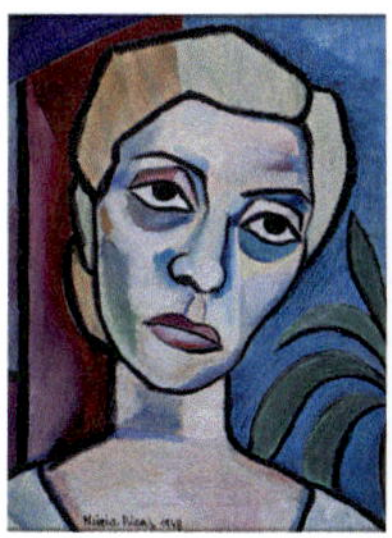

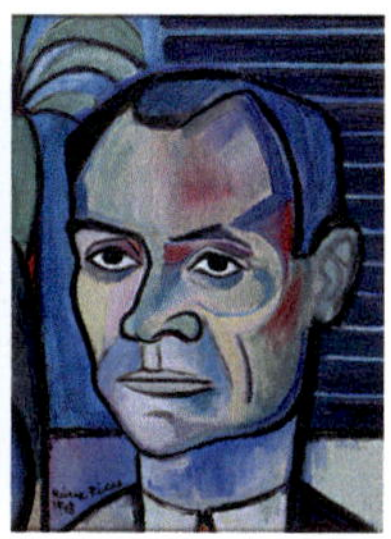

The Contemporary Art section could begin with the constructivist paintings by ***Joaquín Torres Garcia*** *(1875-1949), a Uruguayan painter who established himself in Catalonia. When he started evolving towards a more avantgarde painting, he moved to Paris.*

New York, *1929 (73 x 60cm), donated by X. Busquets.*

The Port, *1928 (38 x 46cm), donated by Martha Daura.*

Another group of works allows us to see how Barcelona assimilated avant-garde painting in the forties and fifties.

Josep M. Garcia Llort *(1921-2003),* **In Martha and Mary's House**, *1950 (100 x 81cm), donated by F.-P. Verrié.*

Núria Picas *(1927),* **Mother**, *1948 (38 x 28cm);* **Father**, *1948 (34.4 x 26.7cm), donated by the artist.*

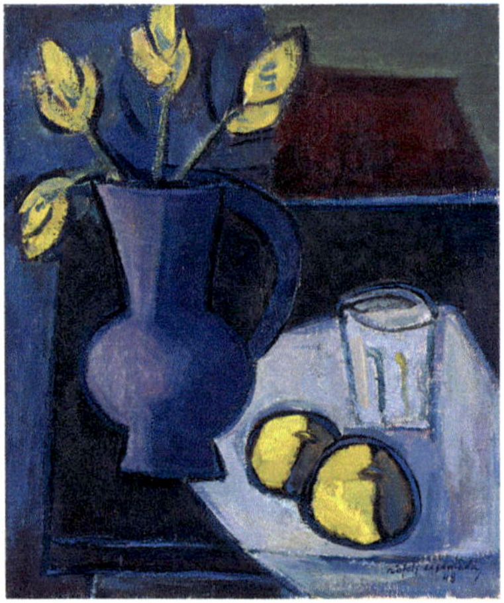

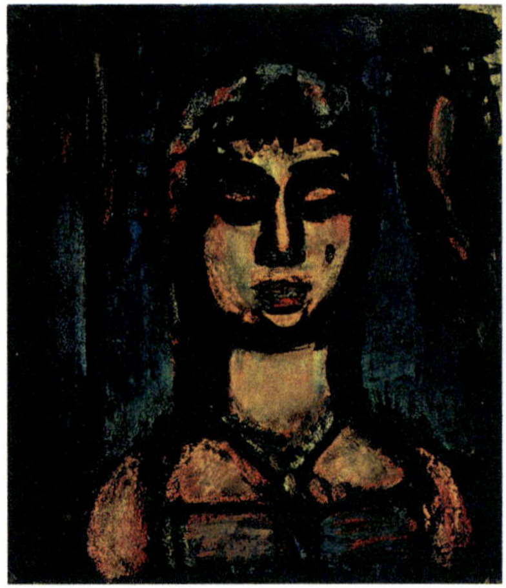

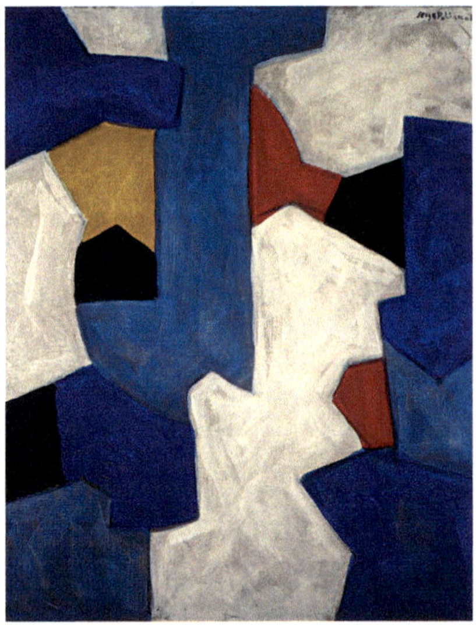

Albert Ràfols Casamada *(1924-2009),* **Still Life***, 1948 (60 x 50,5cm), donated by Jordi Sarsanedas.*

George Rouault *(1871-1958)* **Salomé***, 1932 (35 x 30cm), donated by X. Busquets. He is a first class figure in the international modern art scene and the best representative of the expresionism of humanist and Christian orientation. He had a powerful influence on Catalan Avantgarde Painting from the 40s and 50s.*

Serge Poliakoff *(1904-1969),* **Blue, White, Red, Brown and Black***, c. 1960 (92 x 73cm), donated by X. Busquets.*

Poliakoff's *abstraction is one of the most serious in the Post-war European painting. The chromatic values, highly elaborated, enter into an interactive relationship based on forms that give rise to some very cerebral and considered compositions.*

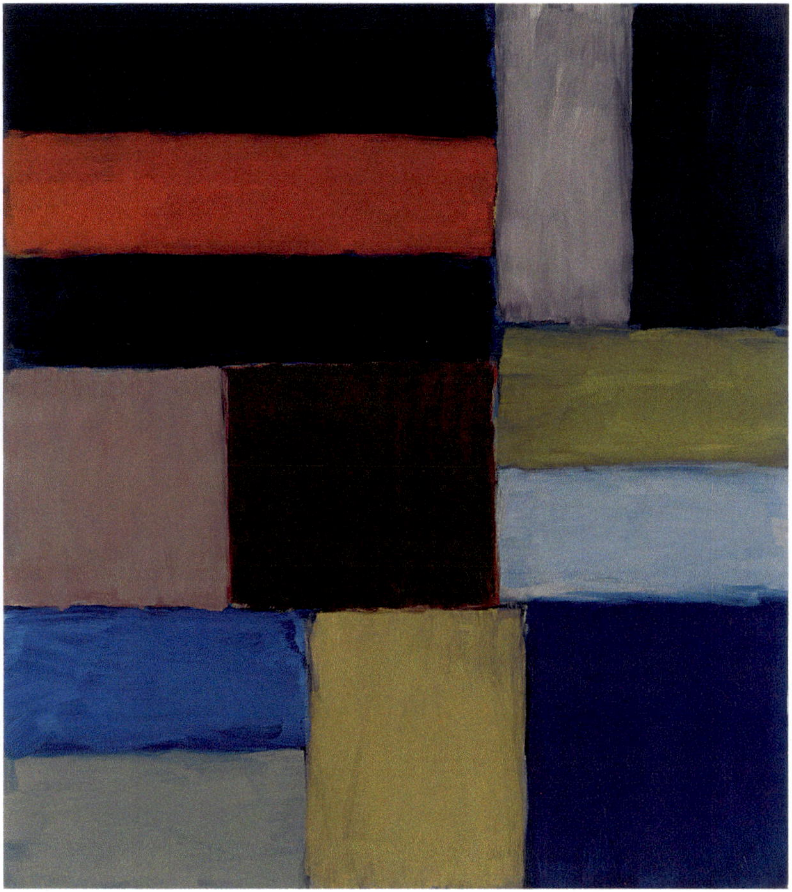

Sean Scully *(1944), an American painter of Irish origin, is one of the best examples of international contemporary painting. His abstract expressionist style is very personal and is appreciated worldwide for the strong yet delicate sensibility, direct and subtle, with which he expresses himself. Scully, who lives between New York, Munich and Barcelona, maintains a cordial relationship with the Monastery of Montserrat and has presented the Museum with a work entitled* **The Mountain of Oisin**, *2010 (225 x 195cm) which commemorates the birth of his son.*

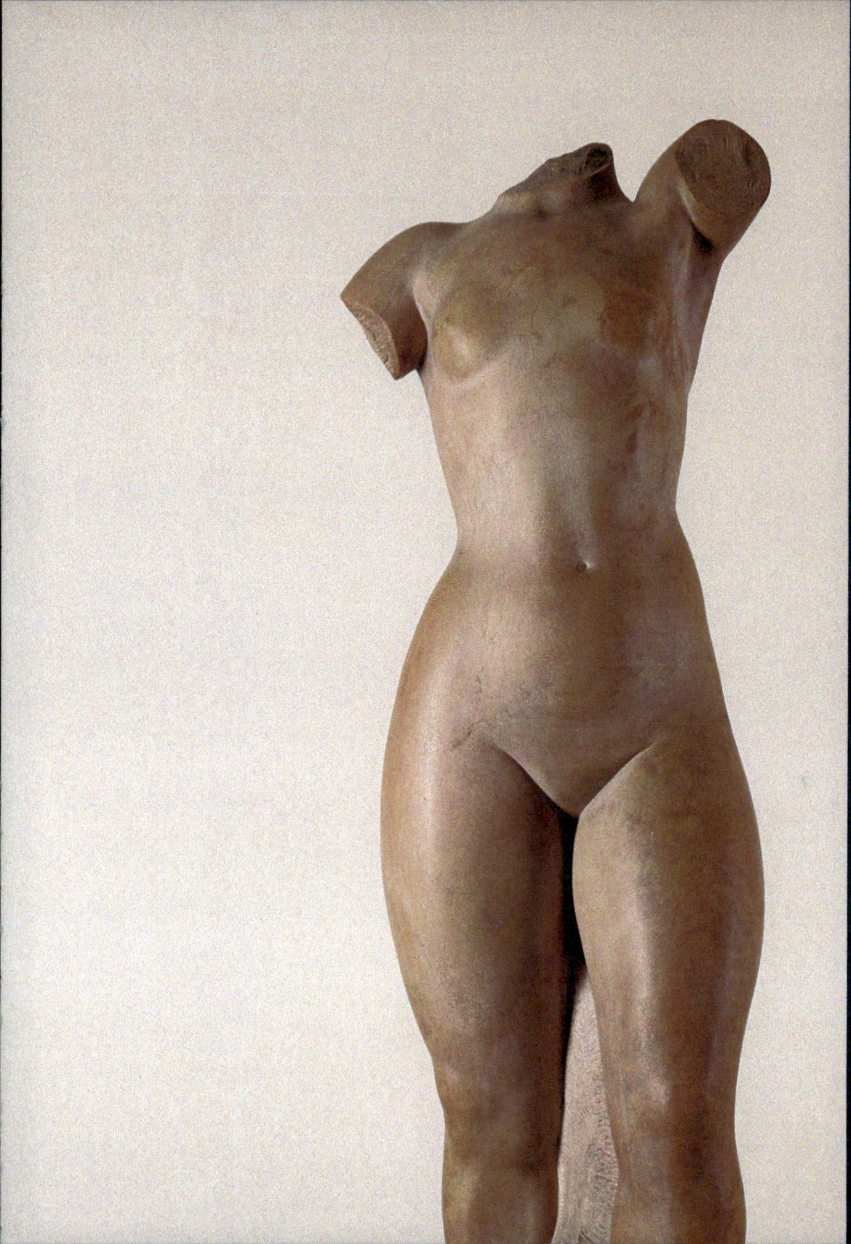

Modern sculpture (19th–20th centuries)

Josep Llimona *(1864-1934),* **Regina Sacratissimi Rosarii**, *1892 (marble, 142 x 60 x 40cm), donated by Margarida Mur i Carreras, is a religious sculpture which follows the most characteristic Modernist aesthetics. Evokes the ideal woman and is a beautiful example of modernist naturalism within the religious context from the end of the century.*

Beauty, *1924 (marble, 120 x 32 x 35cm), donated by J. Sala Ardiz, is a very characteristic example of the delicacy of the sweet, soft and slightly morbid shapes which are typically Modernist. The blur in her face gives the sculpture a halo of mystery.*

The collection of sculptures also allows us to observe the evolution in taste and style in the Catalan art scene from the last two centuries, from the Pre-Modernist years of the Barcelona Universal Exhibition in 1888 with **Joan Roig i Solé** (1835-1918), **Agapit Vallmitjana** (1833-1905), **Rossend Nobas** (1838-1891), until the Modernist period: **Josep Montserrat** (1860-1923) and especially **Josep Llimona** (1864-1934), there exists a great deal of his work in Montserrat.

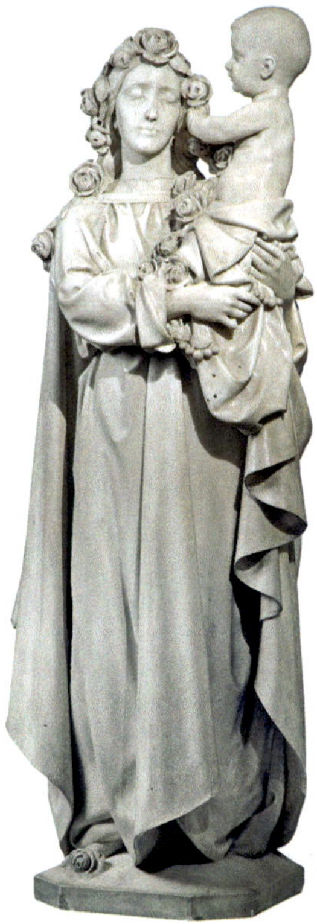

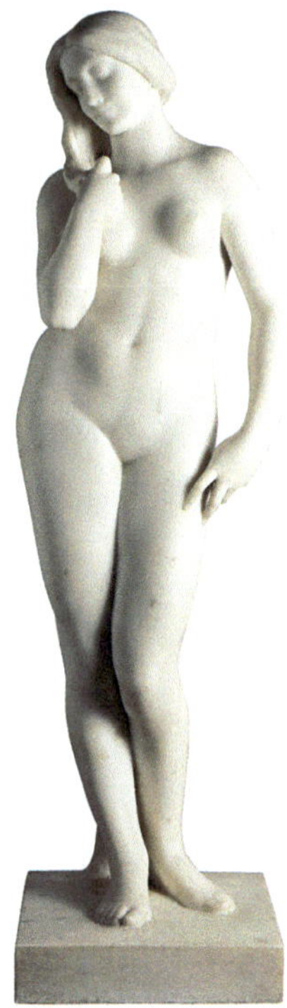

Modern sculptures (mobiles) in Montserrat amount to over one hundred and fifty pieces. The main ones are exhibited in the museum, together with paintings from the same period and style. The smallest ones are located in a glass cabinet and offer a beautiful collection of terra-cotta and bronze pieces which are frequently being renewed.

The main characteristic traits of Noucentista Art can be clearly observed in the work by ***Josep Clarà*** *(1878-1958),* ***Josep Dunyach*** *(1886-1957),* ***Manolo Hugué*****,** ***Enric Casanovas****, etc.*
The Parnassian spirit from Old Greece breathes again from the ideals of balance, grace and from art which goes beyond time and through the centuries without losing its currency.

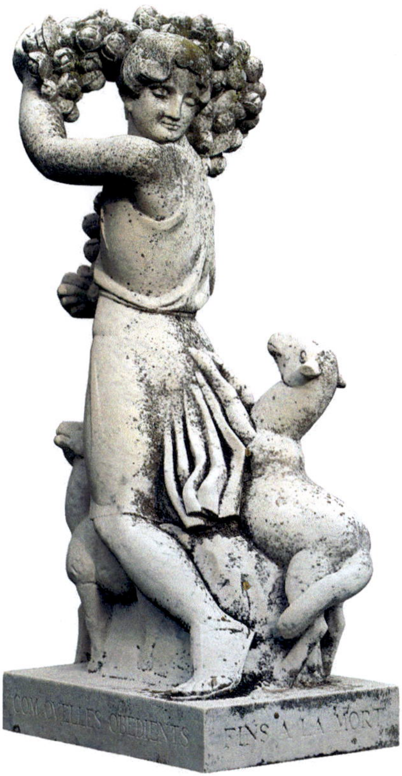

Manolo Hugué *(1872-1945),* **The Good Shepherd***, 1943 (plaster, 127 x 58 x 45cm). It is the first step for the stone sculpture that Abbot Marcet ordered for the garden inside the monastery.*

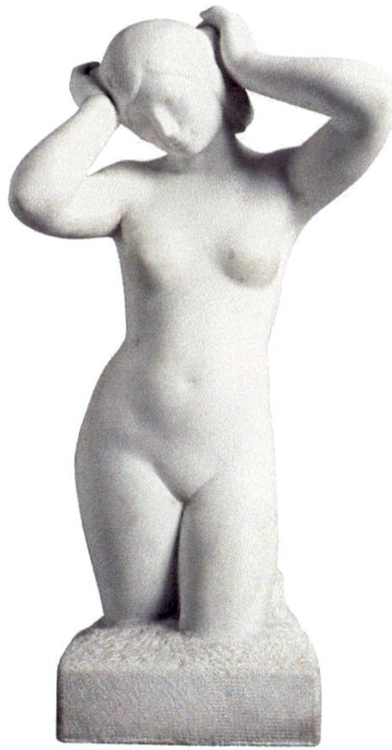

Enric Casanovas *(1882-1948)* **Female Nude***, 1924, (marble, 73 x 24.5 x 24.5cm), donated by J. Sala Ardiz.*

A second generation of Mediterranean sculptors took the principles of Art Nouveau to clearer, lighter and firmer solutions. Each and every one of them had his own personal style. The following ones are worth mentioning: ***Pere Jou*** *(1891-1964),* ***Enric Monjo*** *(1895-1976),* ***Rafael Solanic*** *(1895-1990),* ***Josep Canyas*** *(1905-2001),* ***Josep Viladomat*** *(1899-1989).*

Pablo Gargallo *(1881-1934),* **Female Torso**, *1931 (stone, 84 x 19.5 x 19.5cm), donated by Pere Sensat, is a very emblematic piece for its firm moderation, agility and balance.* **La Petite Volupté**, *1907, (terra-cotta, 23 x 15 x 8.8cm), donated by Pere Sensat. The artist emphasizes the sinuosity of the composition and lines.*

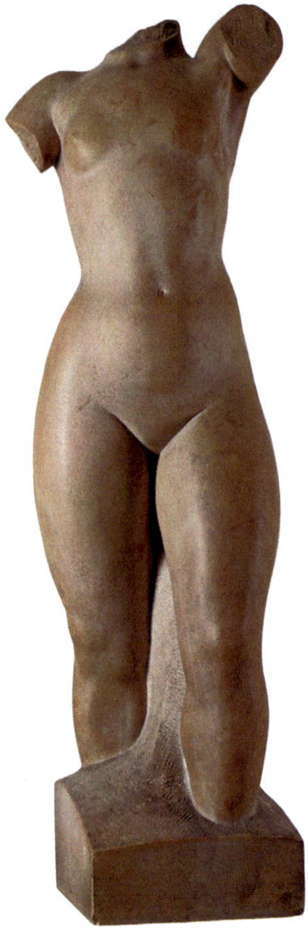

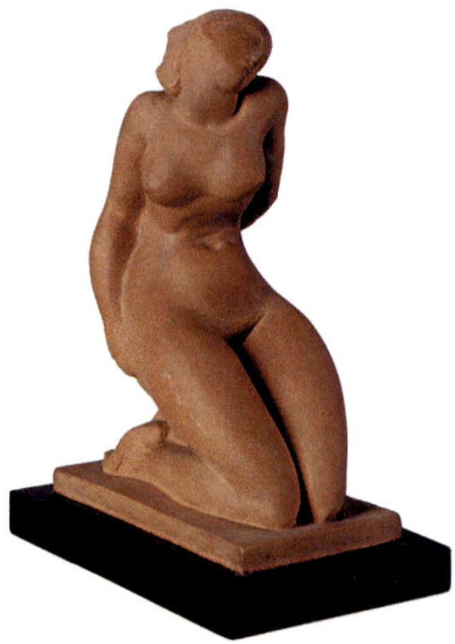

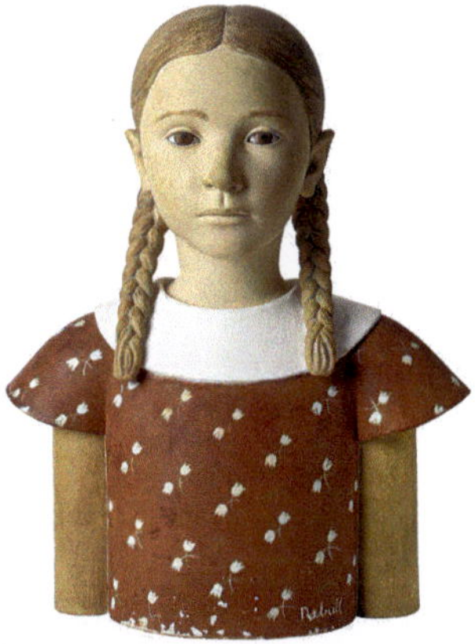

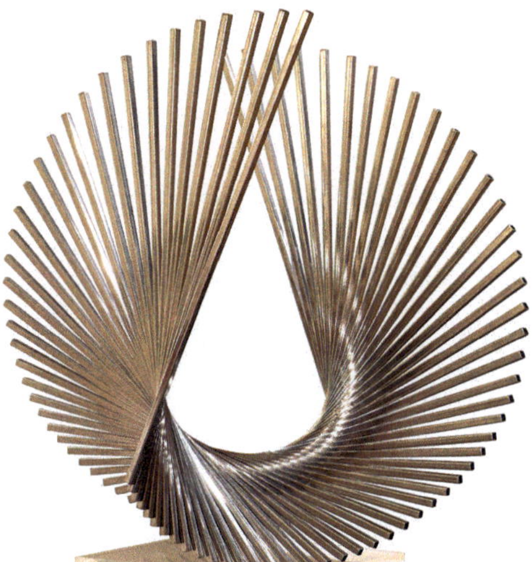

***Joan Rebull** (1899-1981) was one of the artists who was more involved in the reconstruction and beautification of Montserrat from the 40s to the 70s. He was the author of the beautiful reliefs in the façade of the monastery as well as several sculptures in the museum, such as* **Maria Rosa**, *1935/1948, (polychrome stone, 43 x 34.5 x 24cm), donated by J. Sala Ardiz. This piece aspires to the height of effort that Catalonia made in order to educate a whole generation of urban, clean and keen children, showing the calmness learned from the dificulties and events of daily life at the time of the Mancomunidad and the Autonomy in 1931.*

Contemporary art is represented by **Andreu *Alfaro*** *(1929),* **Genitrix**, *c. 1972 (75 x 75 x 48cm), donated by Pere Sensat, and* **Strokes**, *1980-1981, donated by Josep Suñol, very characteristic of this Valencian artist.*

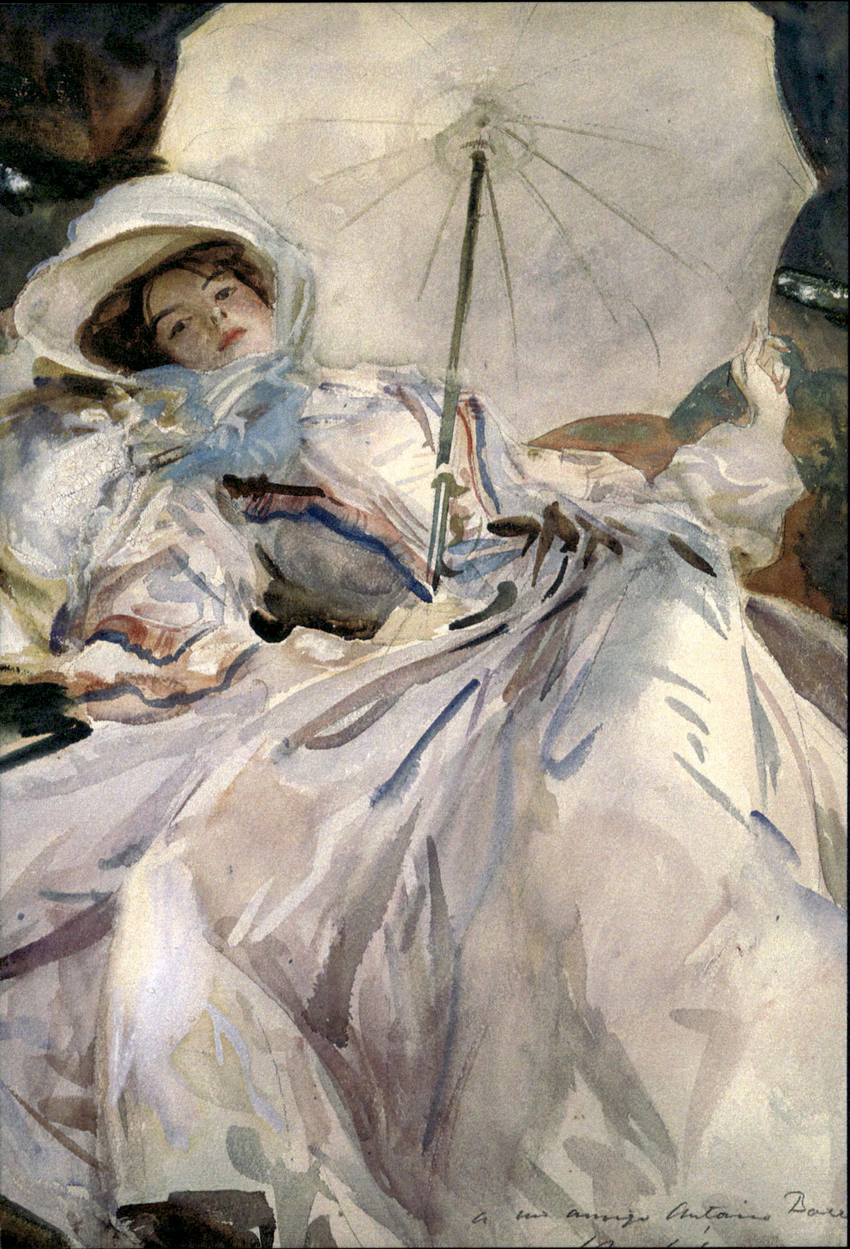

Collection of drawings and watercolours

John Singer Sargent *(1856-1925),* **Lady with Parasol**, *c. 1911, (watercolour, 53 x 40cm), donated by J. Sala Ardiz.*

Mariano Fortuny *(1838-1874),* **The Tapestry Merchant**, *Paris 1870, (watercolour, 59 x 85cm), donated by J. Sala Ardiz. It is a masterpiece by this Catalan artist who became universally famous in his time. The exquisite detail combines with the free trade and secure handling of the work. Eastern painting is one of the most typical themes of this period, which was marked by the North African colonial wars and the discovery of the exotic world of Islam.*

Drawing as well as any painting on paper is very fragile and delicate and they both require special climatic and lighting conditions. Nowadays, due to the lack of space in the museum, this large and outstanding collection cannot be permanently exhibited. Therefore, the best samples are only exhibited in combination with other temporary exhibitions.

The collection exceeds 1,500 examples. The majority are from artists of the 19th and 20th centuries. However, there is no lack of high quality work by older artists.

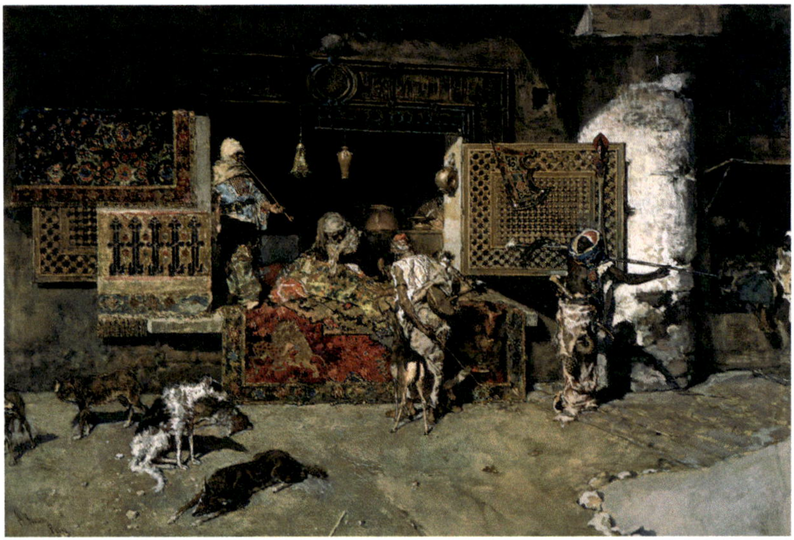

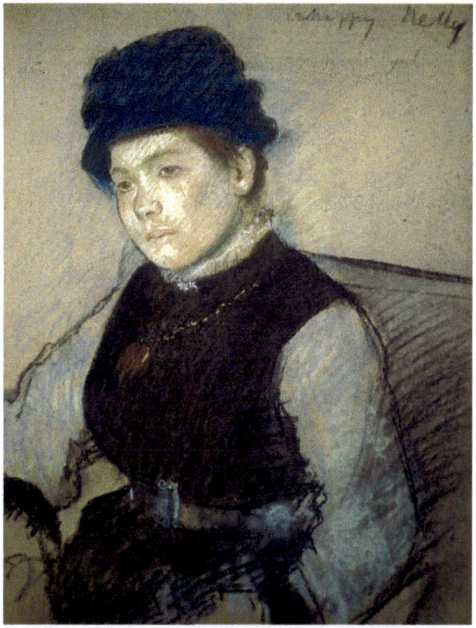

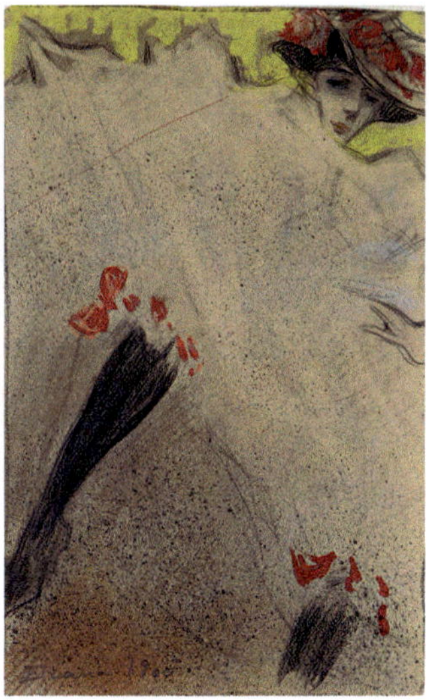

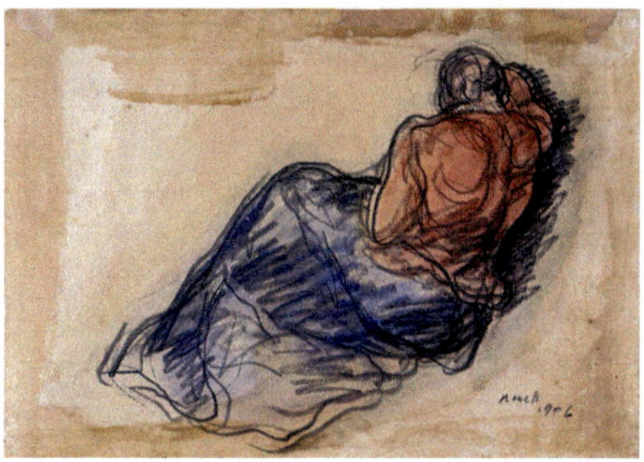

Edgard Degas *(París, 1834-1917),* **Unhappy Nelly**, *c. 1885 (pastel colours, 63.5 x 48cm), donated by X. Busquets. It is an interesting piece within the artistic production of this famous impressionist painter, who specialized in the ballet from the Parisian Opera. The figure is Ellen Cobden, the first wife of Walter Sickert, a friend of Degas.*

Claudi Castelucho Diana *(1871-1932),* **Can-Can**, *1900 (charcoal and pastel, 33.7 x 21cm), Just Cabot donation.*

Isidre Nonell *(1873-1911),* **Gypsy in Repose**, *1906 (pastel colours, 30 x 41cm), donated by X. Busquets.*

Among the most eminent artists whose work is featured in Montserrat, there are: ***Eugenio Lucas Velázquez*** *(1817-1870),* ***Eugenio Lucas Padilla*** *(1824-1870),* ***Lluís Rigalt*** *(1814-1894),* ***Francesc Gimeno*** *(1858-1927),* ***Joan Llimona*** *(1869-1926),* ***Josep Clarà*** *(1878-1958),* ***Ricard Opisso*** *(1880-1966),* ***Pere Ynglada*** *(1881-1958),* ***Ismael Smith*** *(1886-1972),* ***Laura Albéniz*** *(1890-1944),* ***Pere Pruna*** *(1904-1977),* ***Emili Grau Sala*** *(1911-1975), etc.*

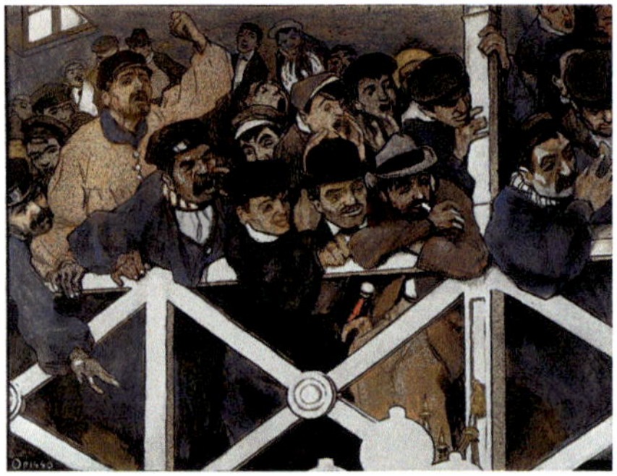

Ricard Opisso *(1880-1966),* **Anarchist Meeting**, *1903 (charcoal and pastel, 35 x 54cm), donated by Montserrat Carreras Jané.*

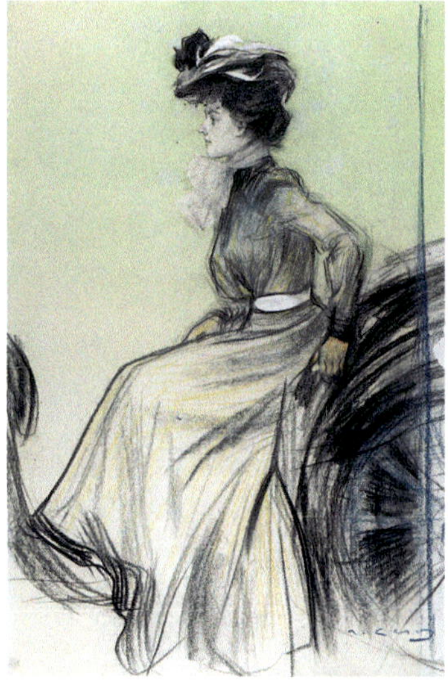

Ramón Casas *(1866-1932),* **Chauffeuse**, *1900 (pastel colours, 63 x 40cm), donated by Montserrat Carreras Jané.*

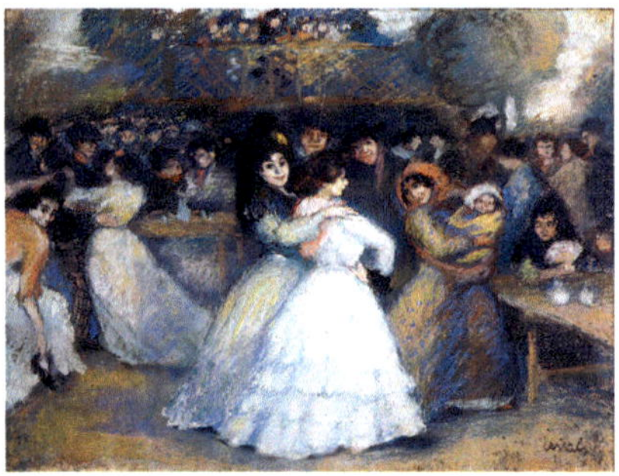

Ricard Canals *(1876-1931),* **The Fête**, *c. 1902 (pastel colours, 50.5 x 66cm), donated by Sala Ardiz.*

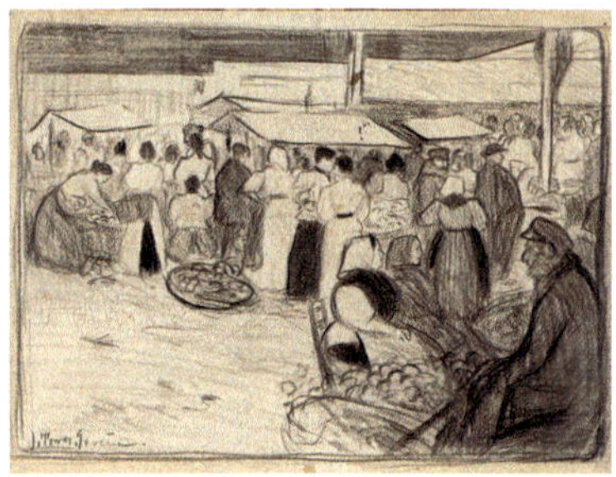

Joaquim Torres Garcia *(1874-1949),* **Market**, *c. 1898 (charcoal, 25 x 35cm), donated by Francesc Carbó i Batet.*

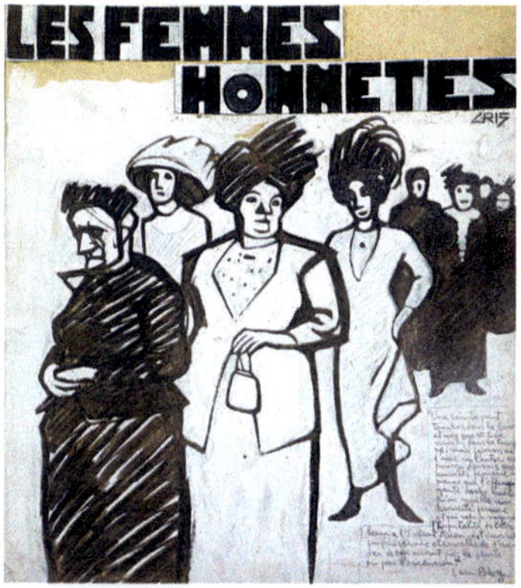

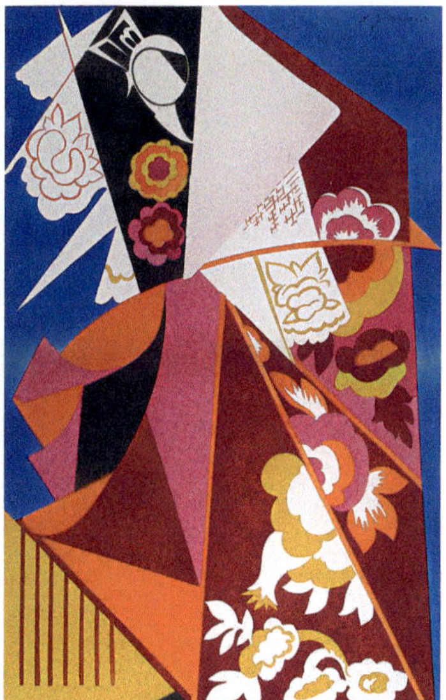

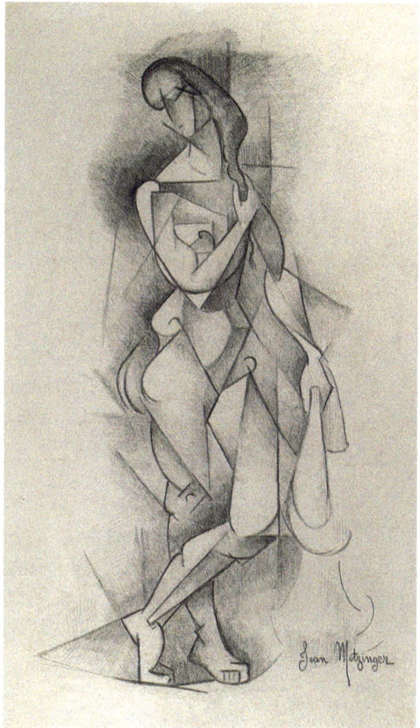

The collection also has originals by famous illustrators of the international press such as the painter ***Juan Gris*** *(1887-1927),* ***Jules Grandjouan*** *(1875-1968),* ***Josep Simont*** *(1875-1968), etc.*

On the avantgarde scene: ***Jean Metzinger*** *(1883-1956),* **Nude Female**, *c. 1916 (charcoal 61 x 58cm), donated by X. Busquets.* ***Natalia Gontxarova*** *(1881-1962) became famous as a costume designer of the Ballets of Diaghilev,* **L'Espagnole**, *1917 ('Pochoir', 42.5 x 26cm), donated by Mark Moloney.*

The Museum of Montserrat has a rich collection of twenty six drawings by ***Salvador Dalí*** *(1904-1989), which cover the period from 1922 to 1927. They come from the famous pharmacist Joaquim Cusí i Furtunet's collection, donated by his daughter Josefina.*
Portrait of the Painter's Father, *c. 1925, (charcoal, 36 x 27cm),* **Female Figure, Back**, *c. 1924 (pencil, 20.7 x 13.8cm),* **Harlequin and Figure Studies**, *c. 1926 (ink, 21 x 27.2cm),* **Maria Carbona**, *1926 (lead pencil, 49 x 43cm), donated by J. Sala Ardiz.*

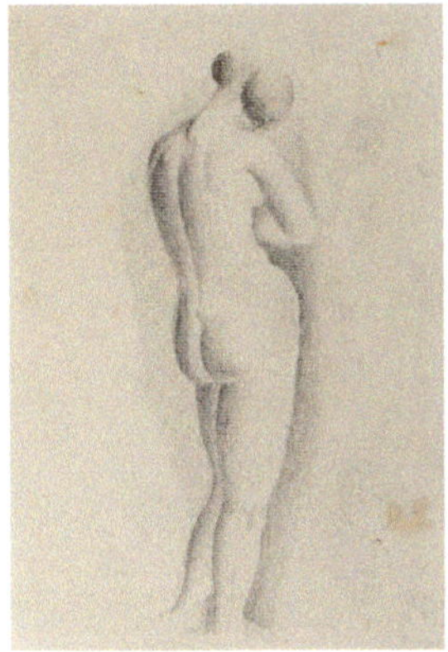

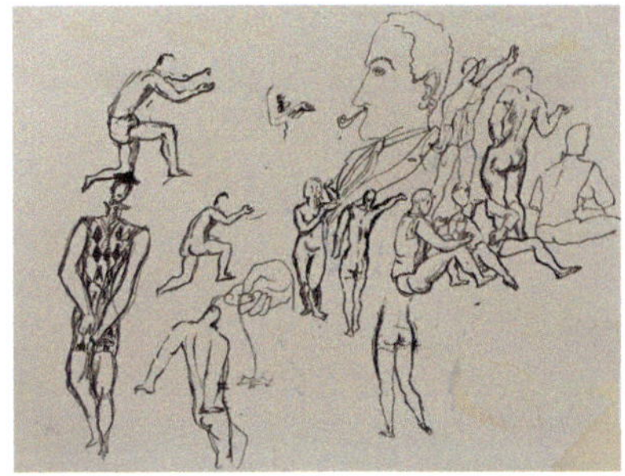

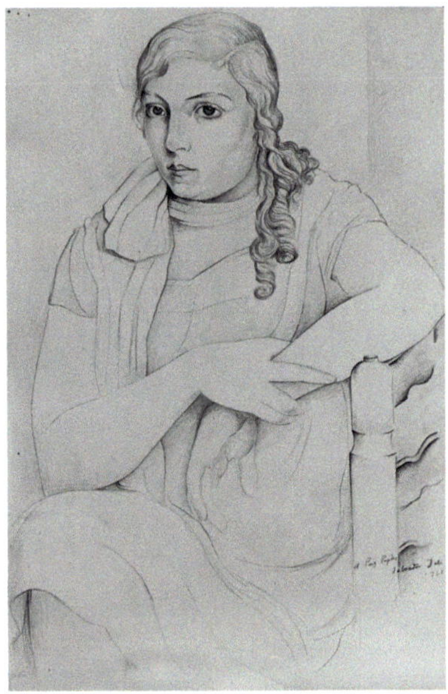

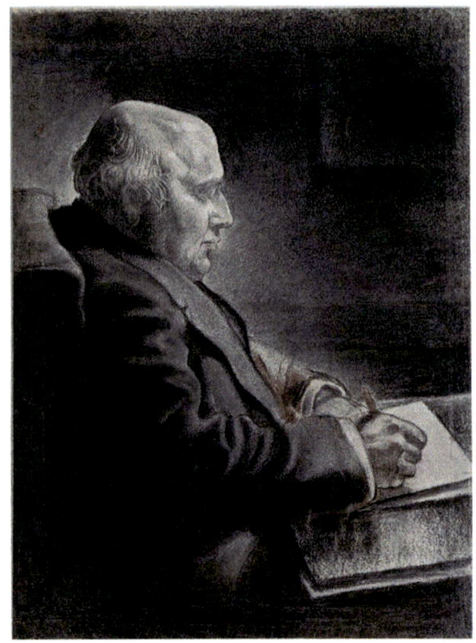

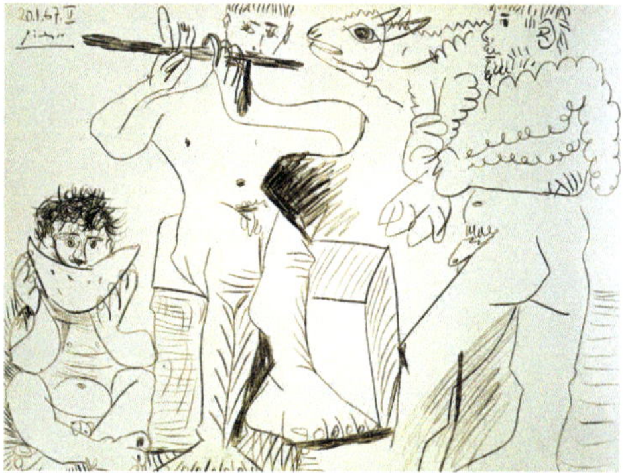

There are five drawings by ***Pablo Picasso*** *(1881-1973). The first one is from the year 1900* **Picador** *(watercolour, 21 x 13.5cm), and the last one is* **Homme à l'agneau, mangeur de pastèque et flûtiste**, *1967 (50 x 65cm), both donated by Xavier Busquets.*

And we end the tale of drawings with two by ***Antoni Tàpies*** *(1923)* **Homage to Picasso**, *1971 (mixed media, 30 x 31cm), and* **Montserrat century XXI**, *1999 (mixed media, 105 x 78cm), which the artist personally gave to the Museum of Montserrat.*

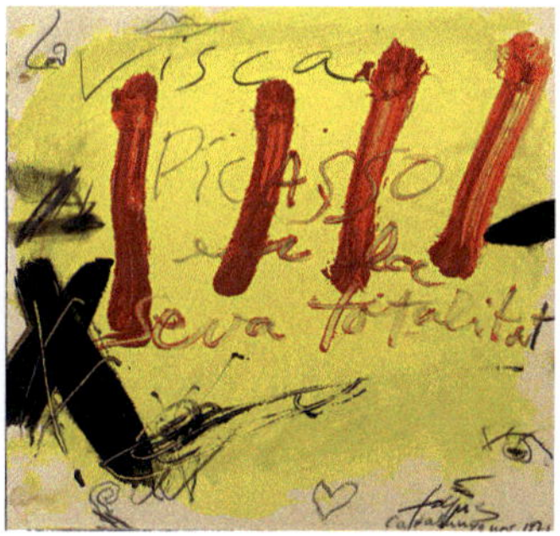

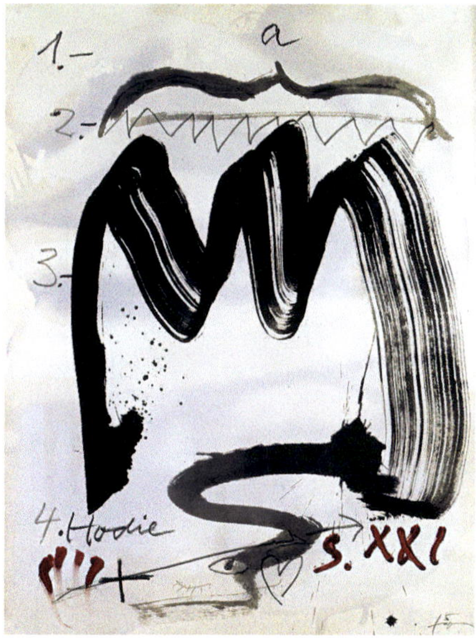

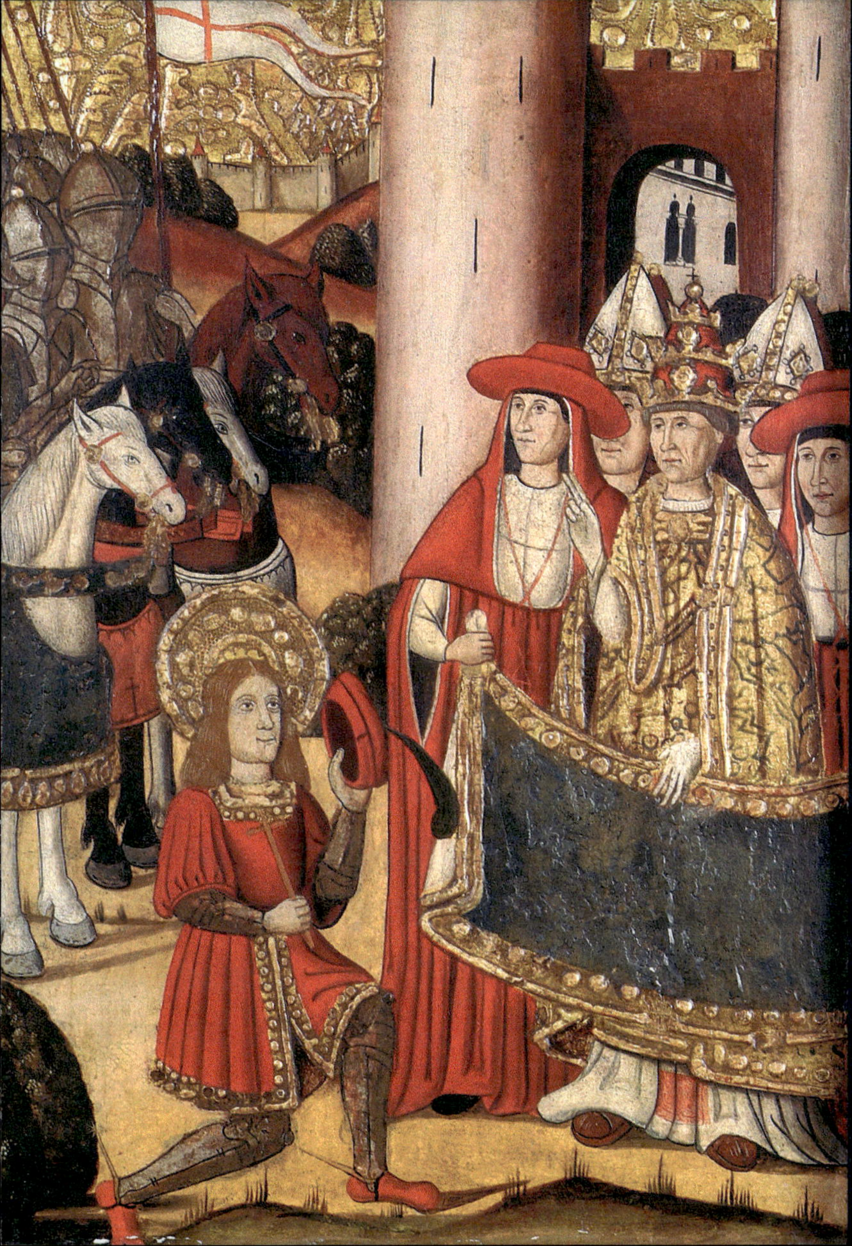

Other Reserve Collections

Prehistory and Iberian culture

The singular morphology of the mountain range of Montserrat has attracted attention since man inhabited this land. The Museum of Montserrat also has an entire section of prehistoric materials which were collected in several sites in the mountains and its surroundings. They range from the Paleolithic right up to the Iberian era, almost without interruption (6000-300 BC). These sites have been named Cova Freda, Cova Gran, Santa Cecilia, Les Soleies, Can Jorba, etc. The excavation works that the Institute of Catalan Studies carried out in 1922 arouse great interest, mainly due to a very peculiar type of cardial ceramic which was called "Montserrat pottery". This section is located in a room inside the monastery where only researchers are allowed in.

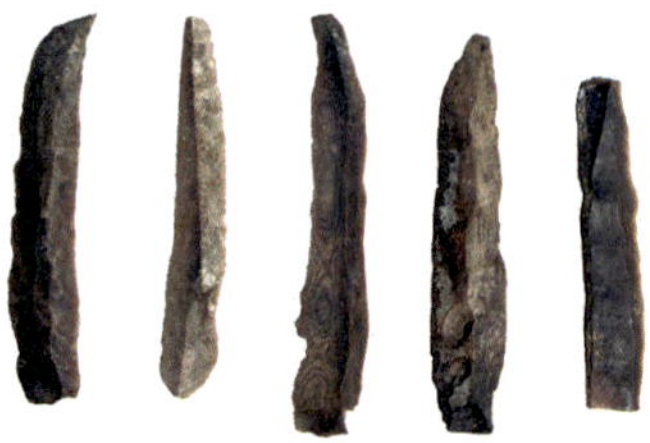

Silica Knives *from the* Cova Gran *site, Calcolithic Age (2500-1800 BC)*

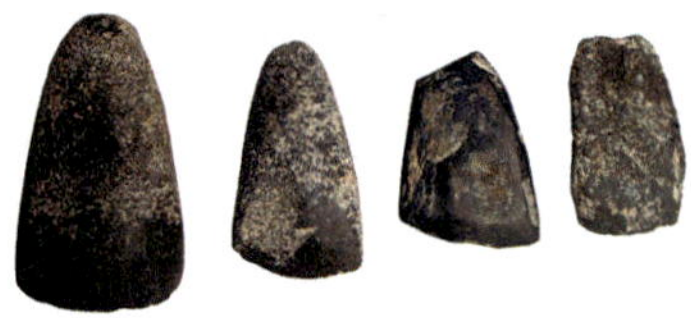

Stone axes *(basalt, diorite) from* Cova Freda. *Calcolithic Age.*

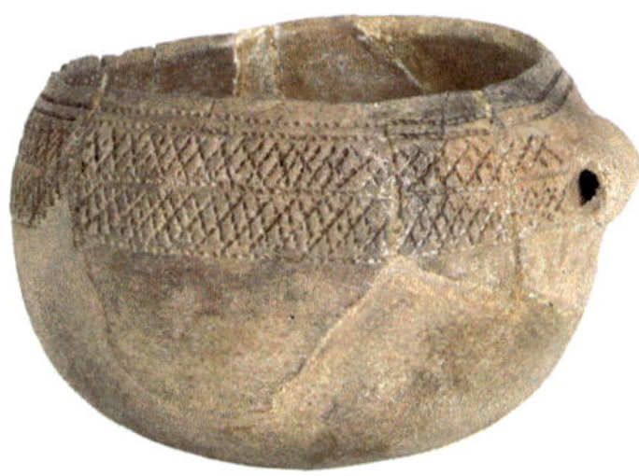

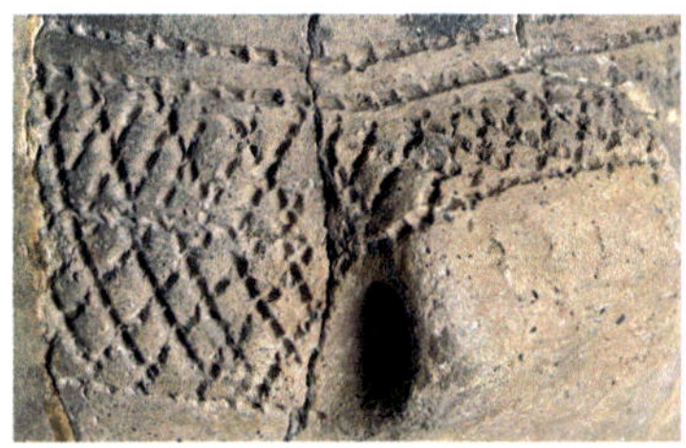

Vessels with cardial incisions *from the* Cova Gran *site, 6000-4000 BC (14 x 15cm). Detail of the handle.*

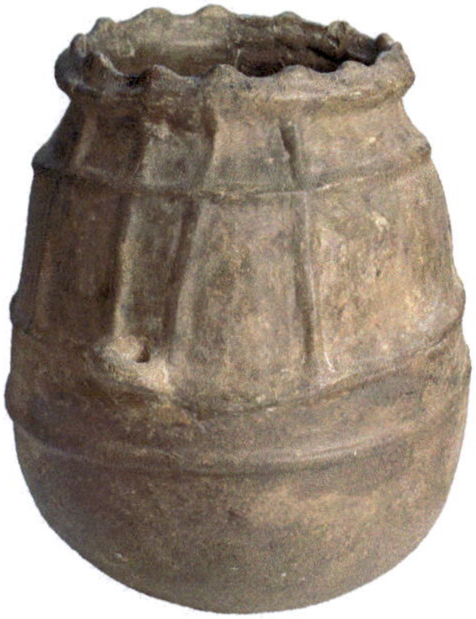

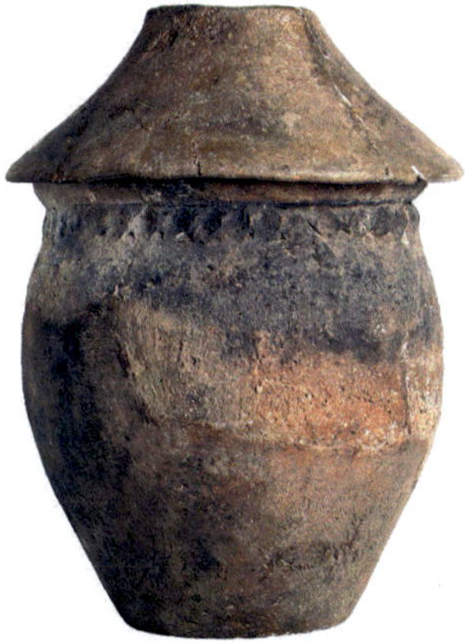

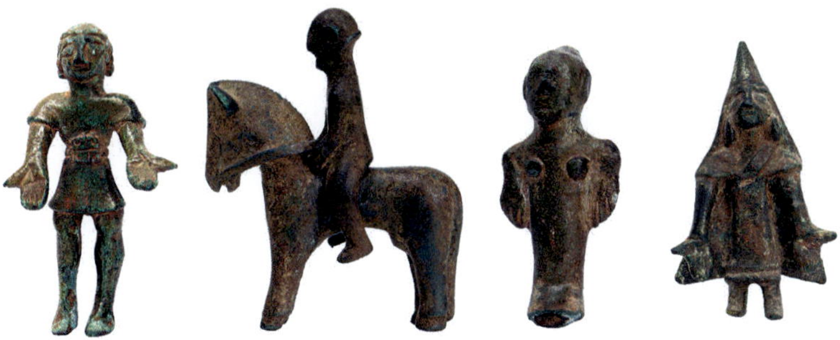

Clay vessel decorated with cords *(59 x 50cm), Iron Age, from the Cova Gran [Great Cave] site.*

Urn*, pottery with cord and fingerprints (33 x 18cm) from the Cova Freda [Cold Cave] site.*

Independently of the Montserrat sites, the Museum of Montserrat has received about twenty ***Iberian bronze figures*** *which have been donated by Sensat and Busquets. They are prayer figures, dressed or undressed men, women with veils, horsemen, itiphallic warriors, etc. which were religious offerings at the time.*

Amerindian Art

The collection of pre-Columbian art came to Montserrat in 2002 as part of a donation by Caja Madrid. It consists of fifty pieces of extraordinary beauty. They clearly illustrate the life, culture and beliefs of the indigenous folk who inhabited the current territory of Mexico, Guatemala, Costa Rica, Colombia, Ecuador, Peru, Argentina and the Easter Island.

__Female figure__, Ecuador, Chorrera, 1800-300 AD. (polychrome ceramics, 30 x 15.5 x 9cm).

__Figure__, Ecuador, Bahía, 500 BC-500 AD (polychrome ceramics, 39 x 22 x 17cm).

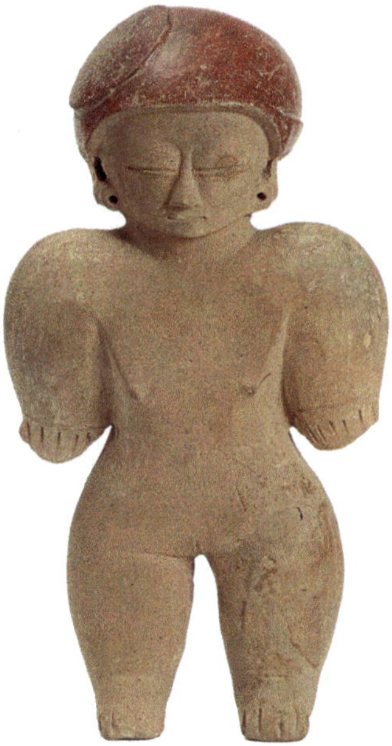

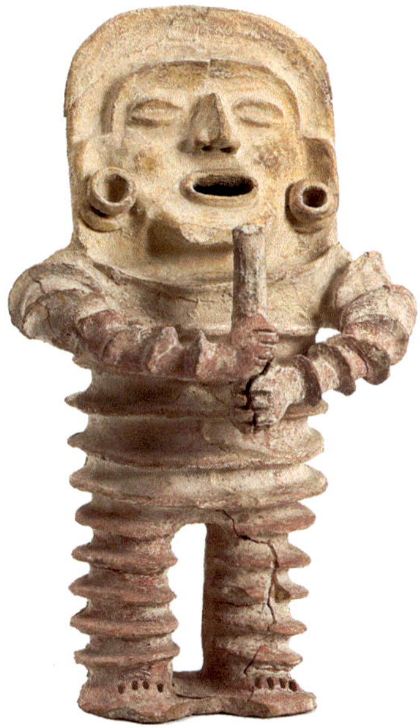

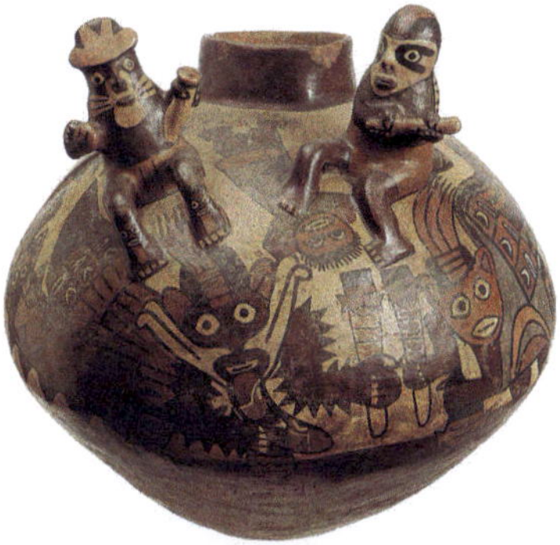

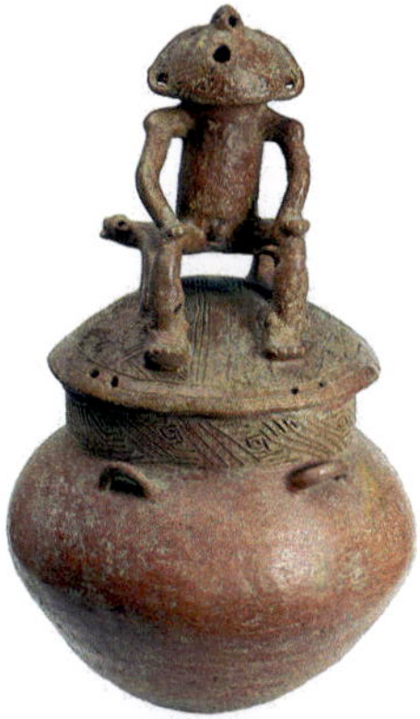

Funeral recipient, *Peru. Nazca, 300-600 AD (polychrome ceramics, 47 x 40 x 40cm).*

Funerary urn with a lid, *Colombia, Quimbaya, 1000 AD (ceramics, 55.5 x 26 x 26cm).*

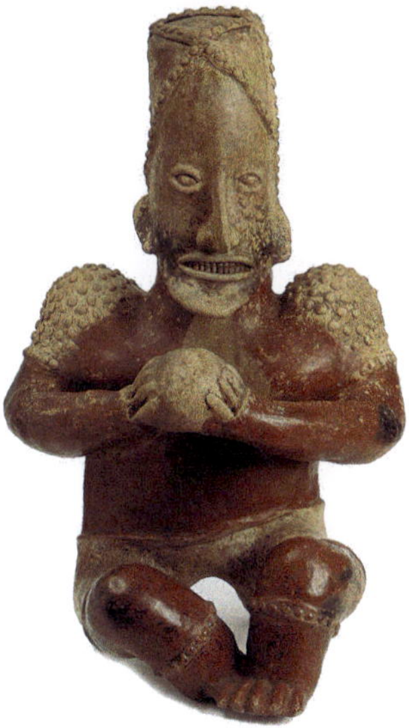

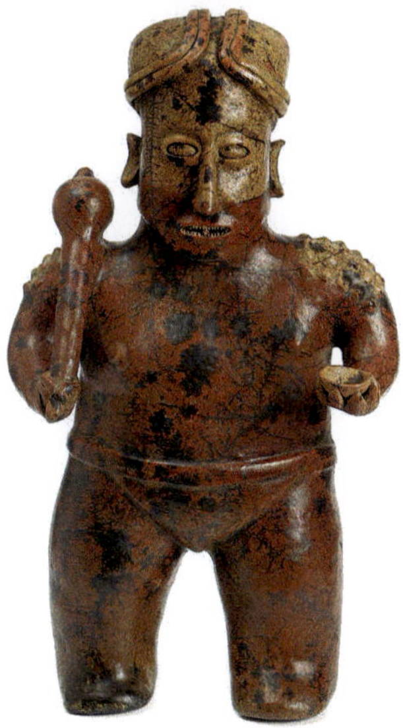

Ball player, *Mexico, Jalisco, recent pre-classical period (polychrome ceramics, 58 x 37 x 24.2cm).*

Warrior, *Mexico, Jalisco, recent pre-classical period (ceramics, 49 x 28.5 x 14.5cm).*

ASIAN ART

The Far East and its different cultures which are impregnated by the spirit of the Hinduism, Buddhism and Taoism have an attractive influence on our Western world due to their spiritual dimension. Their delicate and expressive aesthetics lead to calmness and concentration and they have become a challenge for mankind today, especially when we have lost our deepest cultural roots. The collection of Asian art at the Museum of Montserrat consists of a small collection of sixteen Japanese high quality prints; eight of them by the great artist **Ando Hiroshige** (1797-1858). There is also about twenty outstanding pieces, not counting twenty fine craft items from the end of the 19th century and first half of the 20th, which were given away by western collectionists, such as china objects, large enamel jars, ivory objects, furniture, etc. Their chronology goes from the 4th century BC to the 20th century, and they correspond to the cultures of India, China, Nepal, Thailand, Vietnam, Indonesia and Japan, geographically.

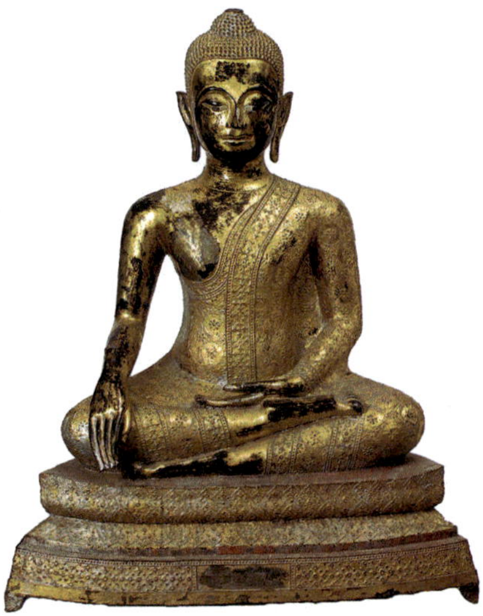

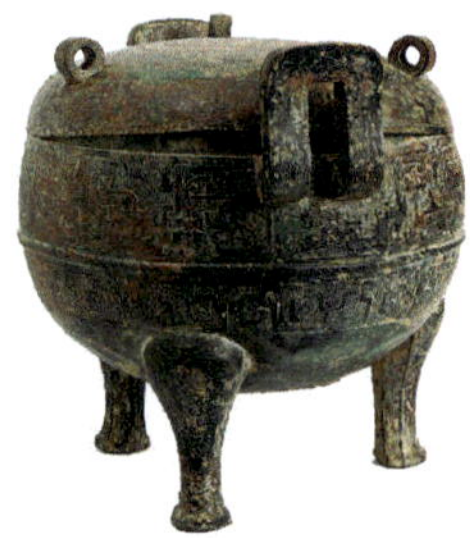

***Sitting Buddha**, Bangkok. Thailand, 20th century (lacquered, golden bronze, 79 x 62 x 40cm).*

***Tripod Jar**, China, East Zhou, 4th century BC, (Ding bronze, 29 x 33.5 x 30cm).*

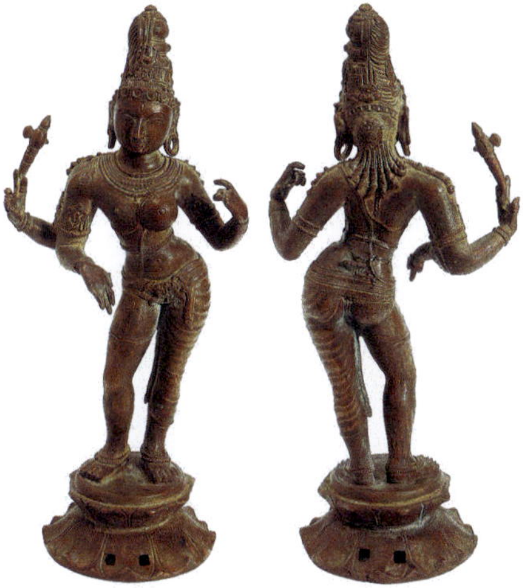

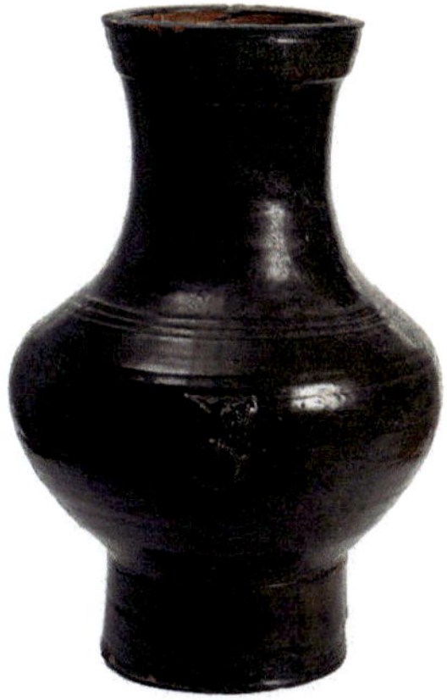

Shiva Ardenari, *India. Vijayanagar, 16th-17th centuries (gilded bronze, 27 x 13 x 9.3cm).*

Chinese Jar, *16th century, (glass ceramics 49cm), donated by X. Busquets.*

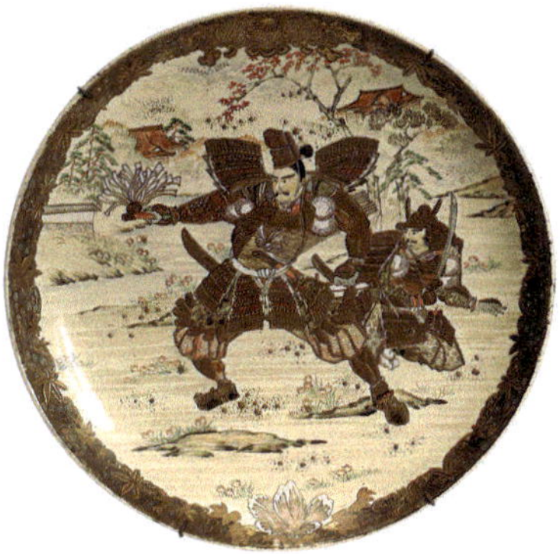

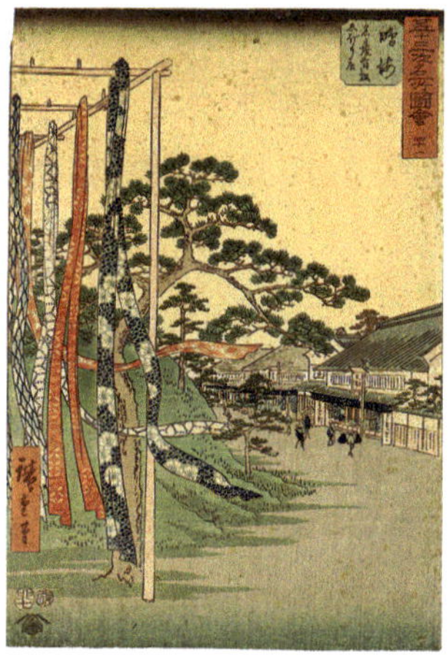

Japanese plate *featuring a* **warrior scene**, *from the first decades of the 19th century. (Satsuma ceramic 38cm), donated by Josep Girbau.*

Ando Hiroshige *(1797-1858),* **Ryogoku bridge**, *from the series "Famous views of Edo" (23 x 35cm).*

Primitive cultures

Some call primitive aboriginal cultures "art in the margins of history", together with pop art, graffiti from all times, children's art and that of the mentally ill, etc. Indeed, time is not an issue in this kind of art and it doesn't evolve. However, each and every one of these primitive cultures has its own personality and different phisonomy. African Art is very different from New Zealand Art. However, all aboriginal cultures show some common expressive traits regarding exuberant, ritual rigidity, repetitive rhythms, which provides a certain previous common denominator, but none the less interesting, of the historic cultures. Primitive cultures communicate certain aesthetic values we can find surprising due to their synthetic nature and the expressiveness of their firm simplicity, precisely because it is basic.

Establishing contact with this art for many avant-garde artists meant a return to the origin of art, that is to say, to the human fundamental creative and instinctive impulses.

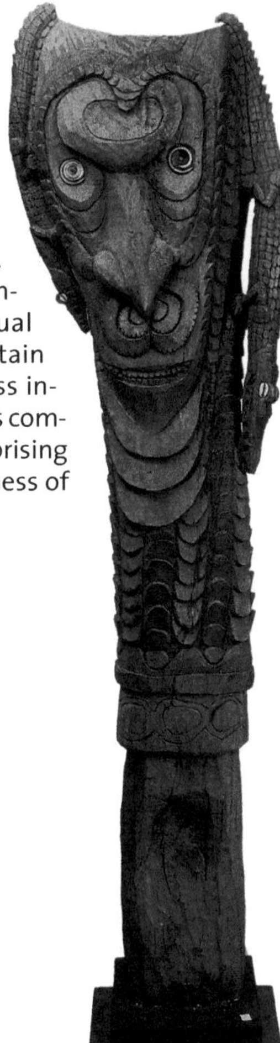

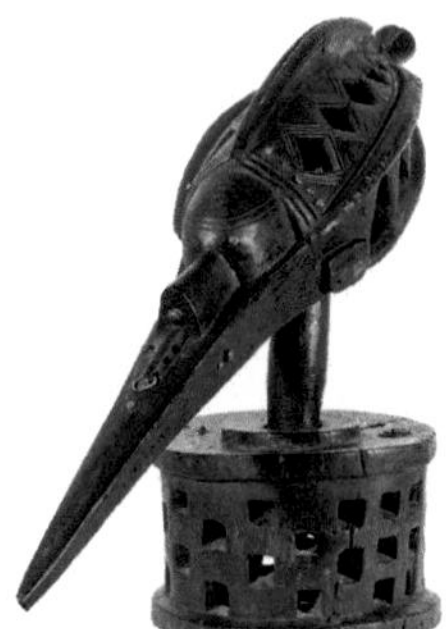

***Beam**, Papua, New Guinea, 20th century (wood and shells, 197 x 60 x 16cm).*

***Aniok**, Baga, Guinea Port (wood and metal, 50 x 76cm), donated by X. Busquets*

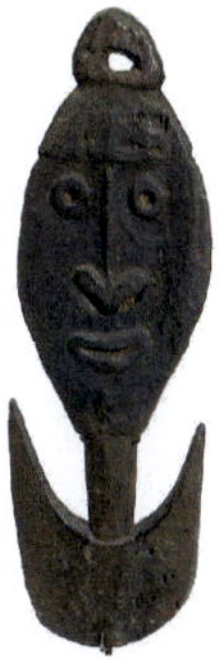

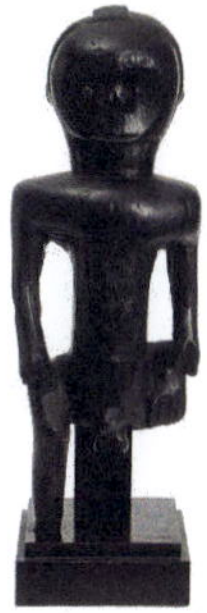

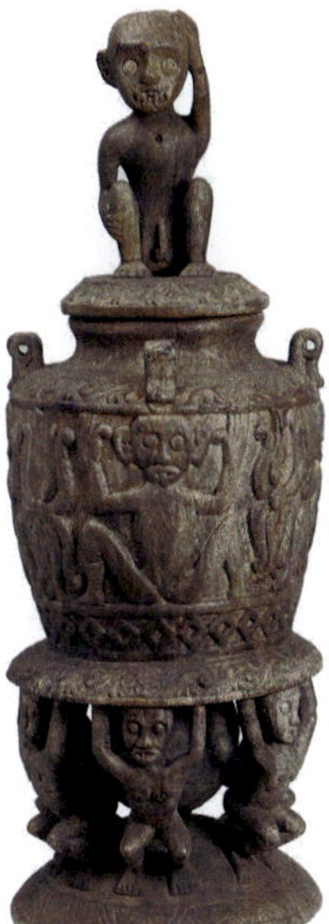

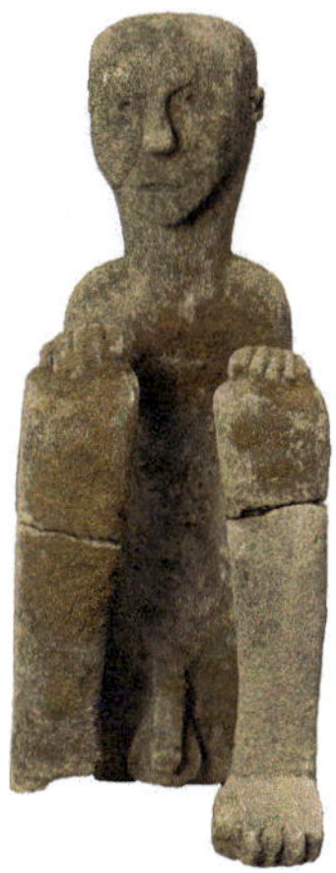

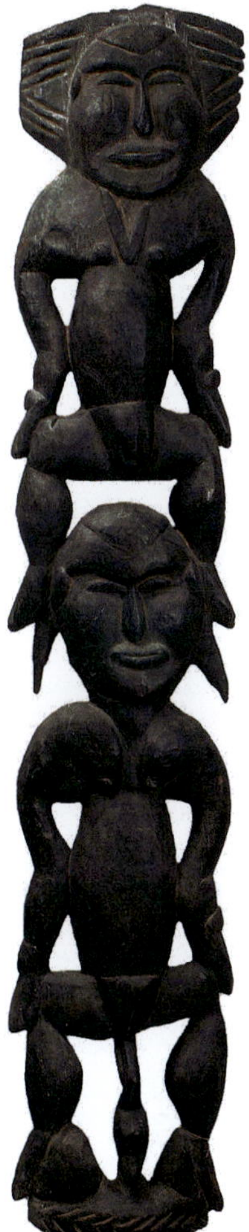

***Coat Rack**, Papua, New Guinea. 20th century (wood, 70 x 21 x 3cm).*

***Antropomorphic figure**, Ecuatorial New Guinea, Fang, 20th century (wood and tin, 42 x 14 x 10cm).*

***Urn with lid**, Indonesia. Dayak, Kalimantan, 20th century (wood 99 x 34 x 34cm).*

***Antropomorphic sculpture**, Papua New Guinea. 20th century (wood 238 x 43 x 19cm).*

***Antropomorphic death figure**, Indonesia. Timor Islands, 20th century (stone, 67 x 26.5 x 28cm).*

Synanogue Torah *from Germany, 18th century. The Torah is the scroll which contains the first five books of the Bible. In Judaism, it is considered the most sacred of objects, after having taken the place of the Sancta Sanctorum from the Old Temple, when this was destroyed. The Torah is usually closed and covered by a rich cloak which is called a mapà.*

The ***Pectoral*** *(*hoshen mishpat*), according to the Ashkenazi tradition, is placed on the Torah. It recalls the one that the Great Priest used to wear during the celebrations in the Temple of Jerusalem. It is made out of silver and it must be particularly rich and decorated with Jewish symbols: the royal crown of David, the Lion of Juda and the scrolls of the Mosaical law.*

Hebrew Culture

As a complement to the Biblical studies which were directed and guided by Father Bonaventura Ubach, a good collection of material from the Holy Land was gathered in Montserrat. They were not only archaeological materials but all kinds of objects which were related to Jewish worship, at home and at the synagogue as well as others related to Jewish customs and adornment. The collection of the Museum of Montserrat is one of the most important of this genre in the Peninsula.

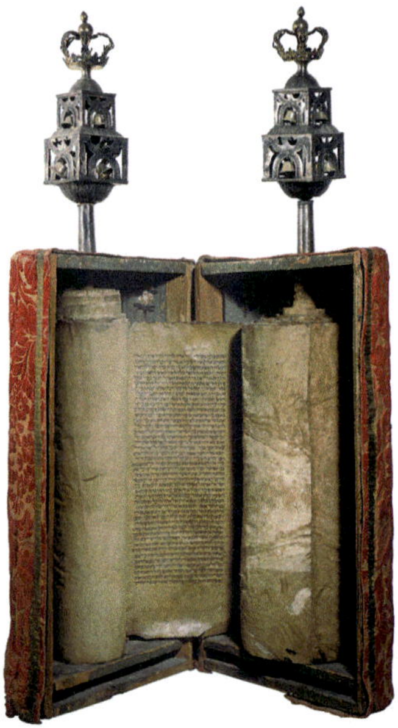

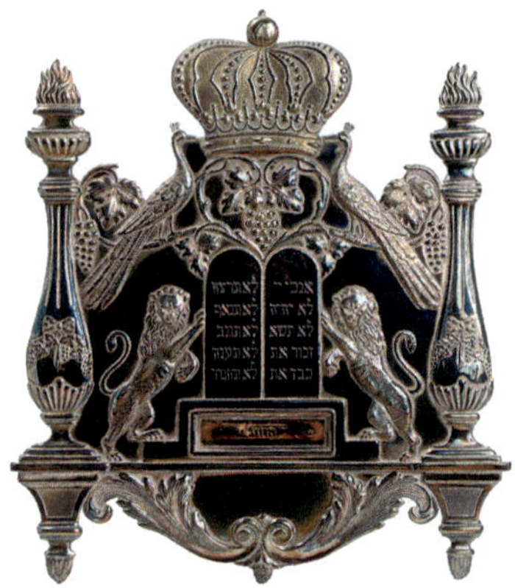

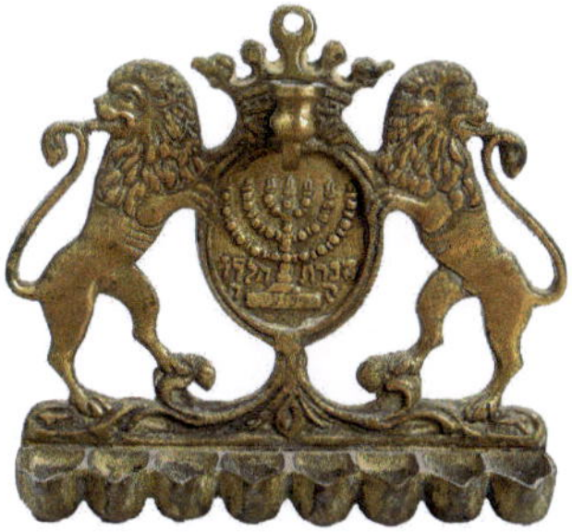
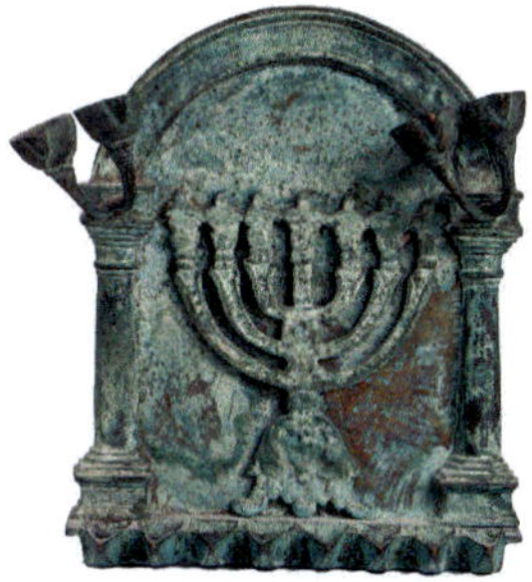
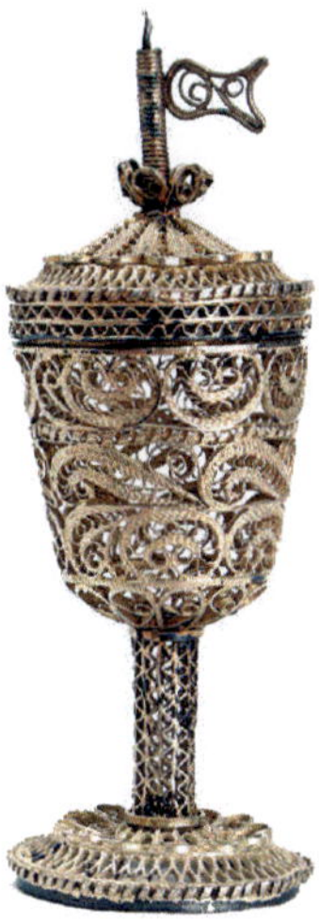
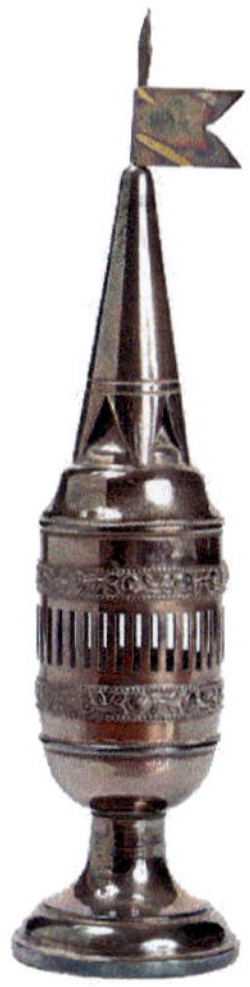

*The **Hanukkiyyah** is used in all Jewish households for the festivity of Hanukkah or temple worship. It consists of a series of little oil lamps which are lit consecutively every day for eight days. They often feature a seven arm candelabra or **Menorá**, typical of Jewish worship.*

***Hadasas** are used to spread perfume and differentiate sacred from secular time.*

The collection also consists of a clothing and embroidery section. The best samples are related to the celebration of the Sabath and Easter (Pesah). There are also other objects which are used in circumcision, weddings and funeral celebrations.

Islamic Culture

The Islamic materials which are preserved in the Museum of Montserrat come mostly from the Middle East. They were acquired to illustrate the ancestral customs of that land, where common traditions with the Biblical world still remain. The holy book of the Koran is the axis and the vital focus of Islamic culture.

The Bedouins' musical instruments have not changed a great deal through the centuries, as well as all the arts which are related to perfumes, such as incense burners, perfumed water jars, etc.

Islam categorically bans imagery. However, as an exception, some cultures from the North East of India, Persia and part of the North of Irak produced beautiful figurative art.

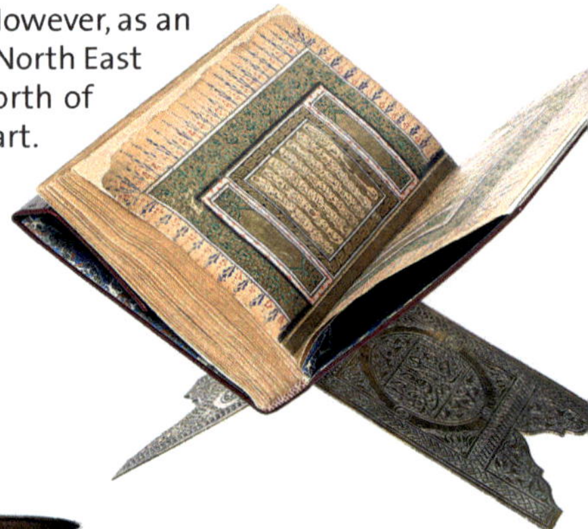

Alkorán *illustrated with miniatures from the 18th century on a folded bronze lectern with rich decoration.*

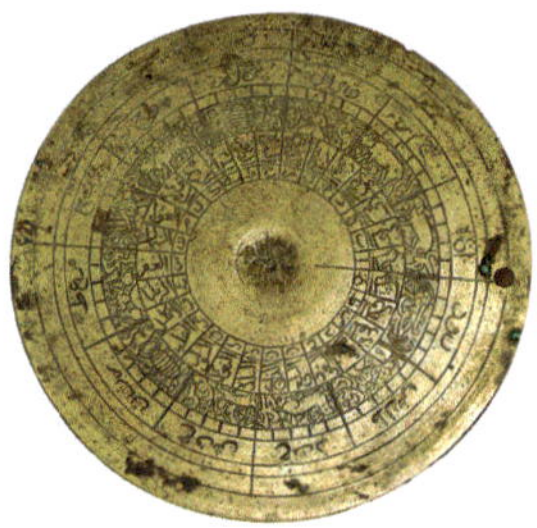

Astral Calendar Chart.

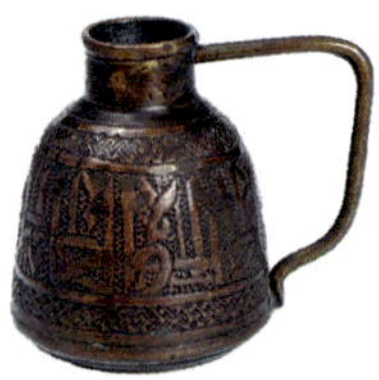

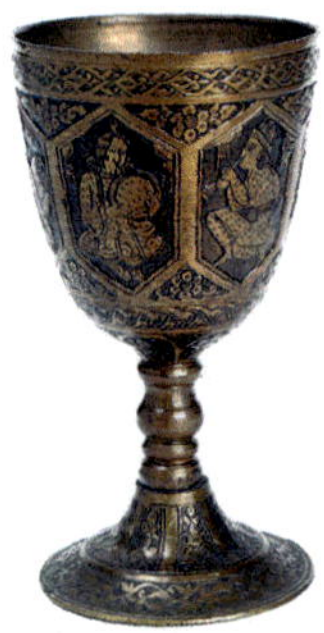

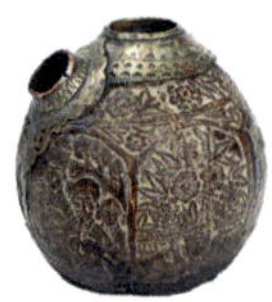

Small *copper* ***Jar***, ***Glass*** *with figures and* ***Narguila'*** *to smoke on pipe.*

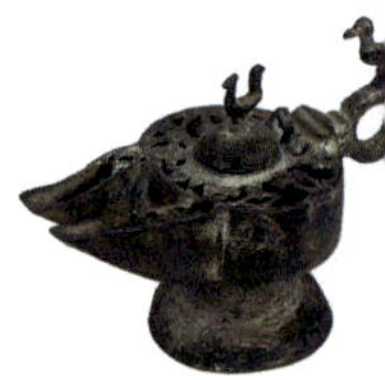

Incense burner, *Iran-Persia, 12th-13th centuries (bronze, 8 x 18.5cm), donated by Caja Madrid.*

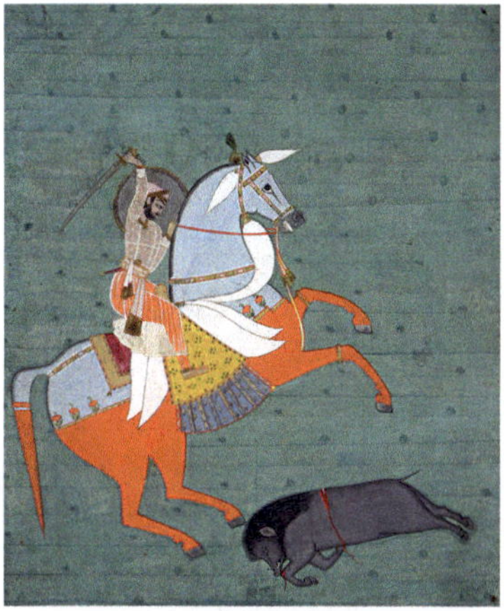

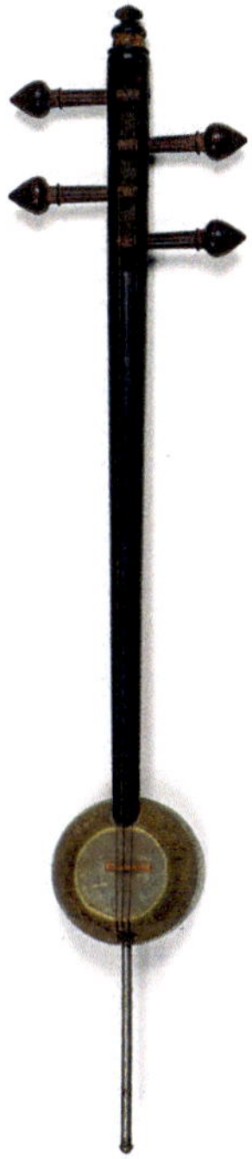

Knight hunting boar, *northeast India, 17th or early 19th century (tempera on paper, 30 x 24.5cm), donated by Just Cabot.*

Four string Lute, *('ud) from the Palestinian Bedouins.*

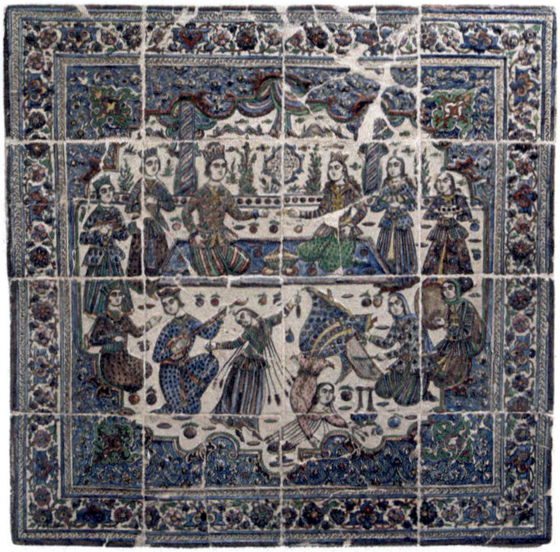

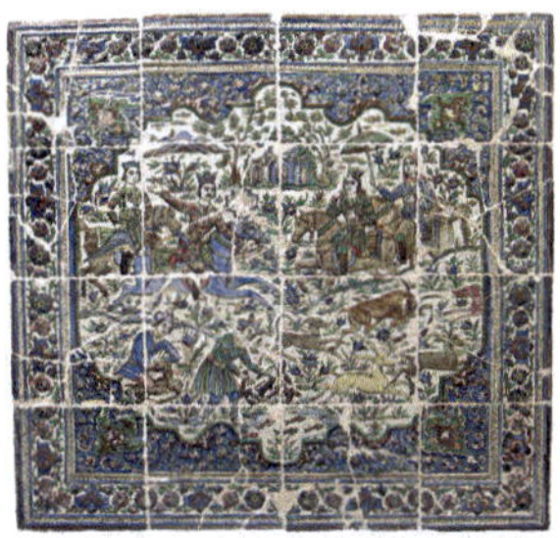

Dance in a garden *and* **Deer hunt**, *border between Persia and Iraq, (Qajar period, 19th century), glazed, glass ceramic with decorations in low relief (107 x 107cm).*

Medieval Art

The collection of medieval art and archaeology conserved in Montserrat is not particularly large. Our pieces come from the old monastery or its surroundings but some of them have also been donated to the museum.

A hundred tombstones and sculptural fragments from old medieval buildings of Montserrat have to be mentioned. The old Romanic facade of the mid 11th century church which was rebuilt in the atrium of the basílica and two wings of the old gothic cloister from 1476 belongs to this period. They remain in situ next to the main facade. A dozen complete sculptures and other loose pieces are also worth mentioning. They illustrate the culture of the time when Montserrat was born and started developing.

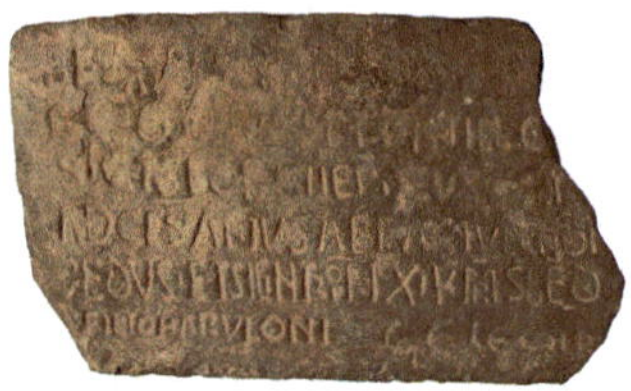

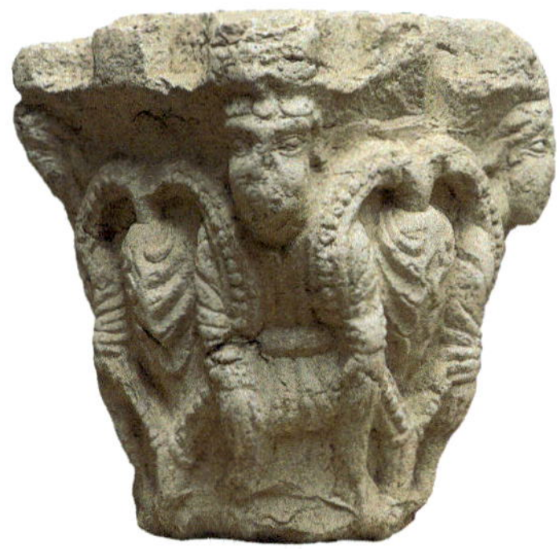

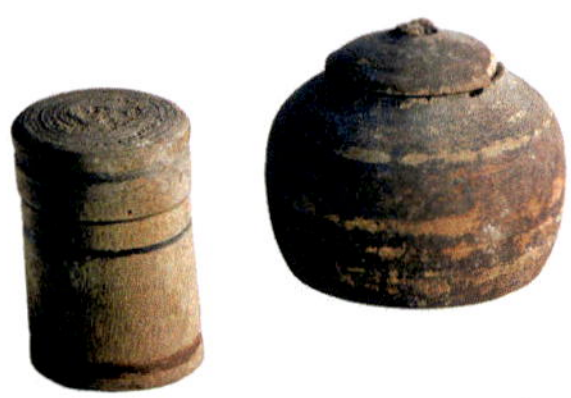

Dedicatetion stone *of Saint Cecili of Montserrat. It was dedicated in the year 957 by the bishop of Vic by order of Abbot Cesarius (stone, 28 x 47cm).*

Relics pots *from the altar of Saint Mary of Banyeres, 13th century (coloured wood, 9 x 5.3 and 8 x 10cm).*

Roman Capital*, 12th century (stone, 35 x 27 x 27cm), donated by X. Busquets.*

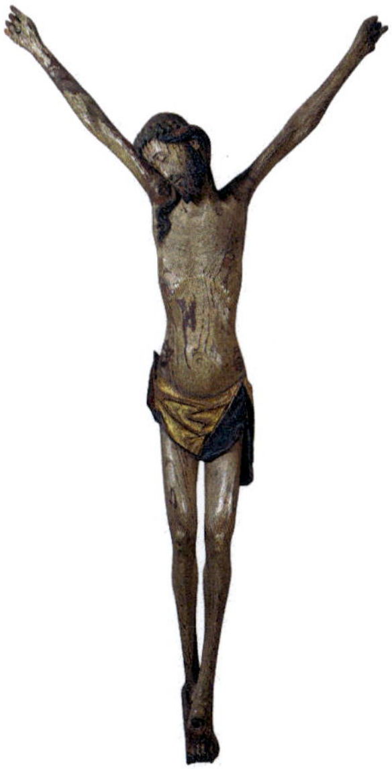

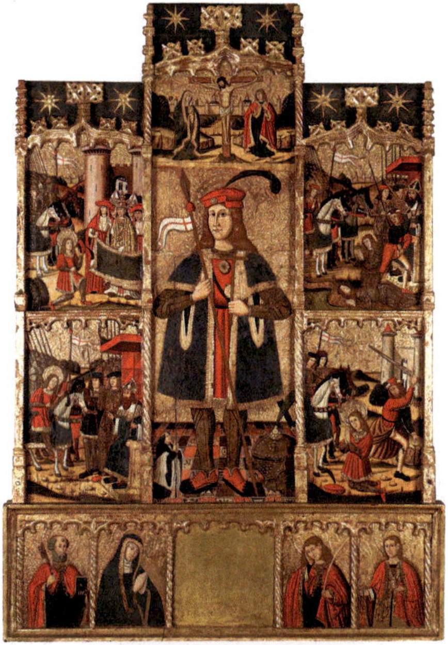

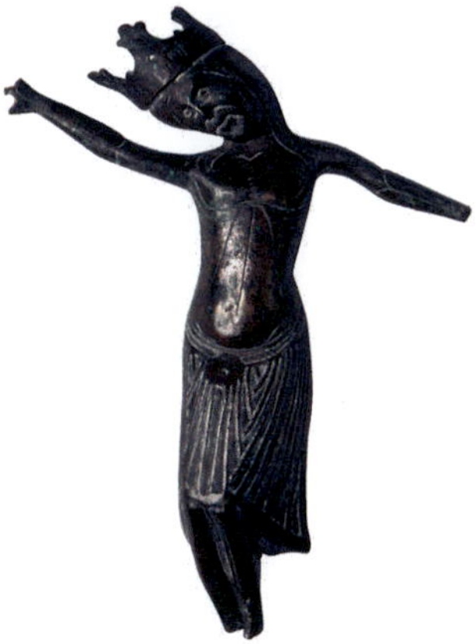

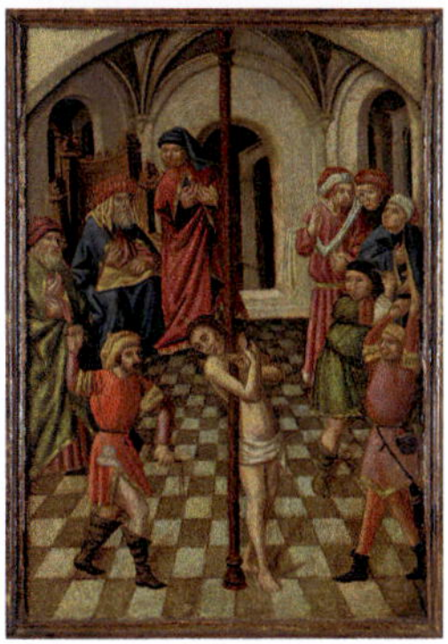

Christ from Renania, *15th century (polychrome wood, 107 x 54cm), donated by X. Busquets.*

Gualba Master
Altarpiece of a Knight Saint, *15th century (tempera on board, 187 x 122cm), donated by Julio Muñoz. It shows four scenes of the life and martyrdom of a saint. Right in the centre, we can see its owner with the patron on his knees.*

Christ of Limoges, *13th century (bronze with traces of enamel, 20 x 15.5cm), donated by Molas-Rifà.*

Flagellation of Christ, *anonymous. Spanish, second half of the 15th century (tempera on panel, 44 x 29.5cm), donated by J. Sala Ardiz.*

Sculpture from the 16th–18th centuries

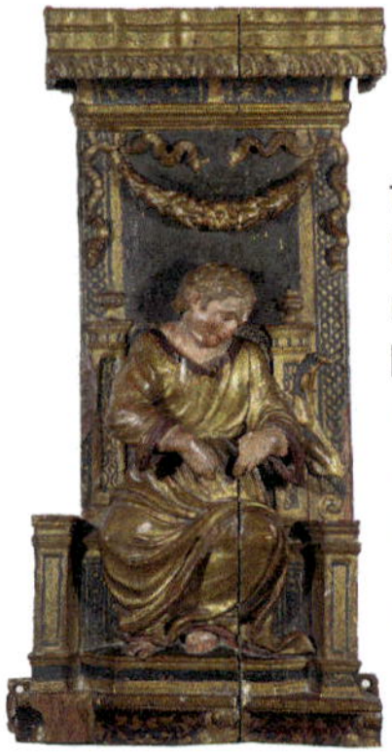

The monastery's heritage also includes several Renaissance and Baroque sculptures. Some of them are the remaining pieces of the great carved altarpieces which were the main decoration of the church of Montserrat before the Napoleonic destruction. It is worth mentioning the two monumental marble tombs which were imported from Naples during the first third of the 16th century by Admiral Bernat de Vilamarí (+ 1516) and the Prince and Viceroy Juan de Aragón (+ 1528), which are located at the entrance of the Basilica's atrium.

Most of the Renaissance carvings and sculptures are still to be studied in the depth they require, but it is obvious that many of them are outstanding pieces of artwork.

To the aforementioned we might add a collection of pieces which have been donated in recent years.

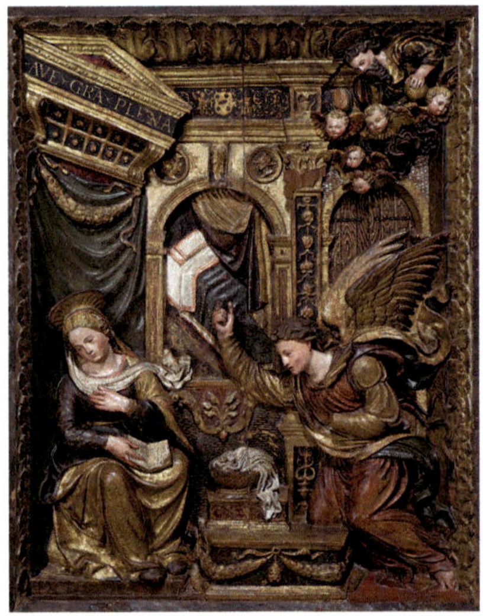

The fragments of the Renaissance altarpiece of Montserrat show the hand of the famous sculptor ***Damià Forment*** *(c. 1475-1540), who worked in Zaragoza, Huesca and La Calzada, but also in Poblet and Barcelona. However, the altarpiece in Montserrat was not made out of alabaster like the others, but polychrome wood. It was paid for by the Empress Isabel, wife of the Emperor Charles, in 1537.*

Child Jesus among the Doctors *(central fragment) (65 x 31.5 x 7cm) and* **Annunciation** *(107 x 83cm), attributed to* ***Damià Forment****.*

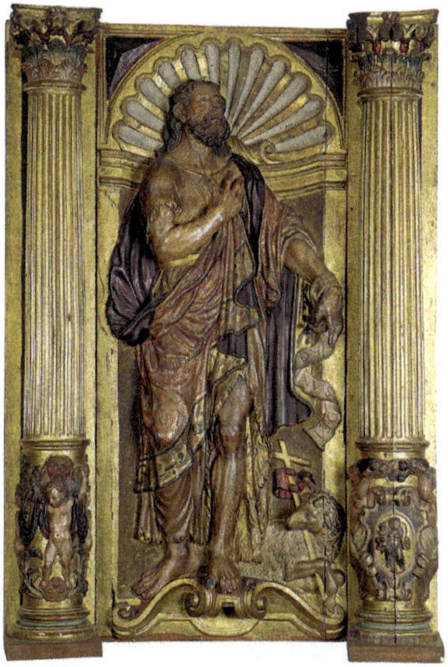

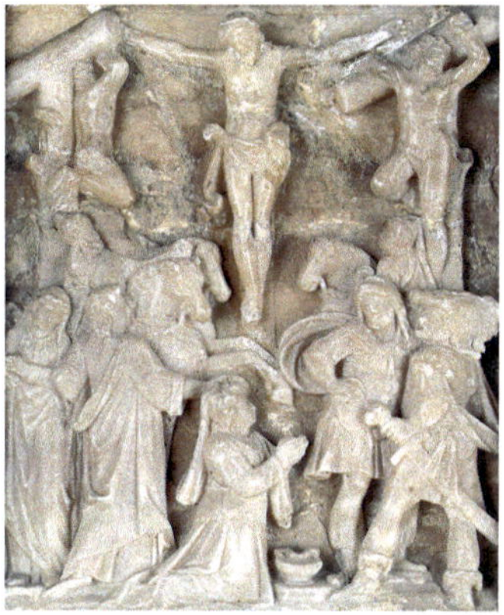

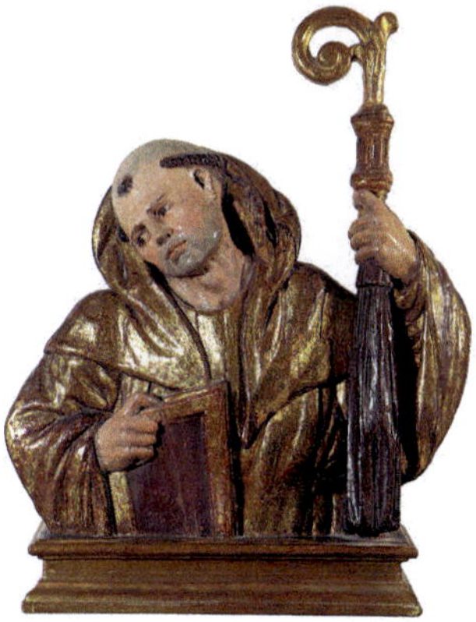

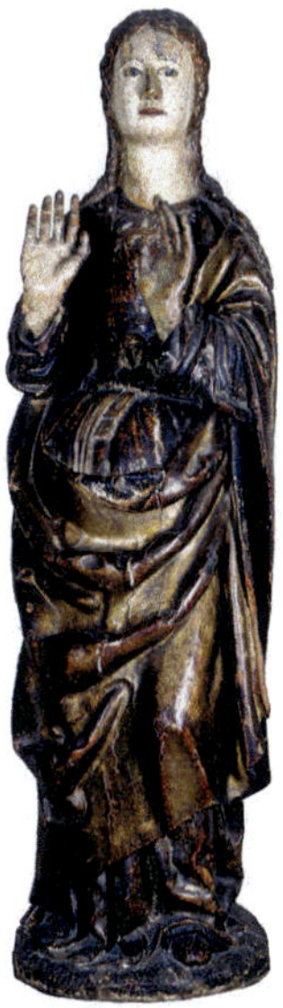

Saint John the Baptist, *16th century (golden polychrome wood relief, 124 x 82cm), It most likely belonged to the upper part of the back of the monastic choir.*

Crucifixion *this is a small altarpiece from Malinas, 16th century (Alabaster, 23 x 18cm). These are small devotional panel which were typical from the city of Malinas. Private buyers obtained different pieces and assembled their personal altarpiece with the scenes and saints of their particular devotion.*

Saint Benedict *long bust, 16th century (golden polychrome carving relief, 37.5 x 35 x 9cm).*

Annonymous from the North of Castille, **Awaiting Birth**, *end of the 15th century (polychrome wood, 114 x 28 x 26cm), donated by Pere Sensat.*

Ceramic, Porcelain and Decorative Art

A very diverse collection of artwork is gathered under the name of decorative and applied arts. They are secondary to drawing, painting or sculpture and they are considered to be minor art but in many cases, they can have extraordinary artistic value. As in many other cases, some of these pieces come from the Monastery itself, but there are also some which have been donated, including some which previously used to belong to the Monastery.

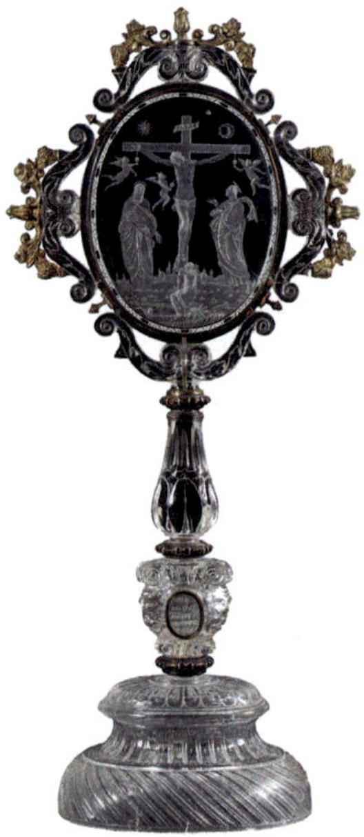

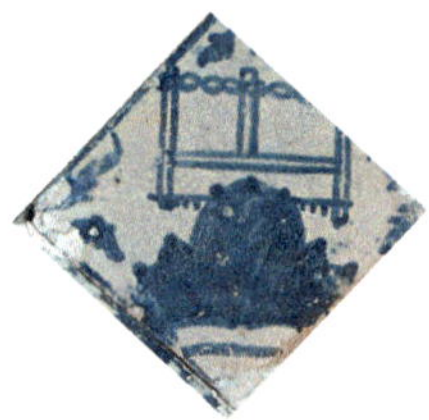

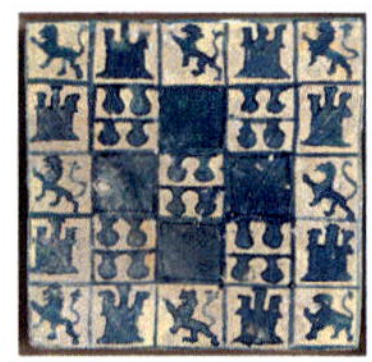

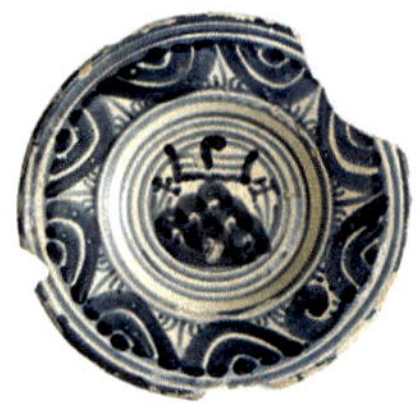

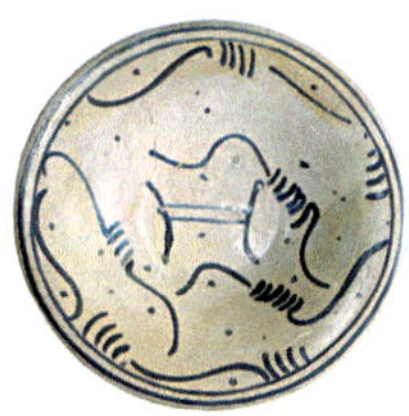

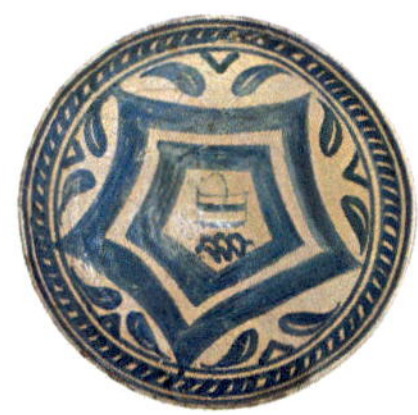

***Offering by the Duke of Mantua**, Vincenzo Gonzaga, 1605 (Carved glass, 62 x 27cm). This devotive object is one of the few ones from the old treasure of Montserrat which has escaped all historical disasters.*

***Tiles with the Montserrat and Castillian and Leon coat of arms** (15.5 x 15.5cm) There are different models and these were mainly used on the pavements of buildings during the period in which Pedro de Burgos was abbot, 1512-1535.*

***Plates with the emblem of Montserrat** (donated by Joan Baltà i Bonet). They are all popular crafts which were very typical in Barcelona. They have friezes and a central circle featuring its characteristic mountains in a graphic and schematic way. The two oldest ones (29 and 20.5cm) date from the 14th century or first third of the 15th century; the middle one (20.5cm) belongs to the encoded model of "diverse orles" and dates from the 17th century.*

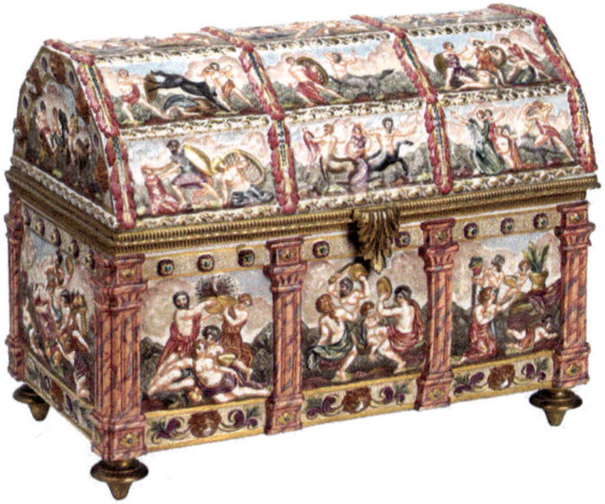

Porcelain chest from Capodimonte, *18th century (31 x 38 x 21cm).*

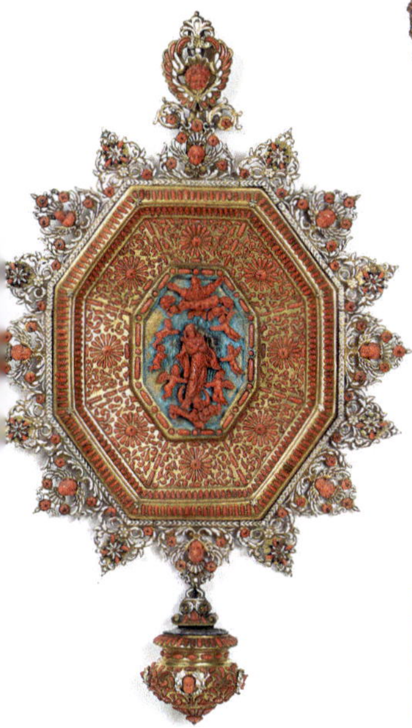

Coral Stoup, *dedicated to the Immaculate Conception, 18th century (copper with enamel and coral, 60 x 36cm). It was an object of devotion which was usually placed in the bedroom to bless oneself before going to sleep.*

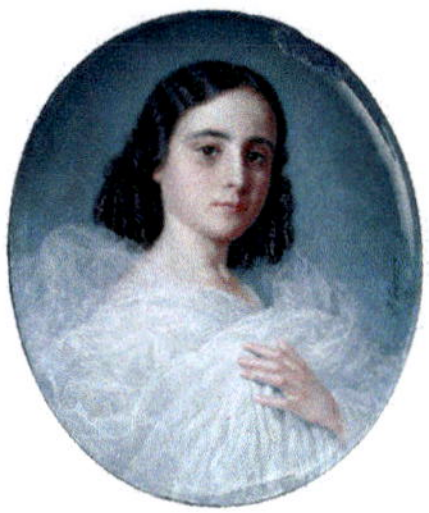

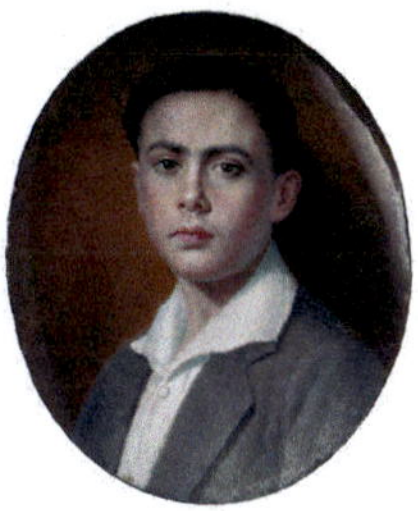

Ferran Guerrero Guimó *(1887-1979).* **The artist's children** *(enamel on porcelain, 6.5 x 5.2cm).*

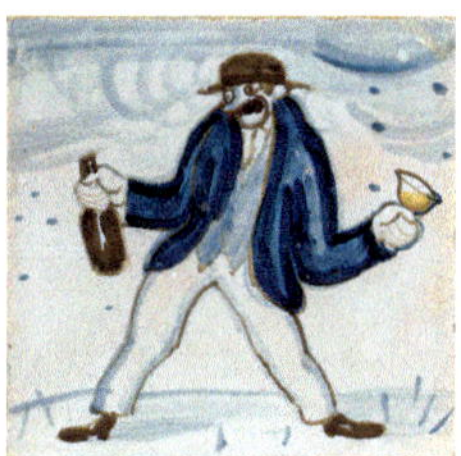

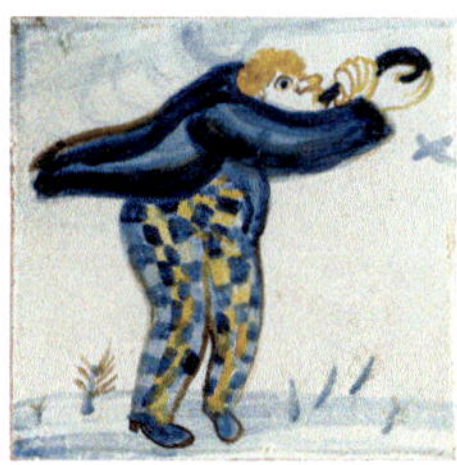

Xavier Nogués *(1873-1940) two tiles with* **grotesque figures of drunkards** *(15.5 x 15.5cm), donated by X. Busquets.*

Clothing, Textiles and Embroidery

Once again we must lament that, owing to the wars and revolutions of the first half of the 19th century, we have lost the many of the rich woven and embroidered liturgical vestments, of the Renaissance and Baroque periods, known from detailed inventories and donors' lists. The pieces included in this section date from the 16th century to the present.

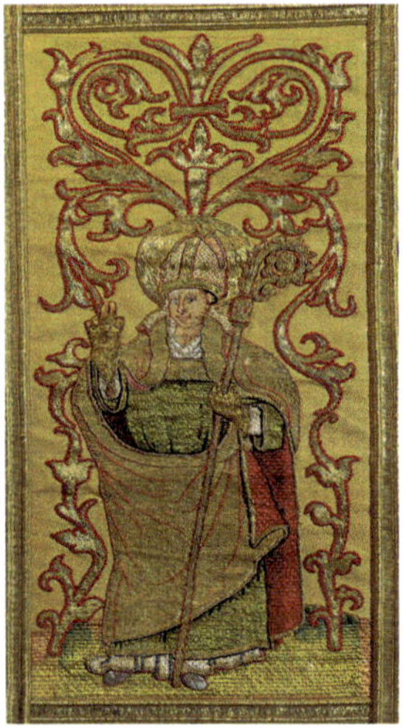

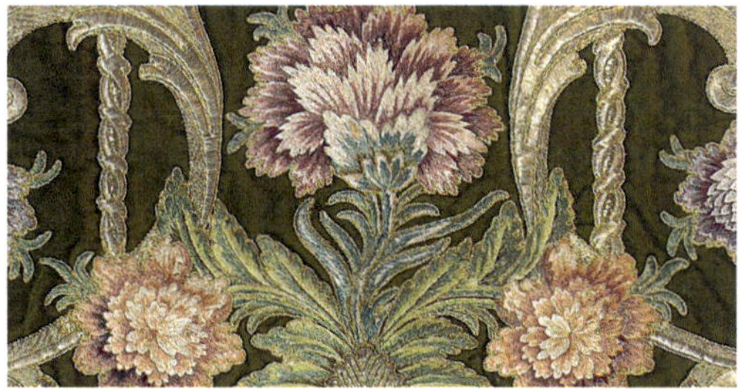

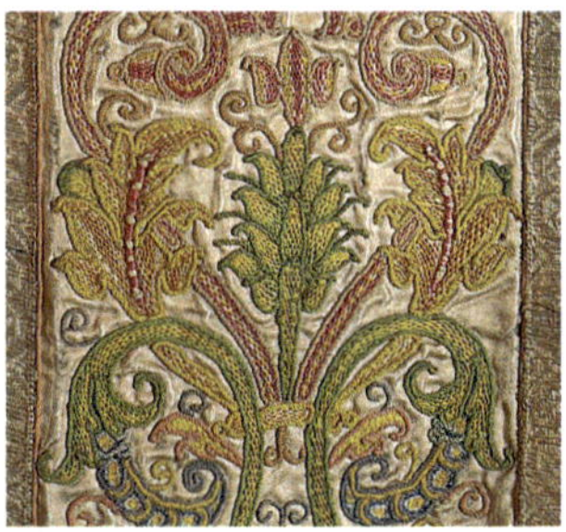

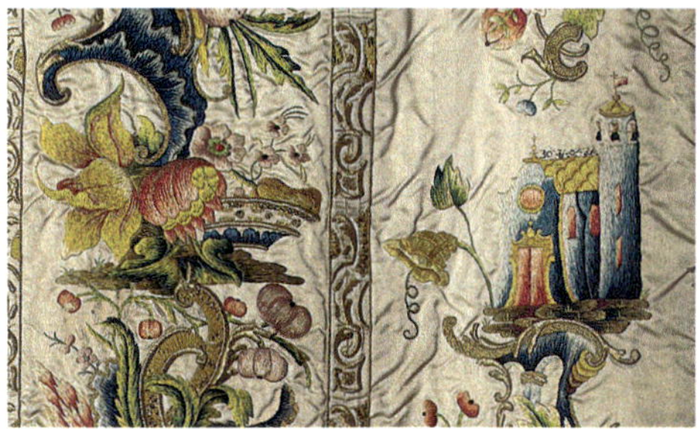

***Holy Bishop**, the central stripe is applied to a chasuble. This piece uses silk and golden embroidery known as "needlework painting", end of the 16th century.*

***Silk Textiles**, with lampas technique, 17th century. Chasuble, detail.*

***Rococo textiles**, silk with gold and polychrome silk textiles, 17th century. Chasuble, detail.*

***Chinese Rococo textiles**, satin, polychrome silk textiles with silver and golden thread, 18th century. Chasuble, detail.*

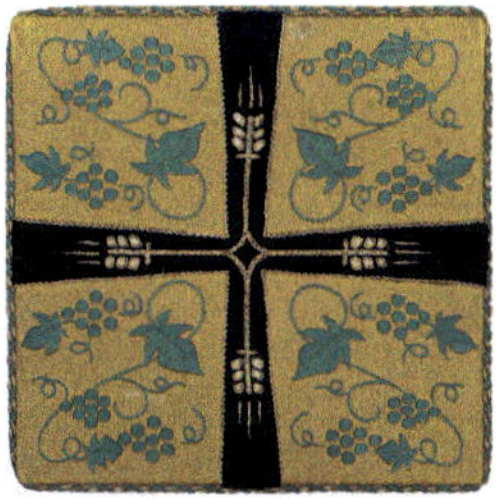
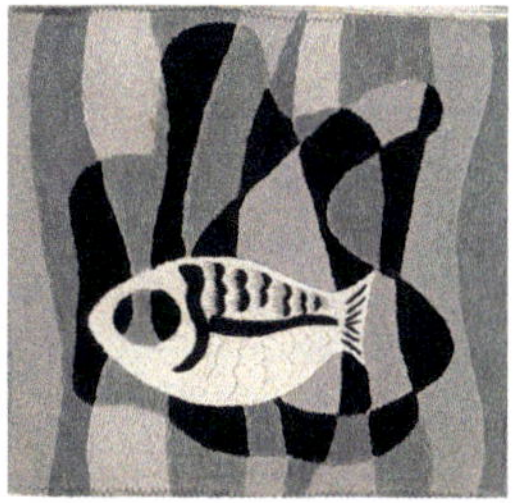
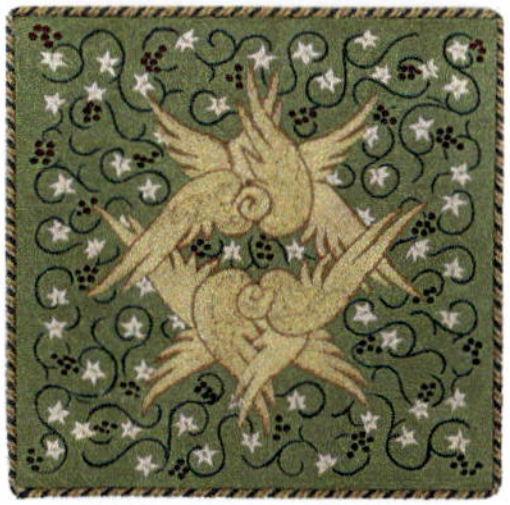
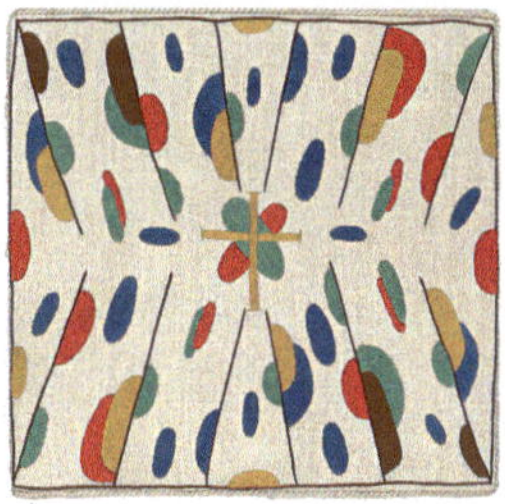
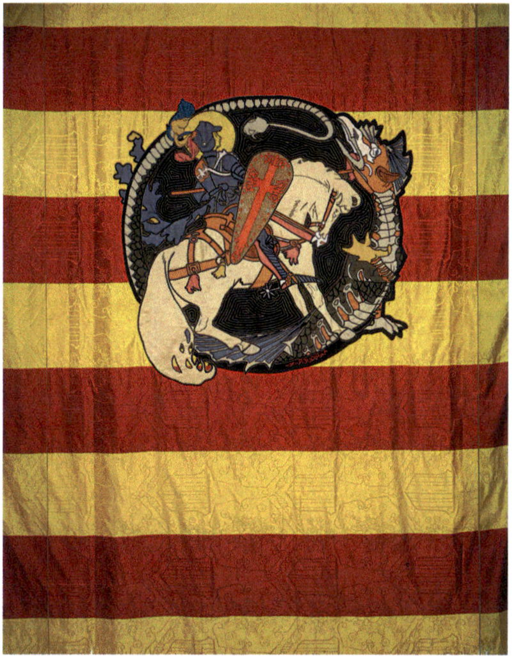

*P**allias** are square shaped liturgic objects. They are made out of a rigid material which is covered by richly embroidered material, since they are often used to cover the chalice containing the holy wine. This collection in Montserrat is very large and contains outstanding pieces.*

*Although **The Flag of the ProCatalan Union** bore the date of 1892, the flag was not actually made until 1904, under the creative direction of the modernist painter **Alexandre de Riquer**, its designer.*

Coin, Medallion and Stamp Collections

The coin collection in the Museum of Montserrat is large and very valuable. Father Bonaventura Ubach started it in order to illustrate the chronology of the last ages and Biblical cities, but soon went beyond those limits. The old coinage of Montserrrat consists of Greek dracmas, didracmas and tetradracmas from the earliest classical period, coins from the Hellenist kings, the Selleucids in the Middle East, the Ptolemeos in Egypt and all the Roman Emperors. The coins from the last Herodian kings have a special interest (Herodes the Great, 37 BC-4 AD and both Agripas) with Greek inscriptions, the Roman generals (including one of Pontius Pilate 26-36 AD), coins from the Jewish riots against the Romans (66-70, and 132-135 AD), from Judaea Capta. The collection is completed by Byzantine and Islamic coins up to the time of the Otoman Empire; but it deteriorates in the Medieval and Modern sections.

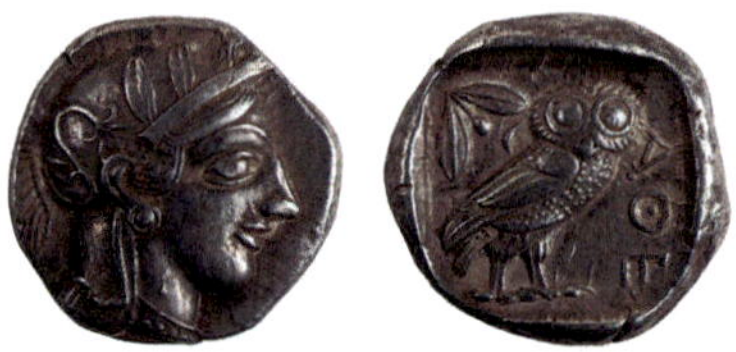

Athenian tetradrachm, c. 440, reverse and obverse (silver, 20mm).

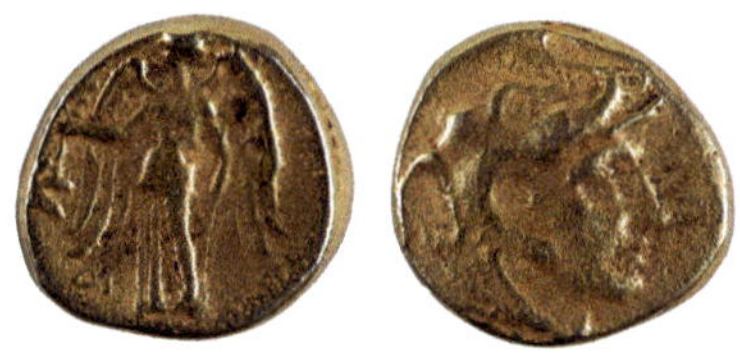

Double stater of Alexander the Great, obverse and reverse.

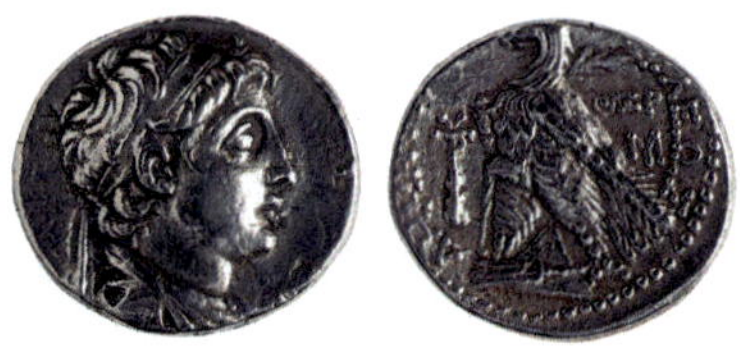

Tetradrachm of Demetrius II Nicator, 145-139 BC, obverse and reverse (silver, 27mm).

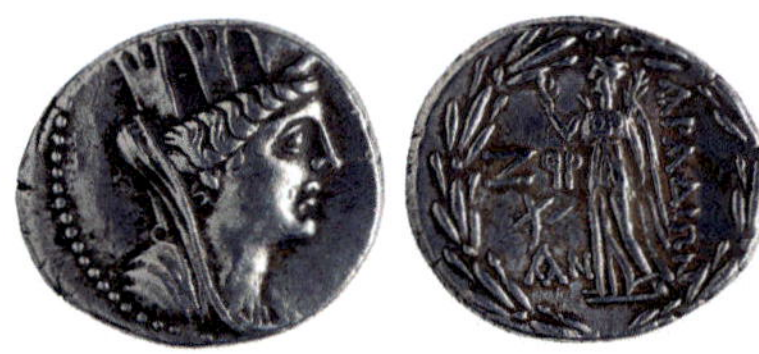

Tetradrachm of Arados, 62 BC, obverse and reverse (silver, 28mm).

The religious medallion collection's highest quality can be appreciated in the large and varied models in relation to the Our Lady of Montserrat, which covers from the 16th century right up to today.

The medallions in commemoration of political, religious and cultural events are also interesting.

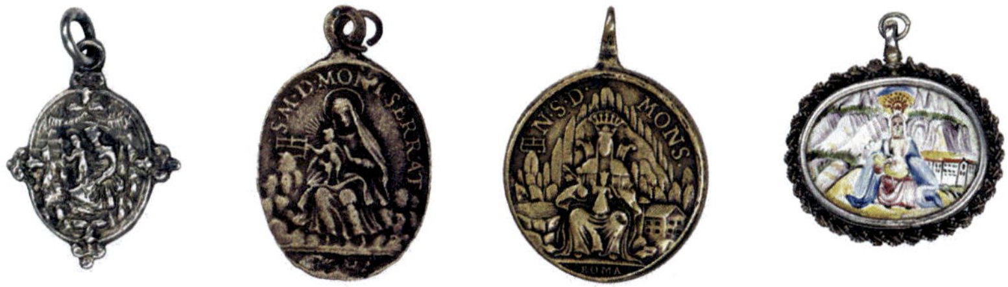

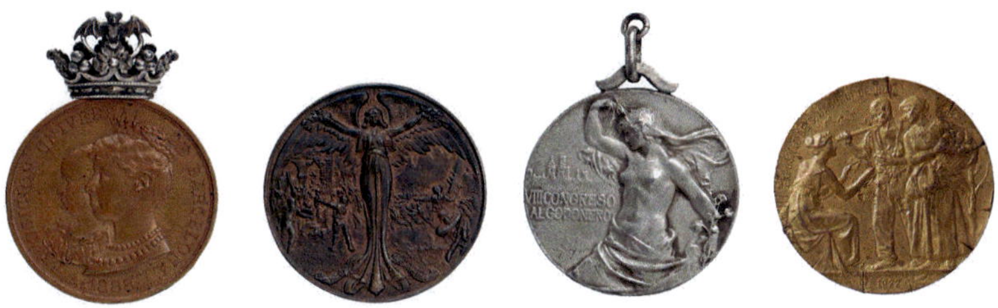

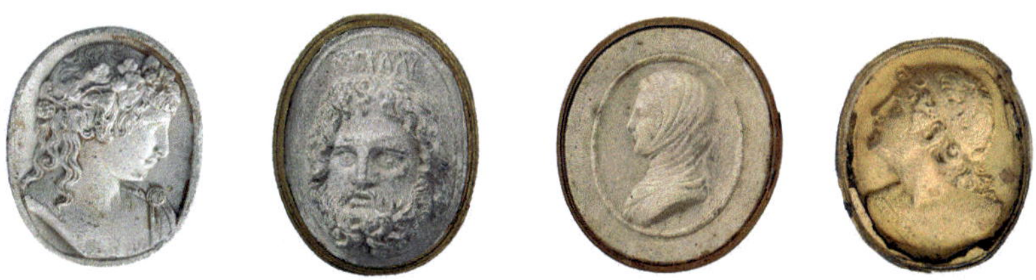

Universal Exhibition of Barcelona, 1888, ***Eusebi Arnau*** (1864-1933) (bronze and silver crown, 50mm).

Centenary of the war of independence, Manresa, 1908. ***Francesc Cuixart i Barjau*** (1875-1927) Tallers Vallmitjana (bronze, 61mm)

8th Cotton Industry Conference, 1911, ***Pablo Gargallo*** (1881-1934) (silver, 34mm).

Catalan Agricultural Institute, 1907, ***Antoni Parera i Saurina*** (1868-1946) (metal, 50mm).

Stamps of hard stone with carvings depicting classical themes, most likely from the 19th century.

The Collection of religious prints

The collection of religious cards and prints consists of about 18,000 pieces which have been properly classified and catalogued. Also in this section, the prints which were made in Montserrat or have its theme are also outstanding. They range from the early ones by Johannes Luschner (1499) and Johannes Rosenbach (1521-1524), until todays.

The **German prints**, the oldest ones, include work by Martin Schongauer (1430-1491), Wilhelm Plydenwürf (+ 1494), Ludwig Krug (1488-1532), Cranach (1472-1553) and Albert Dürer (1471-1528). The **Flemish** section is represented by Lukas van Leyde (1494-1533) Rembrandt and the Collaert, Wierix, Galle and Sadeler families (16th-17th centuries).

Without doubt, the richest and most important section is the **Italian prints** section which covers the period which goes from Mantegna (1431-1506) until Tiepolo (1696-1770) and their disciples and followers. Giovanni Battista Piranesi's (1720-1778) countless religious cards are also very interesting. The Grand Siècle **French prints** are also well represented as well as **Spanish prints** by the work of the best artists.

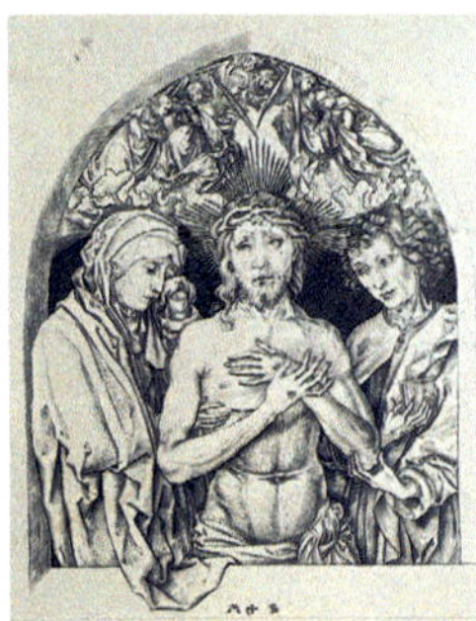

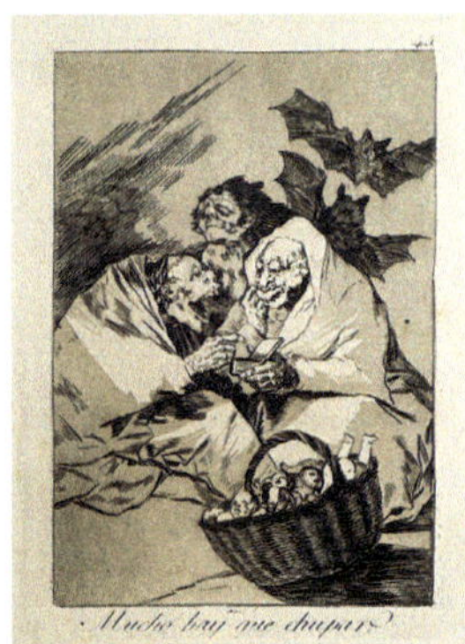

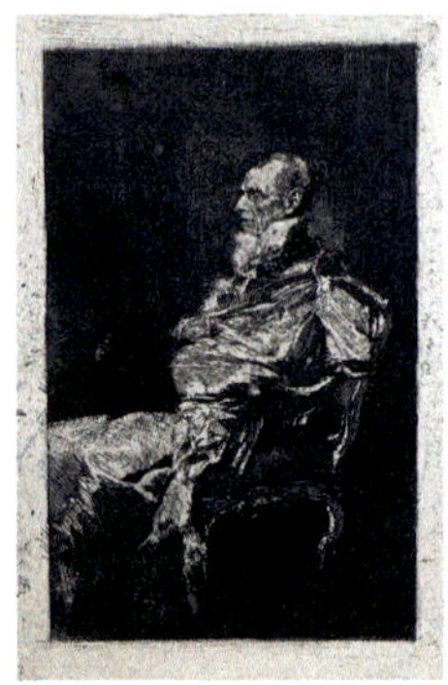

Martin Schongauer *(c.1435/50 -)*, **The Pained Man** *(burin, 18 x 13.5cm)*

Francisco Goya *(1746-1828)*, **There is Plenty to Suck**, *Capricho 45 (etching and aquatinta, 20.5 x 15cm)*

From ***Marià Fortuny****'s (1838-1874) seven religious cards, only the portrait of Meissonier characterized as a* **Diplomat**, *1868 (etching and aquatinta, 26.5 x 16cm) is of particular interest.*

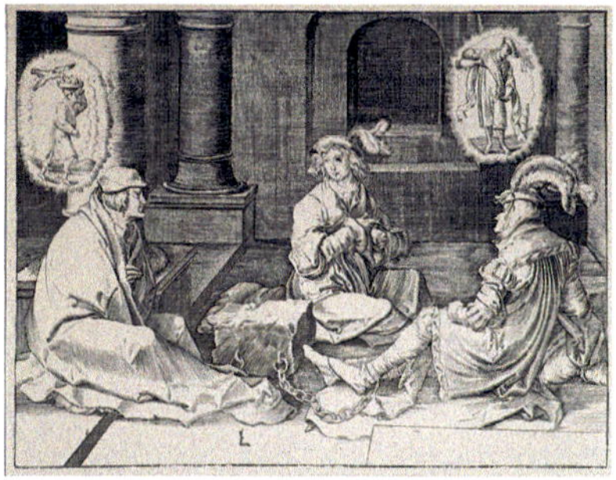

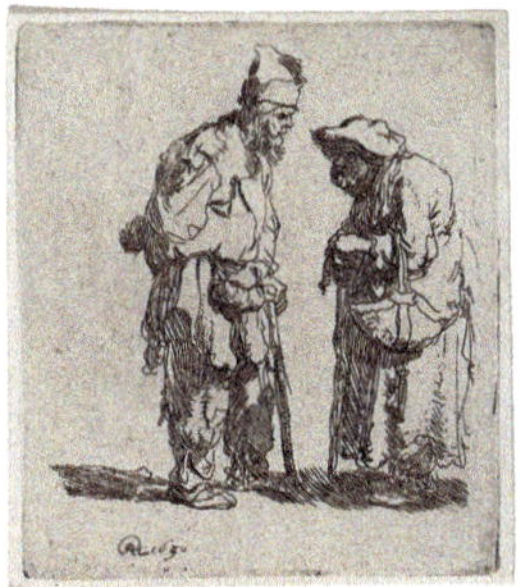

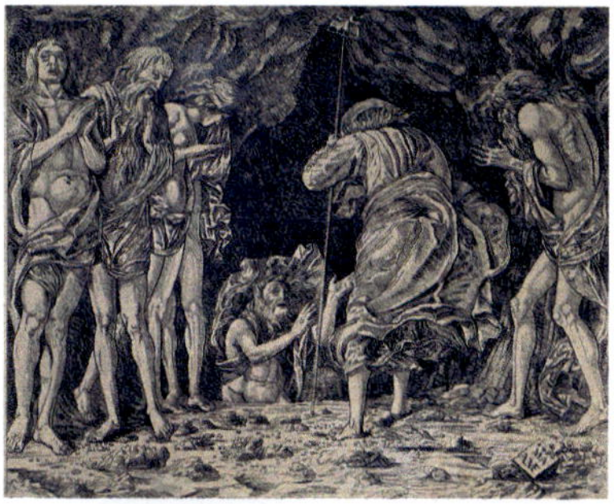

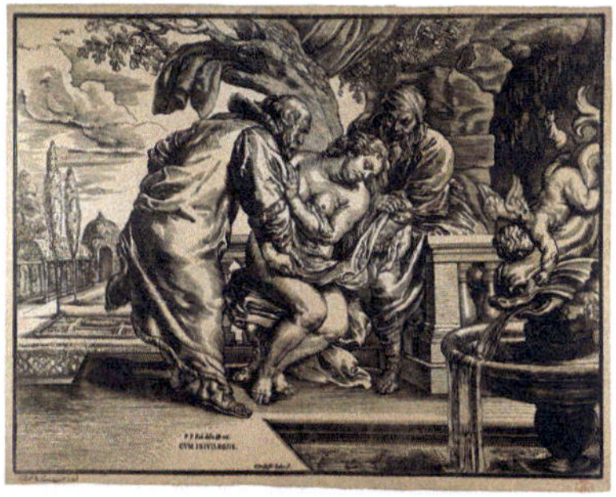

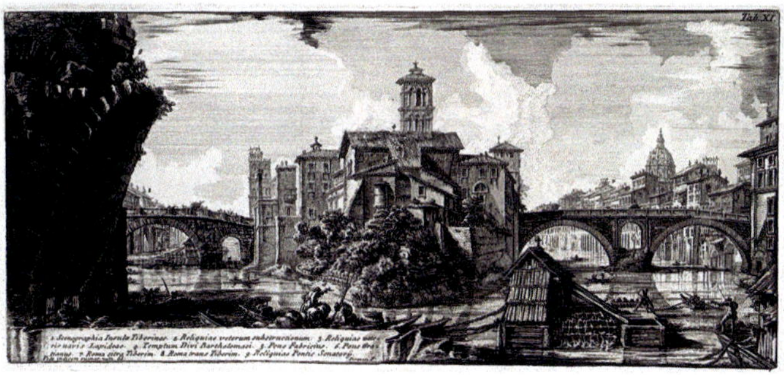

Lucas van Leyden *(c. 1494-1533)*, **Joseph in Prison, Explaining his Dreams to the Pharaoh's Servant** *(burin, 12.5 x 16.5cm)*

Rembrandt *(1606-1669)*, **Poor Conversation** *(etching, 7.8 x 6.6cm).*

Andrea Mantegna *(1431-1506)*, **Christ's Descent into Limbo**, *1492 (etching, 22 x 26.5cm).*

Christoffel Jegher *(1596-1653)*, **Susanna and the Two Elders** *(c. 1633) (44 x 58cm).*

Giovanni Battista Piranesi *(1720-1778)*, **Isola Tiberina**. *Rome 1762 (etching, 20.5 x 44cm).*

__Picasso's__ relationship with Montserrat became stronger from 1963. The painter gave the abbot Aureli Escarré and his community his print **La Sardana de la Pau** *(82.5 x 67.5cm), with an author's dedication in Catalan.*

***Joan Miró** also left some memories of his friendship to the museum, especially after the historical "intellectuals' sit-in in Montserrat" in 1970, which he took part in.*

Modern and Contemporary Graphic Work

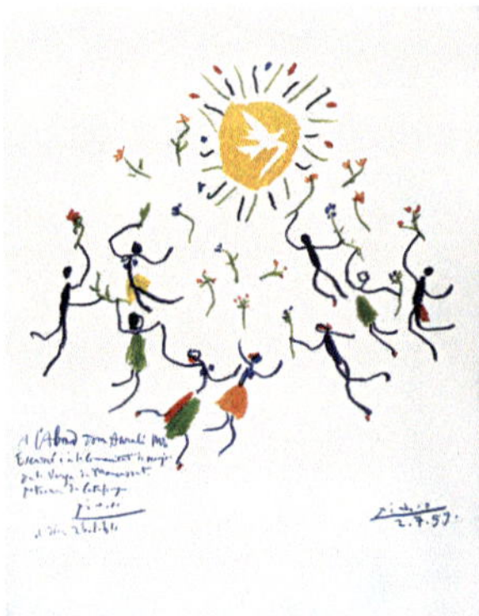

About forty years ago, the Abbey of Montserrat started collecting contemporary artists' graphic work. Some of them have become friends and collaborators in some cultural activities which the museum has organised. Among them, **Joan Miró** (1893-1983) and **Antoni Tàpies** (1923) who gave away "El cántico del sol" (1975) and "Llull-Tàpies" (1985) respectively, and especially **Picasso** who dedicated his 'Sardana de la pau' (Ronde de l'amitié) (1958) to the museum. In this section, Xavier Busquets' contribution should be mentioned. It consisted of the almost complete series of Vallauris' bull posters, also Picasso's, and prints by **Le Corbusier** (1887-1958), **Georges Braque** (1882-1963), **Rouault** (1887-1958), **Max Chagall** (1887-1985), **Hartung** (1904-1989), **Marino Marini** (1901-1980) and **Antoni Clavé** (1913-2005). Many of them were dedicated by their authors.

The list goes on with other artists such as **Georges Braque** (1882-1963), **Max Ernst** (1891-1976), **Salvador Dalí** (1904-1989), **Eduardo Chillida** (1924-2001), **Joan Ponç** (1927-1984), **Josep M. Subirachs** (1924), **Joan Hernández Pijuan** (1931-2005), **Rafael Canogar** (1935), **Josep Guinovart** (1927), **Antoni Llena** (1942), **Perejaume** (1957), **Josep Hurtuna** (1913), **Josep Niebla** (1945), **Alfons Borrell** (1931), **Joan Pere Viladecans** (1948), **Joaquim Chancho** (1943), **Sergi Aguilar** (1946), **Javier Puértolas** (1947), **Agustí Puig** (1957), **Ramiro Fernández Saus** (1961), etc.

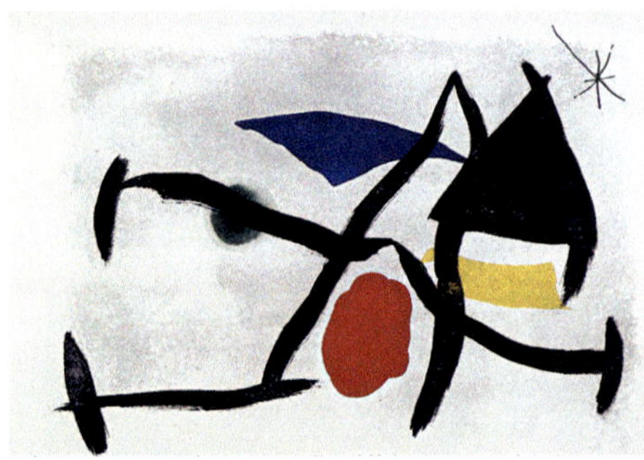

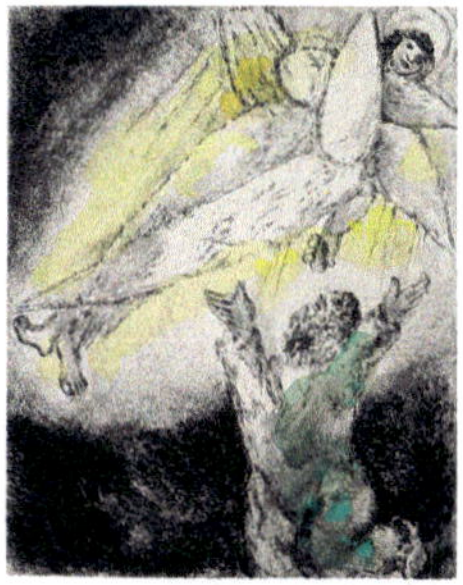

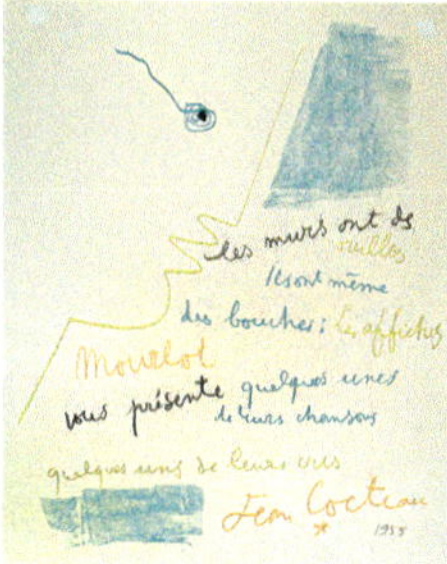

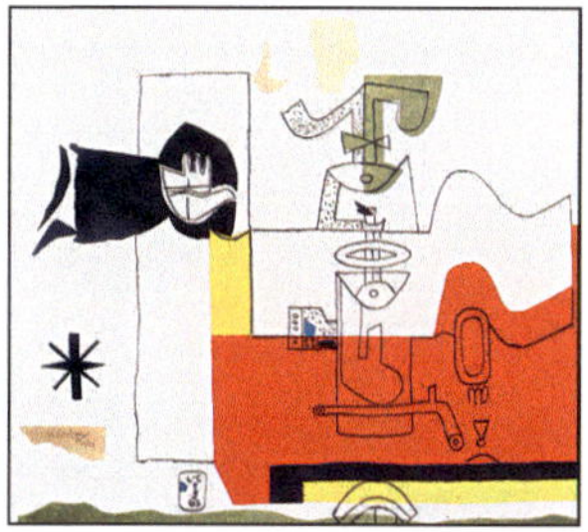

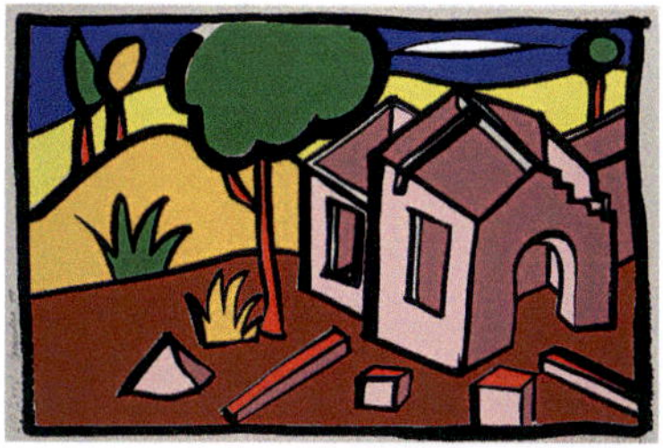

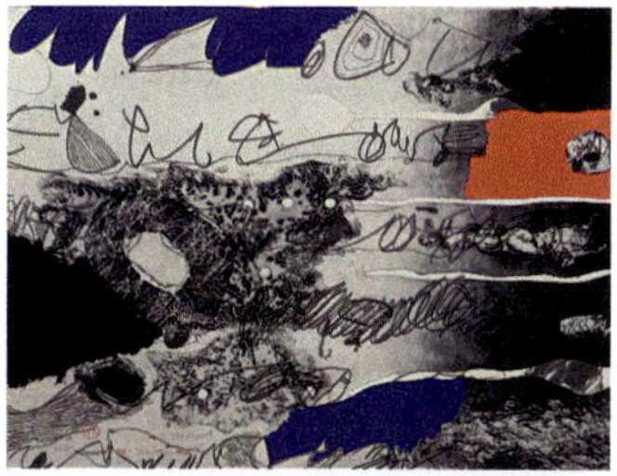

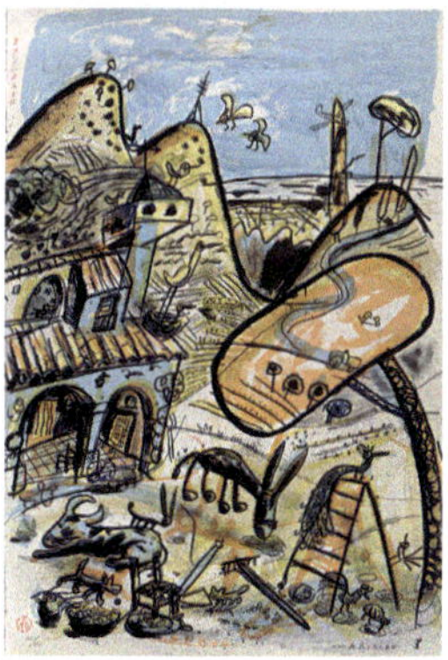

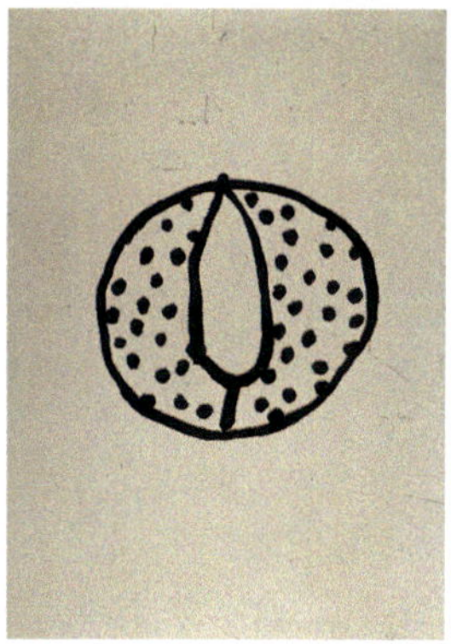

Max Chagall *(1887-1985),* **Vision of Ezequiel,** *(hand-coloured print, 53 x 38.3cm), 85/100, dedicated by the author.*

Jean Cocteau *(1889-1963),* **Les murs ont des oreilles**, *1955 (print, 66 x 50.7cm).*

Le Corbusier *(1887-1965),* **Untitled**, *1963 (print, 72 x 80cm).*

Narcís Comadira *(1942),* **A New House** *(silk screen print, 53.5 x 36cm).*

Josep Guinovart *(1927 -2007)* **Untitled** *(print, 50 x 64.5cm).*

Javier Mariscal *(1950),* **Local Landscape** *(print, 75 x 51cm).*

Joan Hernández Pijuan *(1931-2005),* **Untitled** *(print, 57 x 39cm).*

POSTERS AND *EPHEMERA*

The posters that Montserrat commisioned to be printed during the first half of the 20th century were graphically considered, as very interesting. However, the poster collection at of the Abbey of Montserrat is most famous for their Civil War related background, (1936-1939), which consists of over two hundred pieces of work.

*The **Ephemera** collection of Montserrat comes to over 50,000 pieces. Among them, the postcards are worth mentioning, as well as commercial brand fliers, labels, menus, dance club membership cards, stickers, cut-out (some of these may be peeled off or have some movement), diplomas, letter paper, religious cards, bereavement cards, matchboxes, sugar packets, cigar bands, hotel sticky labels, etc.*

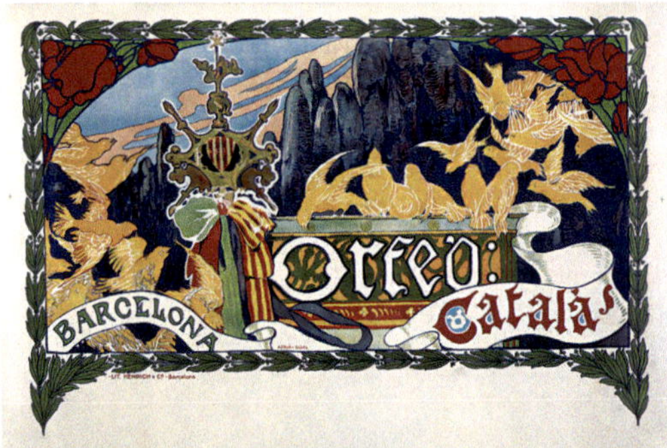

***Adrià Gual** (1872-1944),* **Poster of the Catalan Choral society**, *1904 (print 54 x 93cm), Lit. Henrich, Barcelona.*

The generic name of *ephemera* is used internationally to refer to small size prints. They were both a testimony of the taste and aesthetic ideals of this period and a first class means of mass communication, even though they were not conceived as durable art work. The *ephemera* collection of Montserrat is extraordinarily large and very interesting, especially regarding modernist and turn of the century design. Most of these prints were donated by Carme Carreras Candi (†1985), followed by other later donations.

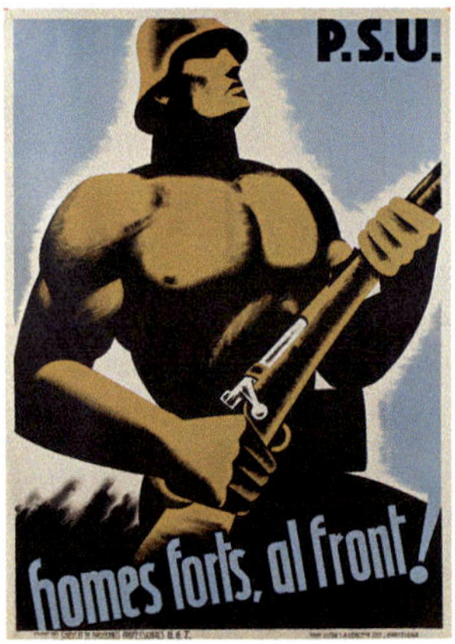

***Martí Bas** (1910-1966),* **Strong men, to the front!**, *1936 (lithograph, 100 x 70 cm), Graf. Ultra, Barcelona.*

An important area in small printing are *Ex Libris*, which constitute a speciality with its own symbolic language and graphic conventions. The Monastery of Montserrat has the good fortune to be home to P. Oriol Diví (1924), an excellent engraver and artist specialising in *ex libris*, whose work in major collections worldwide.

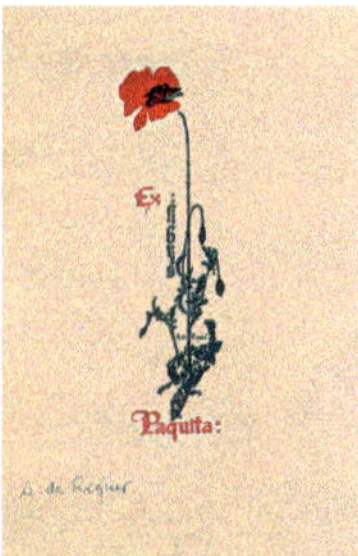

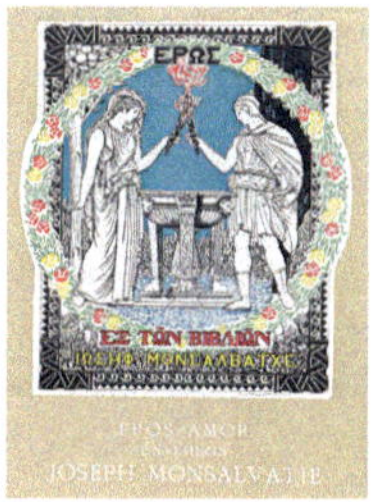

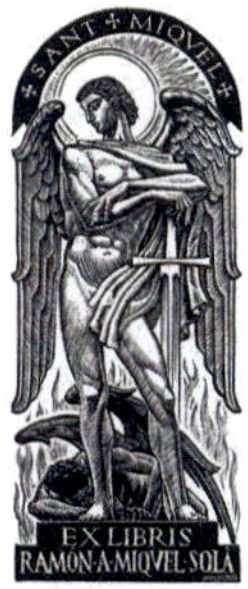

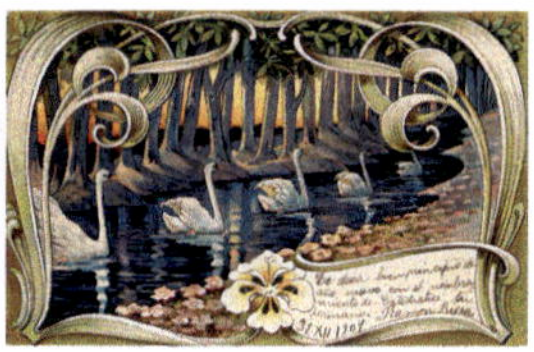

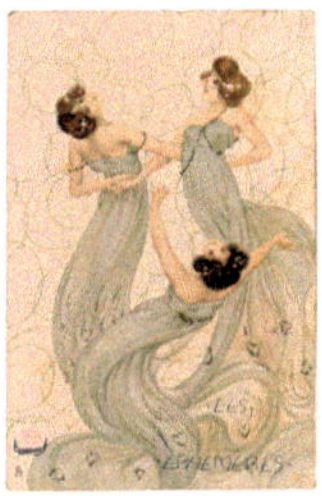

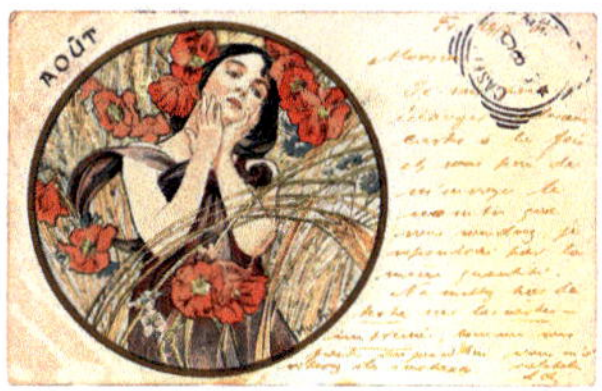

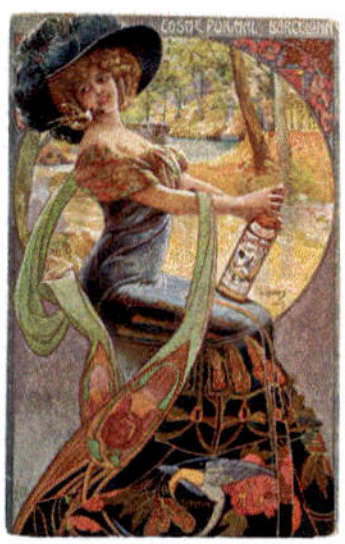

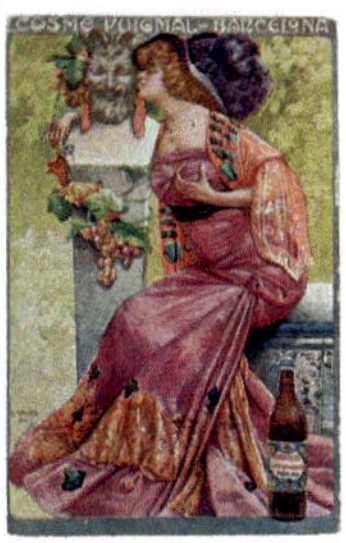

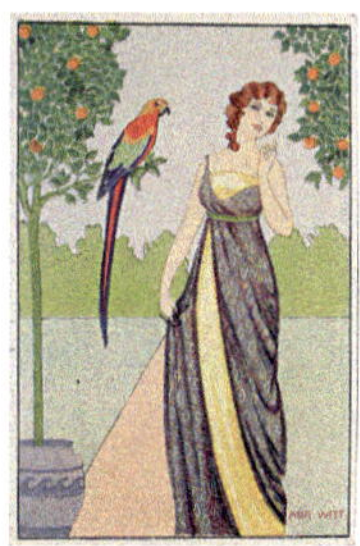

Alexandre de Riquer *(1856-1920)*, **Ex-libris of Francesca Bonnemaison de Verdaguer**, *1904, (ink, dual colour, 8.5 x 2.5cm).*

Ramon Casals i Vernís *(1860-1920)*, **Ex-libris of Joseph Montsalvatje**, *1916, (ink, five colours 11.1 x 9.6cm).*

T.N. Miciano *(1903-1974)*, **Ex-libris of Ramon A. Miquel Solà** *(xylograph, 11.5 x 4.5cm).*

Hans Schulze, **Postcard**, *1900.*

Raphael Kirchner, *postcard*, **Les Ephémères**, *París.*

Alphons Maria Mucha, *postcard* **Août**, *c. 1900.*

Hans Schulze, **Postcard**, *1900.*

Gaspar Camps *(1875-1942)*, **Postcard**, *c. 1903.*

Mia Witt, *Viena*, **Postcard**, *c. 1912.*

The Museum of Montserrat at the service of culture

The Museum belongs to the wider cultural collection of the Abbey of Montserrat. It is a representation of the activity of this institution in the world of archaeology and plastic arts.

It preserves, looks after and restores Montserrat's artistic heritage.

It particularly addresses school children and youths on previously arranged guided visits.

It also welcomes private adult groups, associations, processions, etc who arrange guided visits in advance.

Special weekend activities for individuals or families staying at the Sanctuary of Montserrat's apartments or the Hostel are organised.

It promotes the publishing of its artistic and archeological collection.

It also divulges the Abbey of Montserrat's heritage by means of itinerant monographic exhibitions.

As part of an agreement with the **University of Barcelona**, it promotes humanistic, artistic and archeological **University Symposiums** as well as meetings, national and international conferences on cultural issues related to the Museum and the Abbey of Montserrat.

The Museum of Montserrat is supported by the company **LARSA**, which manages the general services regarding personnel and infrastructure of the Sanctuary and the **Montserrat 2025 Foundation**, which helps to find sponsors who make the Museum's cultural activities possible.

Scholars and researchers can use the Abbey's library (330,000 volumes) for their work.

*The Museum of Montserrat has two temporary exhibition halls: the **Sala Pere Daura**, which hosts large exhibitions, and the **Espai d'Art Pruna**, which features more flexible and experimental possibilities.*

*The lively atmosphere we breathe in in the Museum of Montserrat is reflected in the magazine **El Propileu**, which reports on activities, restorations, donations, loans and exhibition projects. It is accessible from all the Montserrat web pages.*

The Museum itself has a website that provides basic information regarding its contents and activities:

www.museudemontserrat.com

facebook

Museum information

Museum opening times

Open everyday. Times: 10-18 h.
(Summer season: 10-19 h.)

Queries

www.museudemontserrat.com
www.abadiamontserrat.net
www.montserratvisita.com

Library queries

www.bibliotecademontserrat.net

Telephone	938 777 745
Fax	938 777 736
Email	museu@larsa-montserrat.com elpropileu@larsa-montserrat.com

Visitors will also find a comfortable and varied catering services in Montserrat and acommodation at the Monastery, which follows special rules.

Bibliography

Joaquim FOLCH I TORRES, "La pinacoteca de Montserrat", *Destino*, issue 1294, 26 May, 1962, p. 79-81.

Josep de C. LAPLANA, *La col·lecció de pintura catalana moderna de Josep Sala i Ardiz*. Exhibition catalogue *Mestres de la pintura catalana*, Barcelona, Palau de Pedralbes, 1982. Spanish edition with enlargements and details in the catalogue: *Maestros de la pintura catalana*, Madrid, Caixa de Barcelona, 1985.

Alícia SUÀREZ and Mercè VIDAL, "Novetats al Museu de Montserrat", *Serra d'Or*, issue 388, April 1992, p. 44-49.

Josep de C. LAPLANA, "El llegat Xavier Busquets", *Montserrat. Butlletí del Santuari*, 32, January-April 1992, p. 42-46.

Josep de C. LAPLANA, "Unificació dels Museus de Montserrat", *Montserrat. Butlletí del Santuari*, 47, January-April 1997, p. 62-63.

Liliana BARROERO, *Dipinti italiani dal XV al XIX secolo del Museo de Montserrat*, Roma, Istituto Poligrafico e Zecca dello Stato, Libreria dello Stato, 1992.

Josep de C. LAPLANA, "Sobre la funció eclesial dels museus de l'Església", *Qüestions de Vida Cristiana*, issue 202, June 2001, p. 102-110.

Josep de C. LAPLANA, "El Museu de Montserrat, una història, un repte, una missió", *Serra d'Or*, issue 552, December 2005, p. 893-897.

Francesc MIRALPEIX i Joaquim GARRIGA, "La pinacoteca dels segles XVI-XVIII del Museu de Montserrat, un fons ple de sorpreses", *Serra d'Or*, issue 552, December 2005, p. 904-909.

Josep BRACONS CLAPÉS, "La pintura catalana contemporània, nucli del Museu de Montserrat", *Serra d'Or*, issue 552, December 2005, p. 910-913.

Àlex MITRANI, "El Museu de Montserrat i lart contemporani, el sentit de la prospecció", *Serra d'Or*, issue 552, December 2005, p. 914-917.

Josep de C. LAPLANA, "El Museu de Montserrat", en *Història de l'Art Català, Els Grans Museus de Catalunya*, (dir. Jesús Mestre Campi) Barcelona, Ed. 62, 2005, p. 125-131.

Jordi FALGÀS, *Dalí inèdit, Els dibuixos de Montserrat*, Girona exhibition catalogue, September - November, 2007. Fundació Caixa Girona, 103 p.

L'encís de la dona. Ramon Casas al Liceu i a Montserrat, exhibition catalogue with texts by Josep de C. Laplana (superintendent), Francesc Fontbona and Mercedes Palau-Ribes O'Callaghan, Barcelona, September-October 2007, Gran Teatre del Liceu.

Archaeology

J. COROMINAS I ROCA, Dom Beda ESPONA. "Prehistòria de Montserrat", *Analecta Montserratensia*, VI, 1925, p. 225-235

Romuald Mª DIAZ, *Dom Bonaventura Ubach, l'home, el monjo i el biblista*, Barcelona, Aedos, 1962.

Several authors, "Montserrat y la Bíblia", *Montserrat. Butlletí del Santuari*, issue 11, January-April 1985.

Manuel MOLINA, "Tablillas Sargónicas del Museo de Montserrat, Barcelona", *Aula Orientalis*, IX, 1991, p. 137-154.

Romuald Mª DÍAZ, "Orígenes y vicisitudes históricas de la colección de textos cuneiformes del Museo de Montserrat", *Aula Orientalis*, XV, 1-2. 1997, p. 11-20.

Guiu Mª CAMPS, "Egipte en el pensament del P. Bonaventura Ubach", *Montserrat, Butlletí del Santuari*, issue 50, 1998, p. 39-45.

Pere VILLALBA I VARNEDA, "Vidres del Museu Bíblic de Montserrat", *Empúries*, issue 45-46, Barcelona 1983-1984, p. 104-221.

Ester PONS MELLADO, *Terracotas egipcias de época greco-romana del Museu del Oriente Bíblico del Monasterio de Montserrat*, Sabadell, Ausa, 1995, *(Aula Orientalis-Supplementa - 9)*,

I. MÁRQUEZ ROWE – M. MOLINA, "Catálogo de textos cuneiformes publicados conservados en el Museo de Montserrat", *Aula Orientalis*, XV, 1-2. 1997, p. 21-31.

Manuel MOLINA, *Tablillas administrativas neosumerias de la Abadia de Montserrat, copias cuneiformes*, Roma, 1993, *(Materiali per il vocabolario neosumerico - 18)*.

Manuel MOLINA, *Tablillas administrativas neosumerias de la Abadia de Montserrat, transliteraciones e índices*, Sabadell, Ausa, 1996, 483 p. (*Aula Orientalis Supplementa* - 11).

Manuel MOLINA, "Inscripciones reales conmemorativas neosumerias", *Aula Orientalis*, XV, 1-2. 1997, p. 63-67.

Carmen VALDÉS, "Catálogo de terracotas mesopotámicas del Museo de Montserrat", *Aula Orientalis*, XV, 1-2. 1997, p. 223-296.

I. MÁRQUEZ ROWE, C. WUNSCH, "The kudurru fragment of the Montserrat Museu", *Aula Orientalis*, XV, 1-2. 1997, p. 195-200.

Pedro BARBADO MARISCAL, "Museo de Montserrat. Sección de Arqueología del Oriente Bíblico", *Revista de Arqueología*, XVIII, issue 196, August 1997, p. 48-53.

Salvador COSTA I LLERDA, "L'arqueologia de l'Orient bíblic al Museu de Montserrat", *Serra d'Or*, issue 517, January 2003, p. 42-47.

Lluís TURELL COLL, "Los tejidos coptos del Museo de Montserrat: Presentación de la colección", *Antiquité Tardive*, issue 12, *Tissus et vêtements dans l'Anchitée Tardive*, Brepols, Turnhout, 2005, p. 145-152.

Lluís TURELL COLL, "El coleccionismo de tejidos coptos en Cataluña y la formación de la colección del Museo de Montserrat", *Bulletin, Assotiation pour l'Antiquité tardive*, issue 15, Brepols, Turnhout, 2006, p. 100-106.

Lluís G. TURELL COLL, "Història antiga i Arqueologia al Museu de Montserrat. Fòrum d'encontre i escola oberta", *Serra d'Or*, issue 552, December 2005, p. 900-903.

Publications

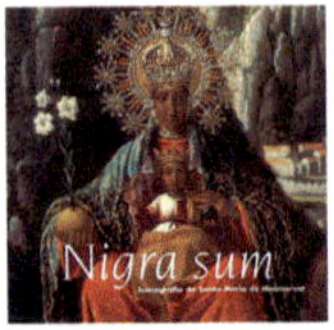

Nigra Sum. Iconografia de Santa Maria de Montserrat, Texts by Josep de C. LAPLANA and Teresa MACIÀ, Museum of Montserrat, 1995 (translations into Spanish, English and German), 306 p., illustr.

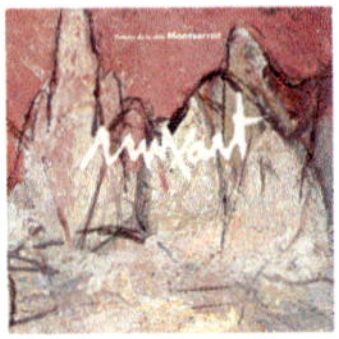

Montserrat de Jaume Muxart, text by Josep de C. LAPLANA, Museum of Montserrat, 1998, 24 p. Illustr.

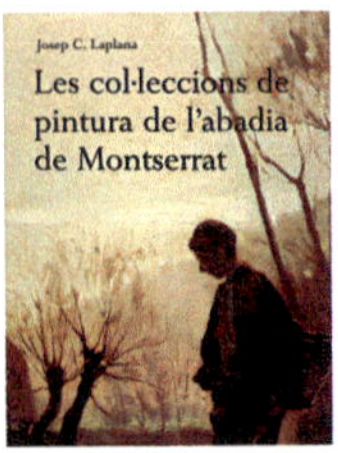

Josep de C. LAPLANA, *Les col·leccions de pintura de l'abadia de Montserrat*, Publicacions de l'Abadia de Montserrat, 1999, 248 p., illustr.

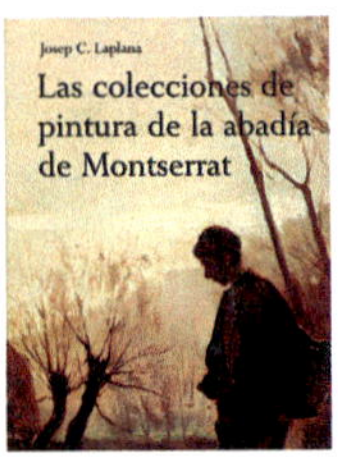

Josep de C. LAPLANA, *Las colecciones de pintura de la abadía de Montserrat*, Publicacions de l'Abadia de Montserrat, 1999.

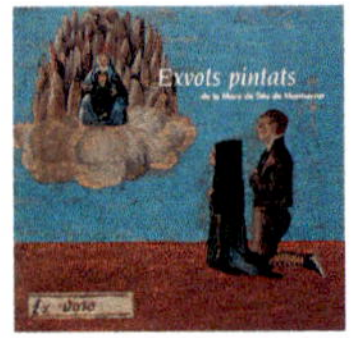

Exvots pintats de la Mare de Déu de Montserrat, texts by Jordi MOLAS i RIFÀ, Museum of Montserrat, 1999, 71 p. illustr.

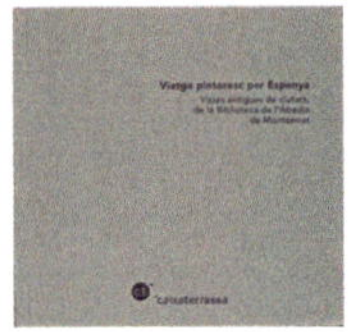

Viatge pintoresc per Espanya. Vistes antigues de ciutats de la Biblioteca de l'Abadia de Montserrat. Texts by Pilar VÉLEZ and Oriol DIVÍ. Cataloguing and commentaries by Josep de C. LAPLANA, Museum of Montserrat, Caixa de Terrassa, 1999, 178 p, illustr.

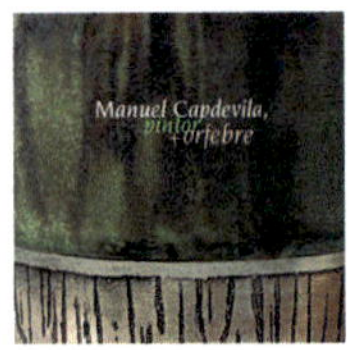

Manuel Capdevila, pintor + orfebre, Texts by Teresa MACIÀ, Pilar VÉLEZ, Jordi A. CARBONELL, Josep de C. LAPLANA, Museum of Montserrat, 2000, 95 p., illustr.

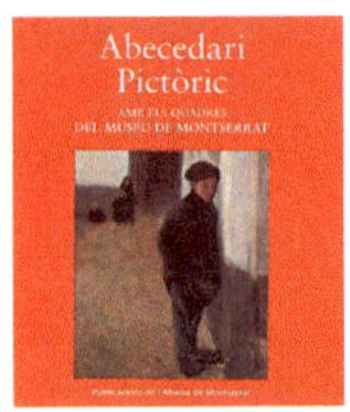

Abecedari pictòric amb els quadres del Museu de Montserrat, Publicacions de l'Abadia de Montserrat, 2001, 60 p., illustr.

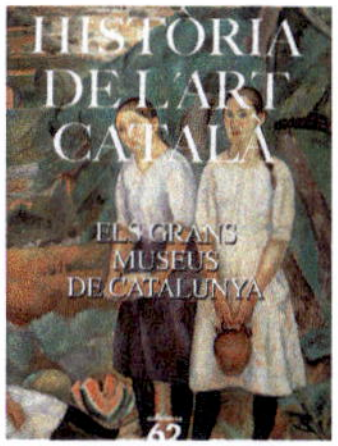

Josep de C. LAPLANA, *Museu de Montserrat*, dir. Jesús MESTRE CAMPI, en *Història de l'Art Català*, ***Els Grans Museus de Catalunya***, Barcelona, Ed. 62, 2005, illustr., p. 125-131, 239 p., illustr.

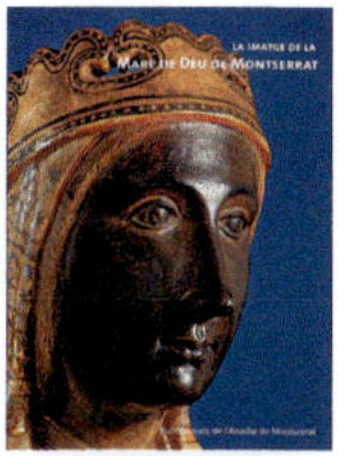

Several authors. ***La imatge de la Mare de Déu de Montserrat***, Publicacions de l'Abadia de Montserrat, 2003, 190 p., illustr. (*Bibl. Abat Oliba. Sèrie il·lustrada - 18*).

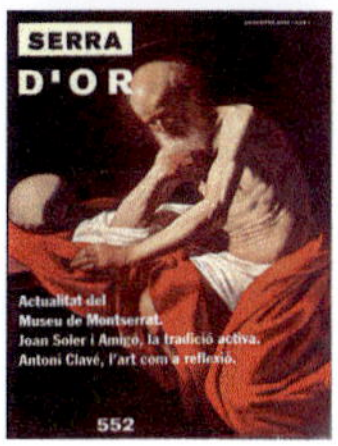

Actualitat del Museu de Montserrat, by several authors, special issue of *Serra d'Or*, issue 552, December 2005, p. 29-53, illustr.

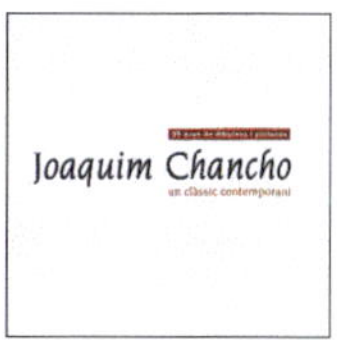

Joaquim Chancho, un clàssic contemporani. 36 anys de dibuixos i pintures. Text by Josep Mª SOLER, Abbot of Montserrat, and 12 unedited text by Joaquim CHANCHO selected and sequenced by Teresa BLANCH, Museum of Montserrat and Banc Sabadell, 2005).

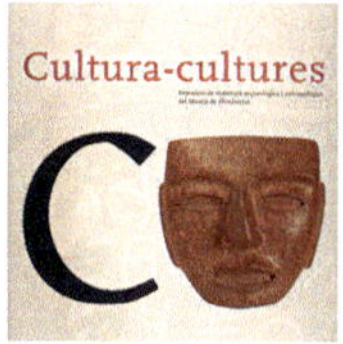

Cultura-cultures. Donació d'art i arqueologia de Caja Madrid al Museu de Montserrat, Museum of Montserrat, 2006, (*El Gussi, 1*), 237 p, illustr., 25 €. Spanish edition, Museum of Fine Art, La Coruña, 2007.

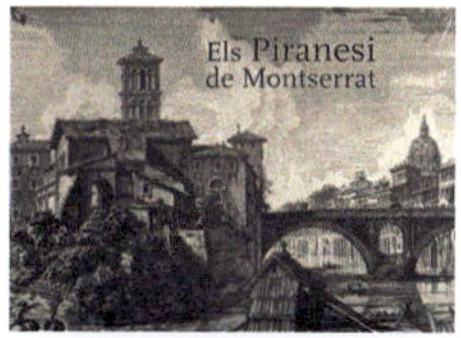

Artur RAMON i NAVARRO, ***Els Piranesi de Montserrat***, Museum of Montserrat, 2006, (*El Gussi, 2*), 200 p, illustr.

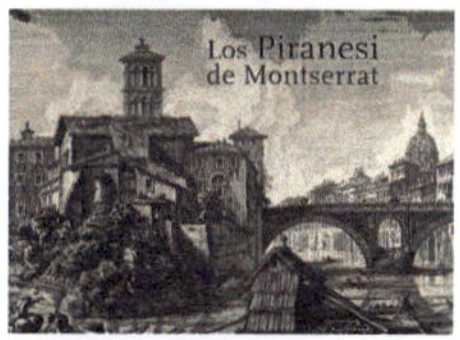

Artur RAMON i NAVARRO, ***Los Piranesi de Montserrat***, Museum of Montserrat, 2006, (*El Gussi, 2*) 200 p. Illustr.

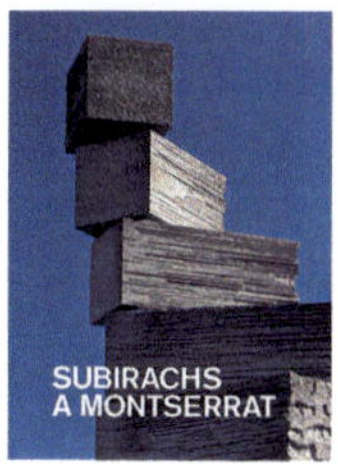

Judit SUBIRACHS, *Subirachs a Montserrat*, catalogue of the exhibition, Museum of Montserrat, February 17 – May, text by Josep M. SOLER, Abbot of Montserrat, Jordi PLA i MASMIQUEL, Artur RAMON NAVARRO and Ignasi MORETA, Editorial Mediterrània, 2007, 142 p., Spanish translation.

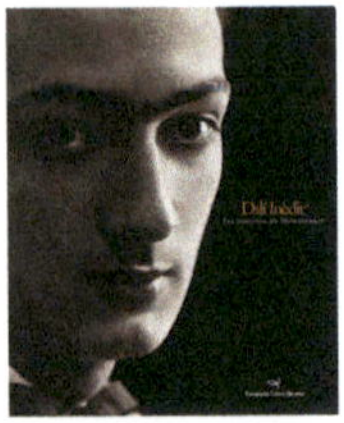

Jordi FALGÀS, *Dalí inèdit, Els dibuixos de Montserrat*, catalogue of the exhibition at La Fontana d'Or, Girona, September – November, Girona, Fundació Caixa Girona, 2007, 103 p.

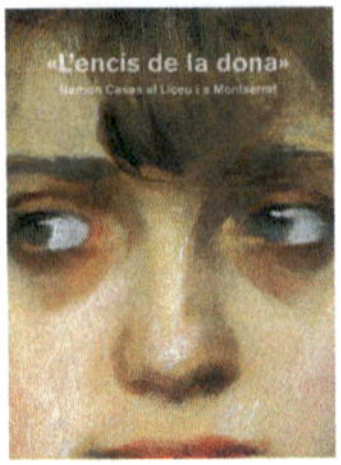

L'encís de la dona. Ramon Casas al Liceu i a Montserrat, catalogue of the exhibition September 20 – October 21 2007, whit texts by Josep de C. LAPLANA (curator), Francesc FONTBONA and Mercedes PALAU-RIBES O'CALLAGHAN, Barcelona, Gran Teatre del Liceu, 2007, 271 p., Spanish and English translation.

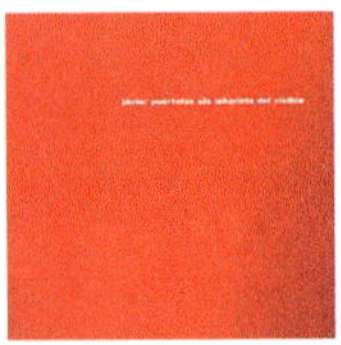

Javier Puértolas als laberints del visible, text by Àlex MITRANI, Museum of Montserrat, 2007, 36 p. illustr.

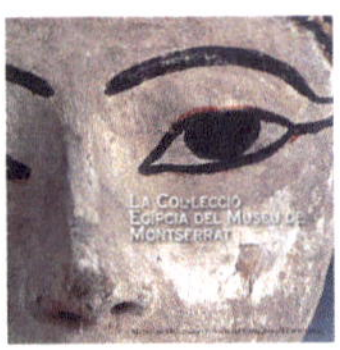

La col·lecció egípcia del Museu de Montserrat, Xavier URIACH and Jaume VIVÓ (dir.), Museum of Montserrat and Catalan Society of Museology.

Jubany, text by Josep de C. LAPLANA and Carles HAC MOR, catalogue of the exhibition February 22 – June 2, Museum of Montserrat, 2008, 36 p., Spanish and English translation.

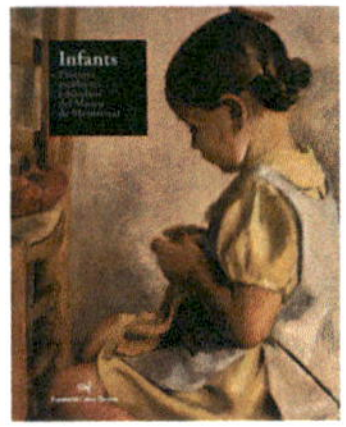

Josep de C. LAPLANA, *Infants. Pintures, escultures i dibuixos del Museu de Montserrat*, text by Arcadi CALZADA, president Caixa Girona, Josep M. SOLER, Abbot of Montserrat and J. CORREDOR-MATHEOS, catalogue of the exhibition, Fontana d'Or, Girona, May 9 – June 15, Caixa de Girona, 2008, 176 p., Spanish translation.

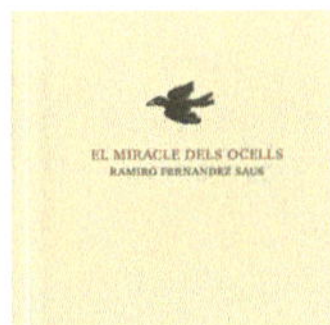

El Miracle dels Ocells. Ramiro Fernández Saus, text by Josep M. SOLER, Abbot of Montserrat and Àlex MITRANI, art critic, catalogue of the exhibition, November 28 – February 17, Museum of Montserrat, 2007-2008, 56 p., Spanish translation.

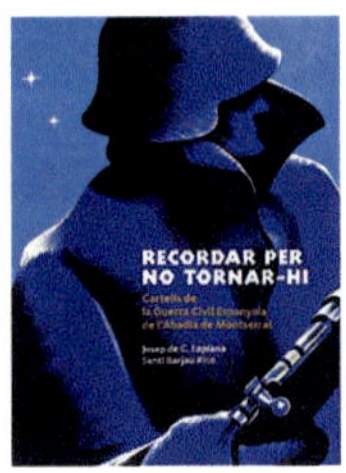

Josep de C. LAPLANA i Santi BARJAU RICO, *Recordar per no tornar-hi. Cartells de la Guerra Civil Espanyola de l'Abadia de Montserrat,* introduction by Marc TAXONERA, catalogue of the exhibition, March 14 – August 26, Museum of Montserrat, 2008, 438 p.

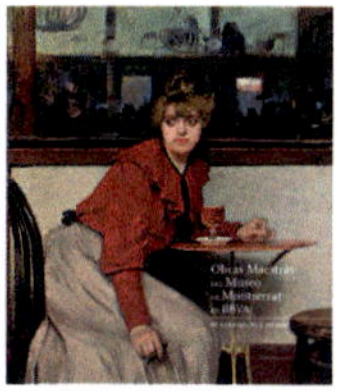

Obras Maestras del Museo de Montserrat en BBVA. De Caravaggio a Picasso, text by Josep M. SOLER, Abbot of Montserrat, Francesc FONTBONA de VALLESCAR, Josep de C. LAPLANA and various authors of the monographies; catalogue of the exhibition, Madrid, Palau del Marquès de Salamanca, October 9 – December 7, Museum of Montserrat - BBVA, Madrid, 2008, 302 p.

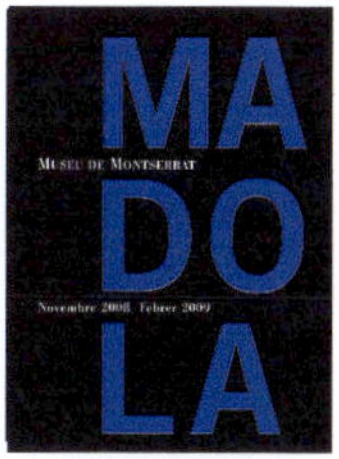

Madola, Vasos sagrats, text by Josep de C. LAPLANA and Àlex MITRANI, catalogue of the exhibition, November 22 – February 17, Museum of Montserrat, 2008-2009, 64 p., Spanish and English translation.

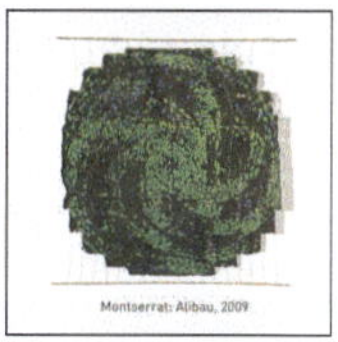

Montserrat: Alibau 2009, text by Josep de C. LAPLANA and Àlex MITRANI, catalogue of the exhibition, April 1 – June 14, Museum of Montserrat, 2009, 44 p.

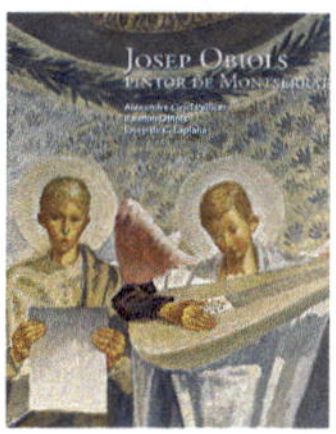

Alexandre CIRICI PELLICER, Raimon OBIOLS, Josep de C. LAPLANA, *Josep OBIOLS, pintor de Montserrat*, with and introduction by Josep M. SOLER, Abbot of Montserrat, catalogue of the exhibition, March 25 – October 25, Museum of Montserrat, 2008, 288 p., Spanish translation.

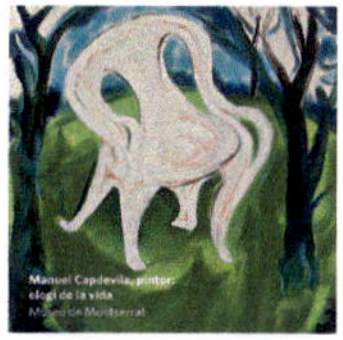

Manuel Capdevila, Painter: In Praise of Life, texts by Josep M. SOLER, Abbot of Montserrat, and Àlex MITRANI, exhibition catalogue, December 4 – March 28, Museum of Montserrat, 2010-2011, 28 pp.

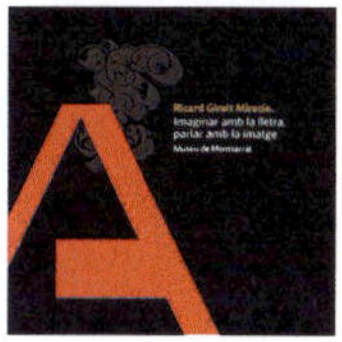

Ricard Giralt Miracle. Imagining with the Letter, Speaking with the Image, texts by Josep M. SOLER, Abbot of Montserrat, and Àlex MITRANI, exhibition catalogue, December 4 – March 28, Museum of Montserrat, 2010-2011, 32 pp.